Simon's Cat

Simon's Cat

by Simon Tofield

GRAND CENTRAL
PUBLISHING

New York Boston

Grand Central Publishing
Hachette Book Group
237 Park Avenue
New York, NY 10017

Visit our website at www.HachetteBookGroup.com.

Printed in the United States of America

First Edition: September 2009
10   9   8   7   6   5   4   3

Grand Central Publishing is a division of Hachette Book Group, Inc.
The Grand Central Publishing name and logo is a trademark of
Hachette Book Group, Inc.

ISBN: 978-0-446-56006-1
LCCN: 2009930514

To Mum, thank you for everything.
This book is for you.

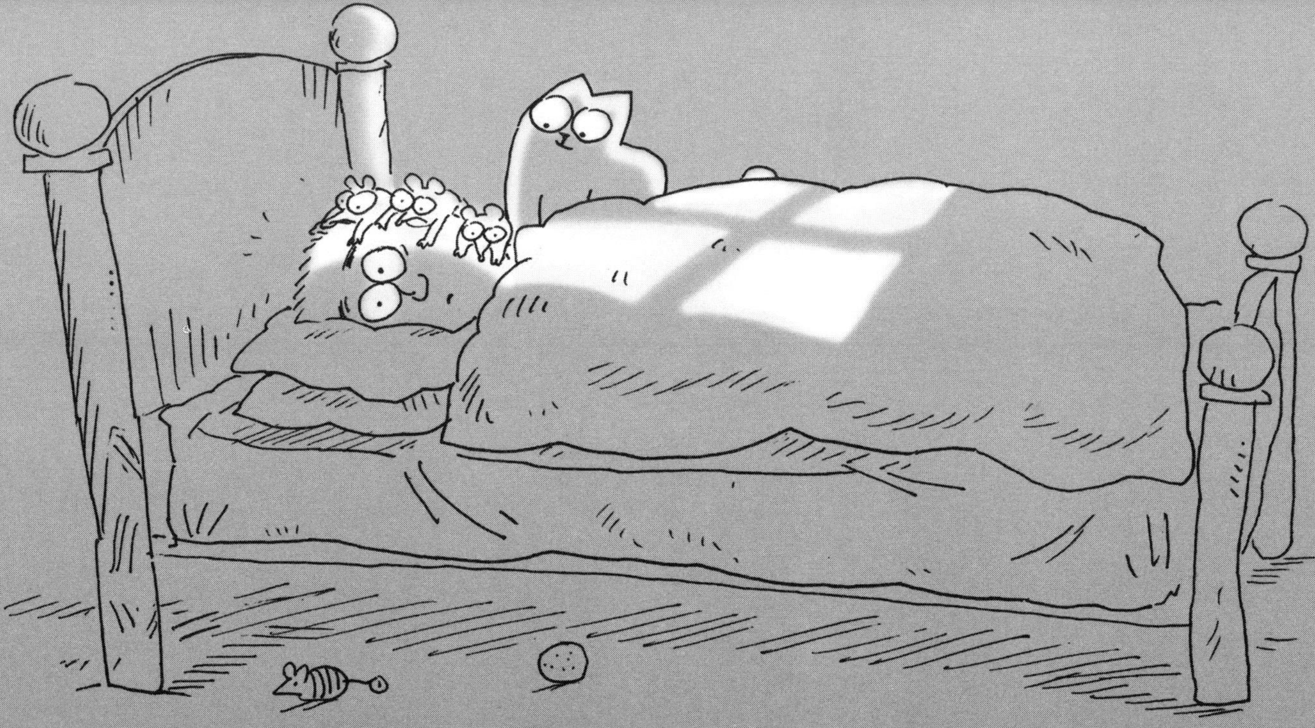

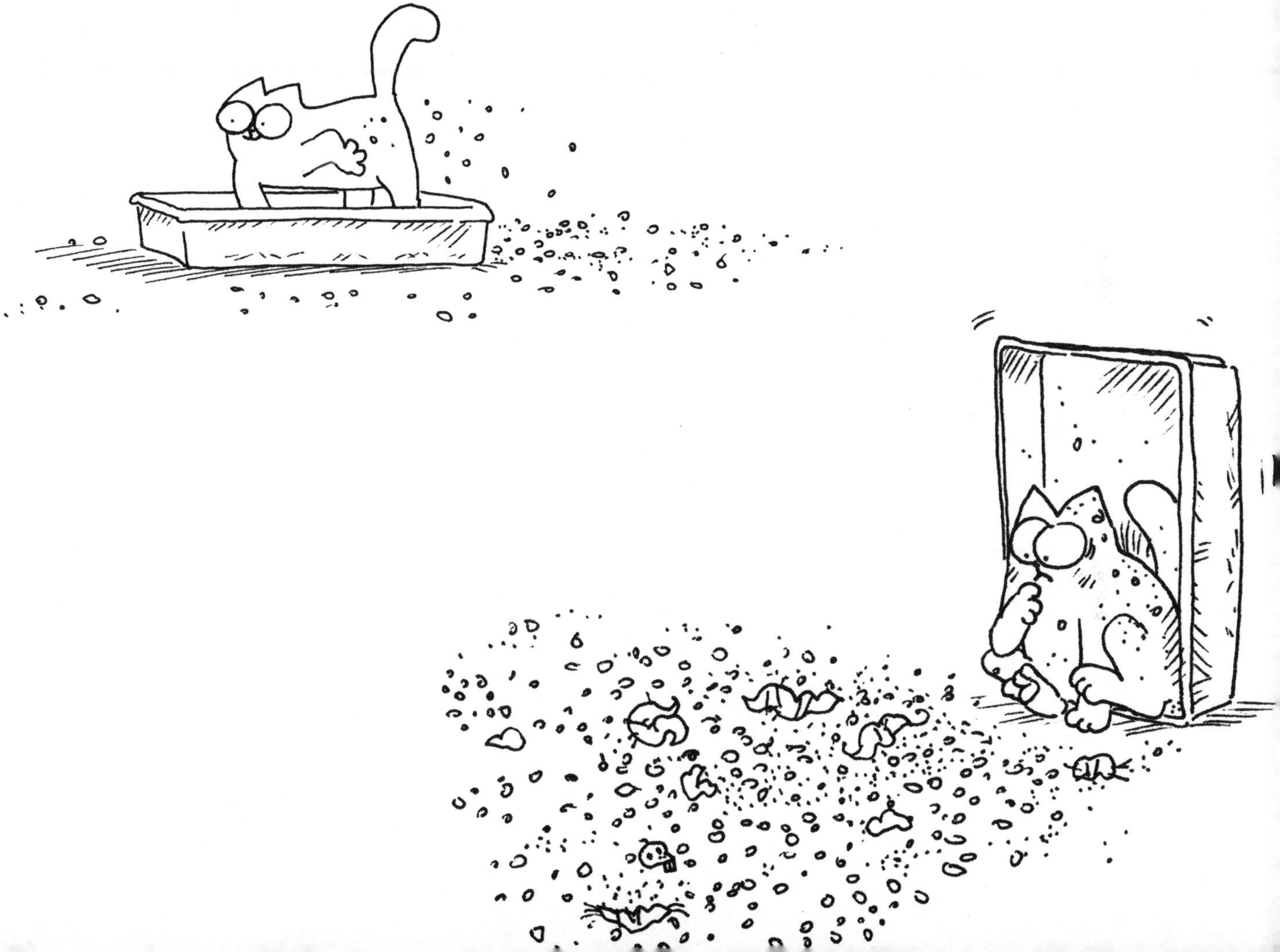

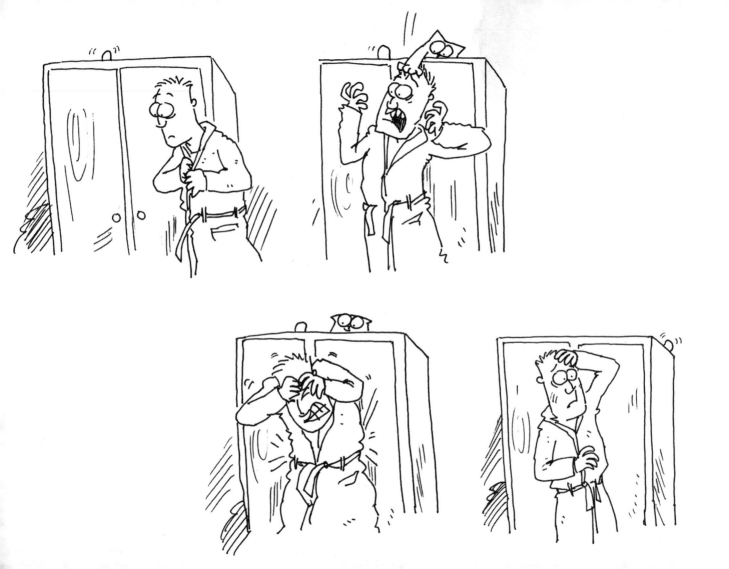

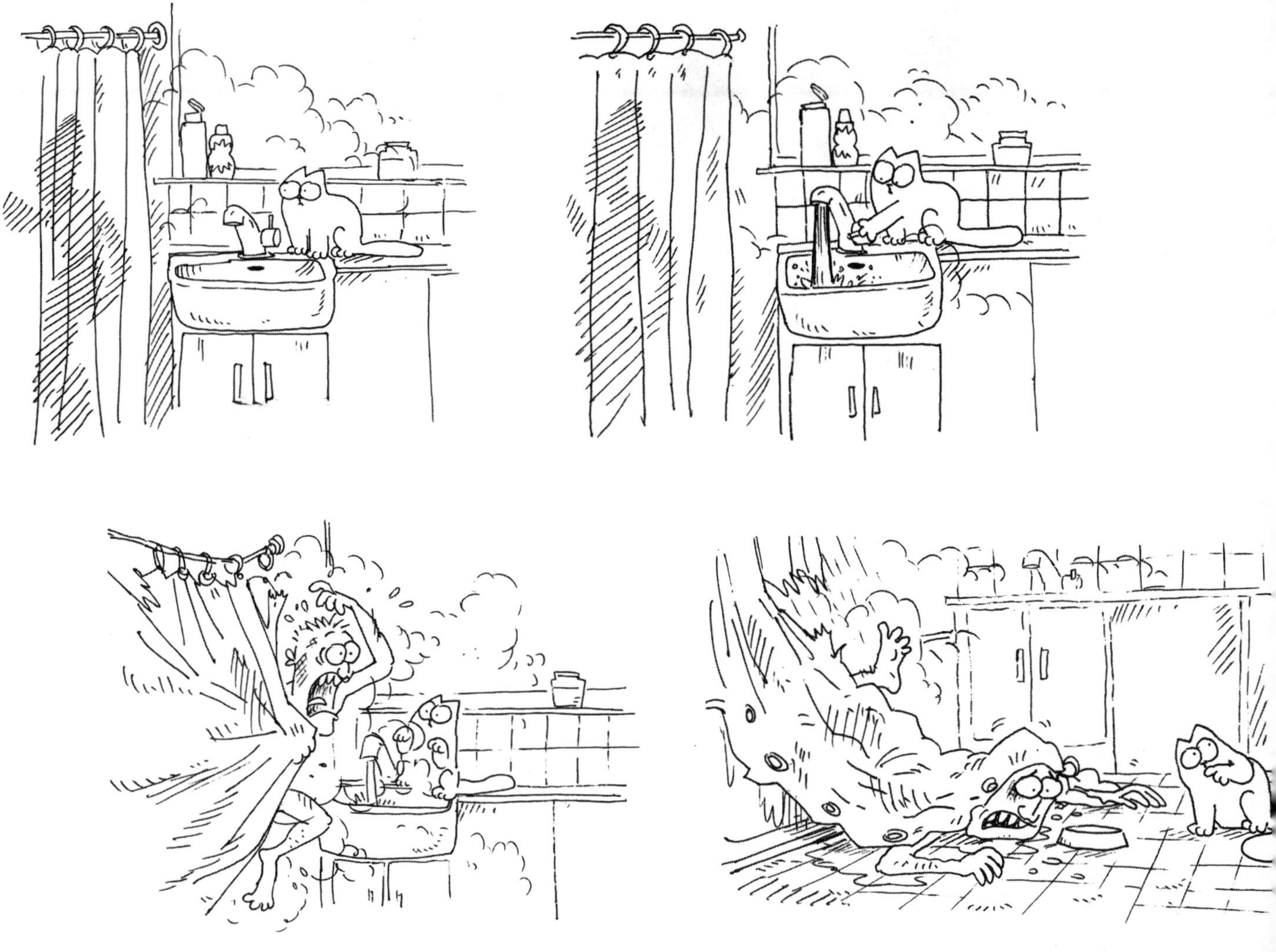

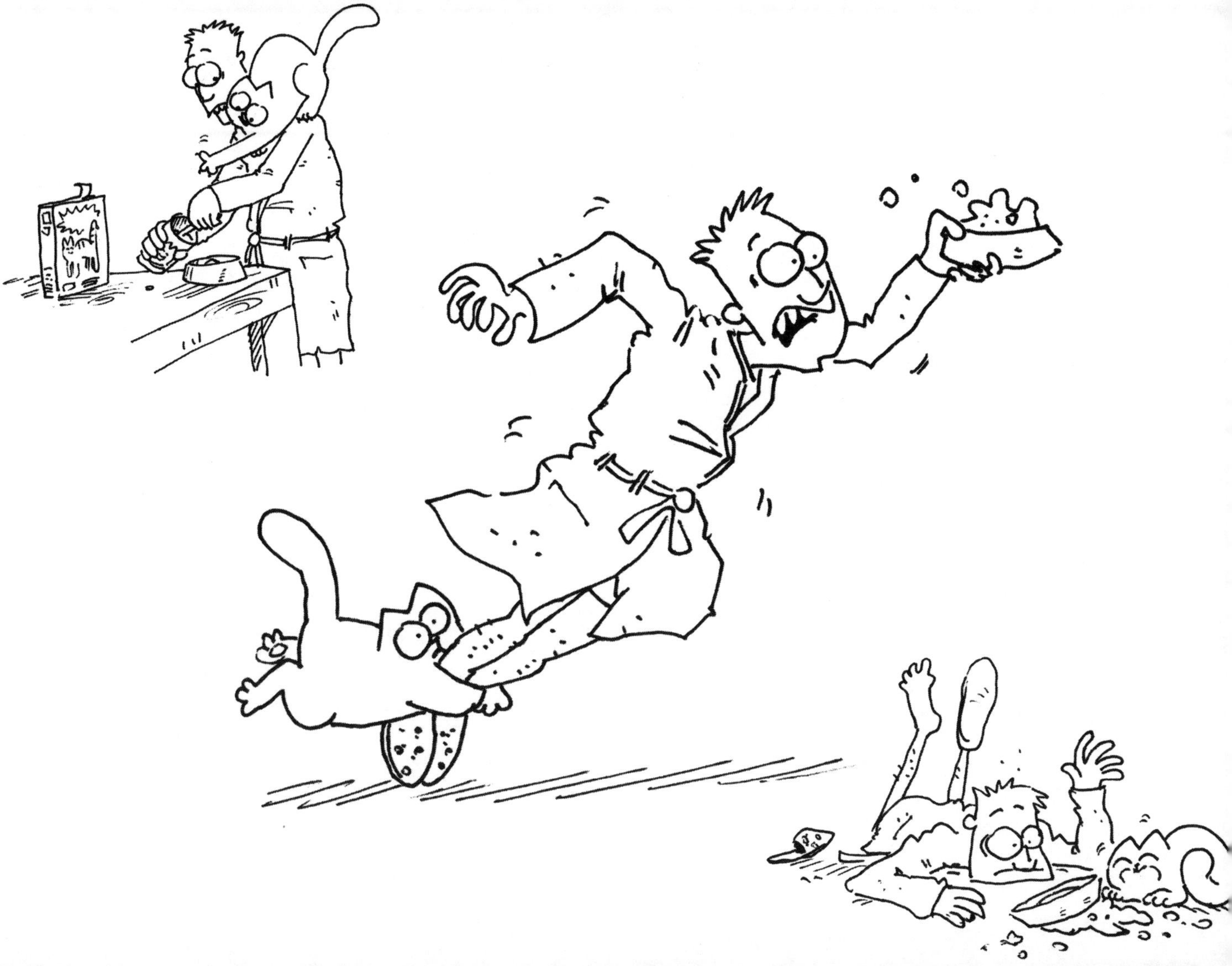

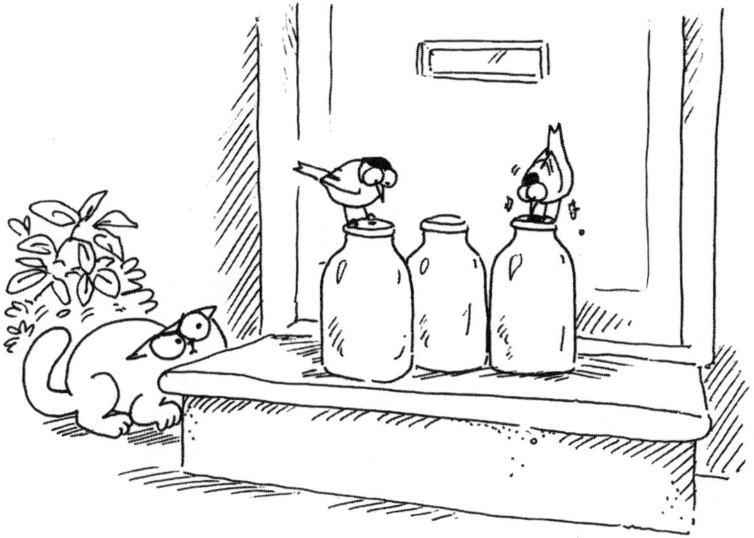

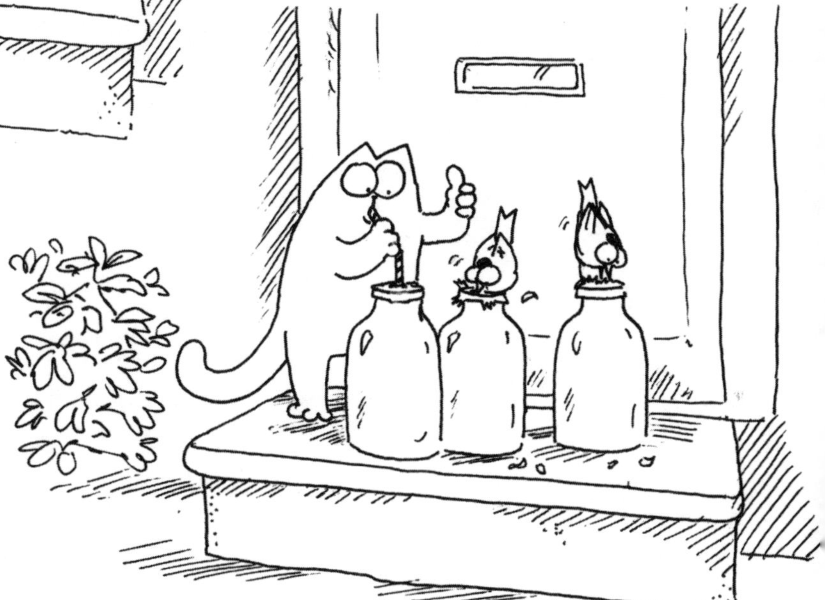

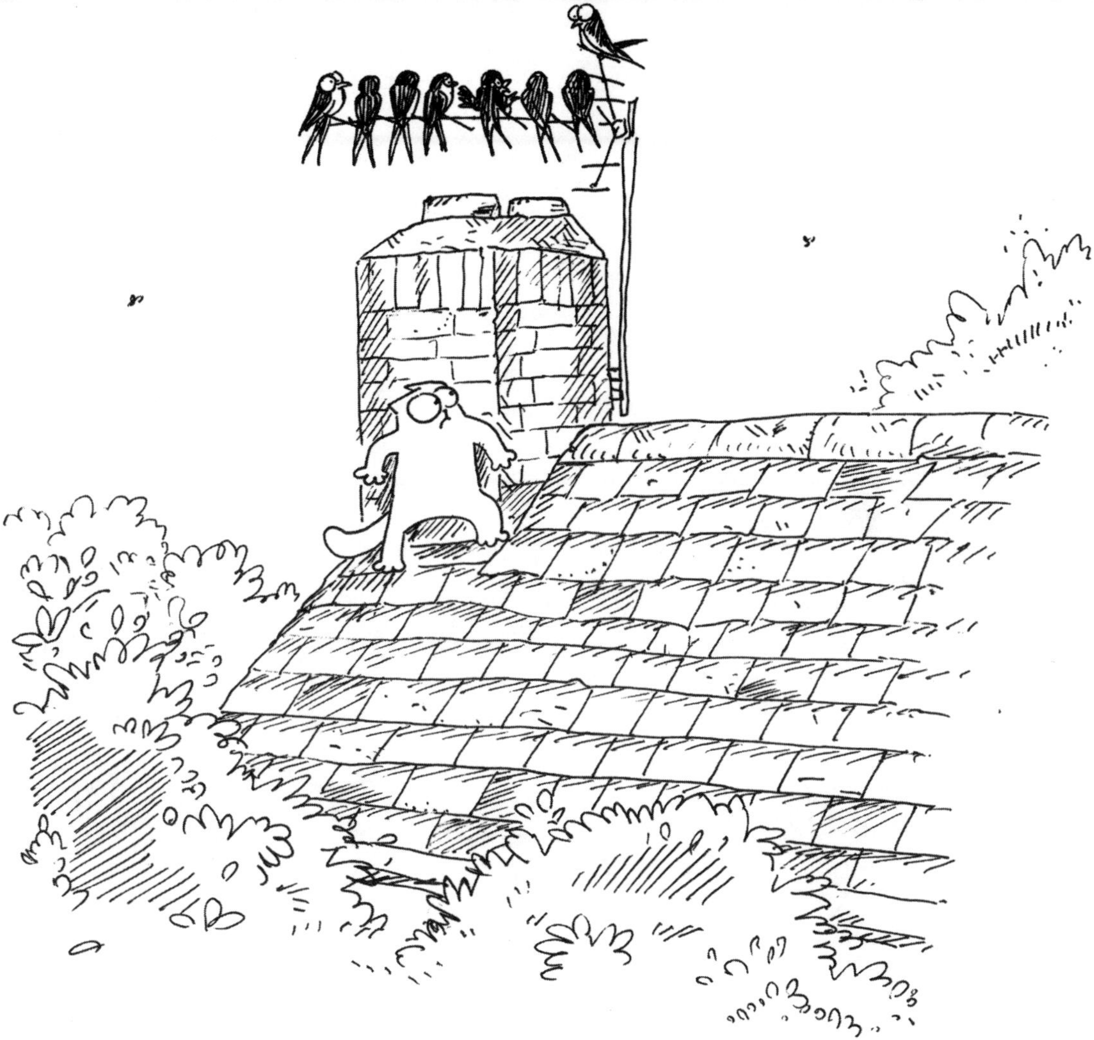

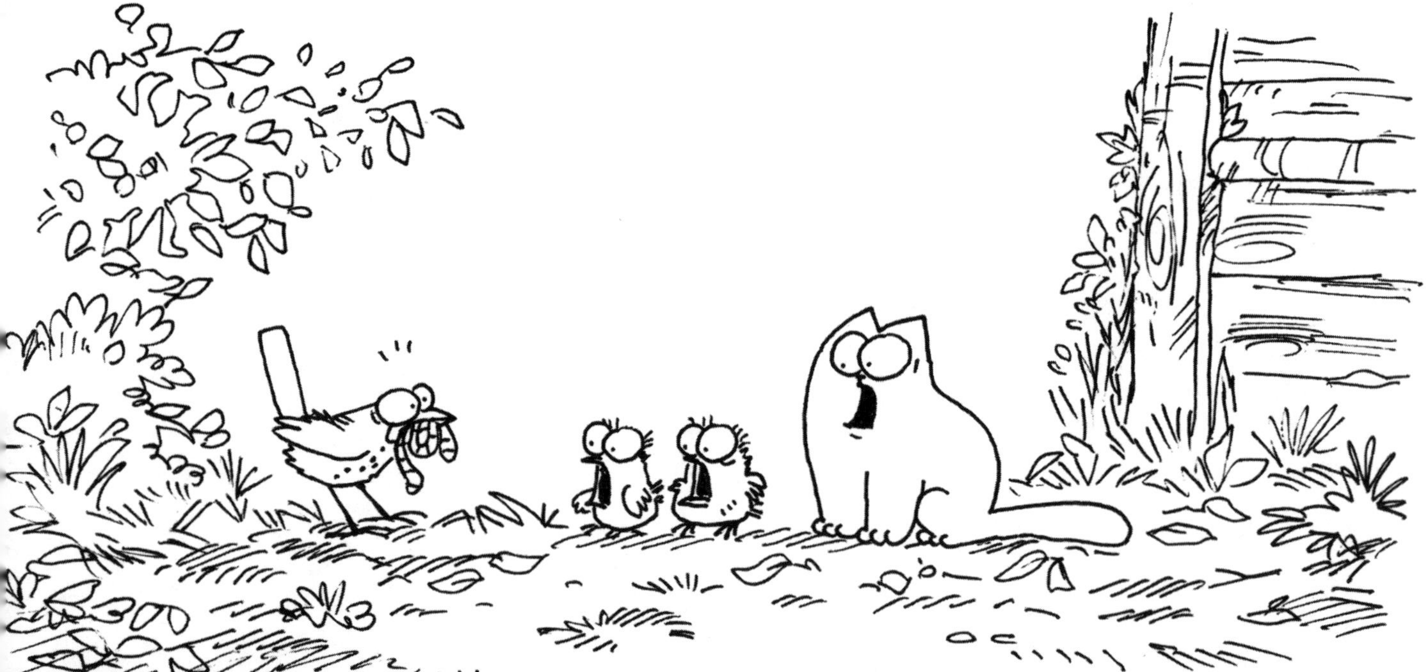

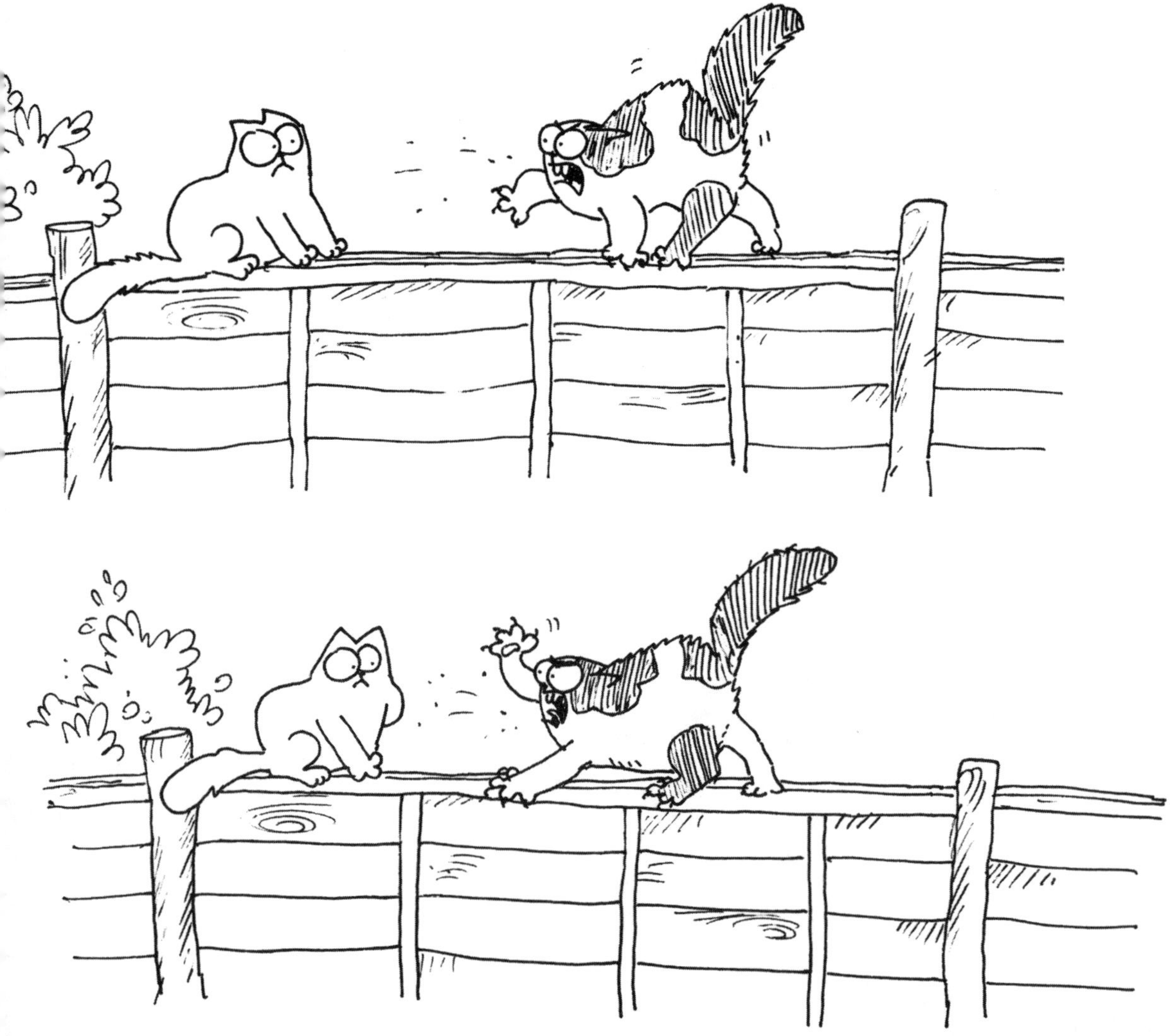

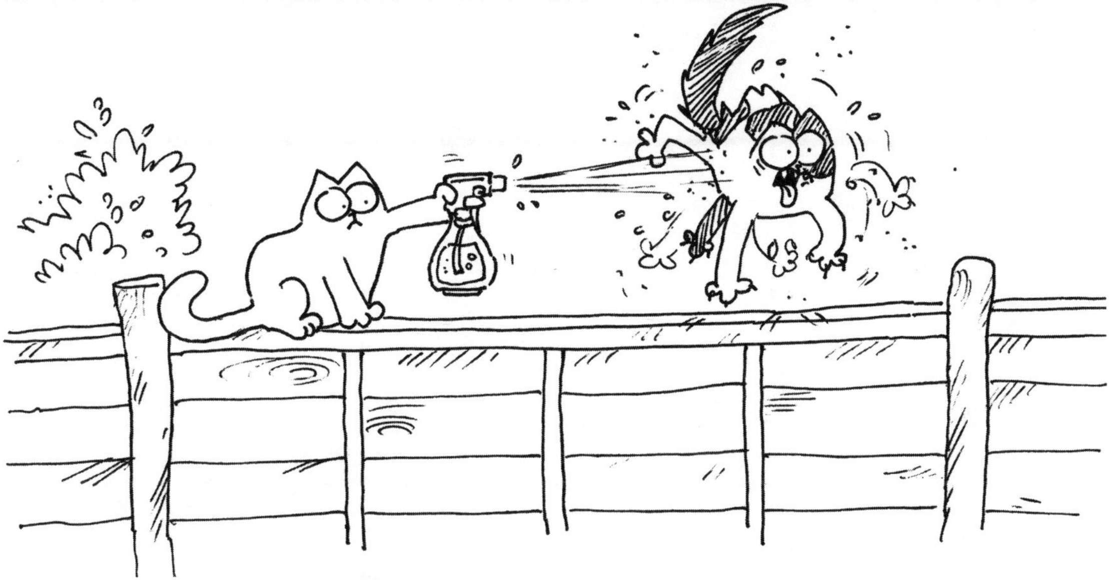

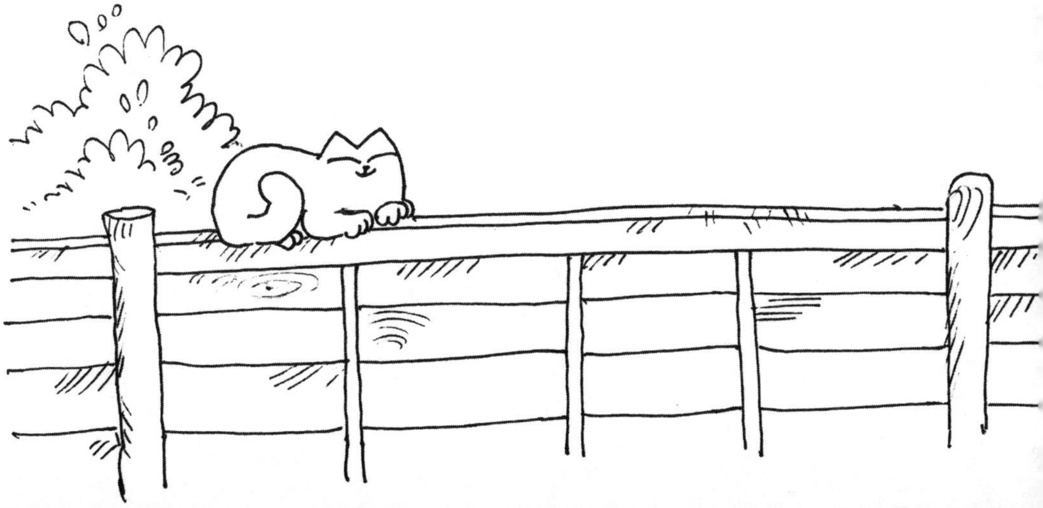

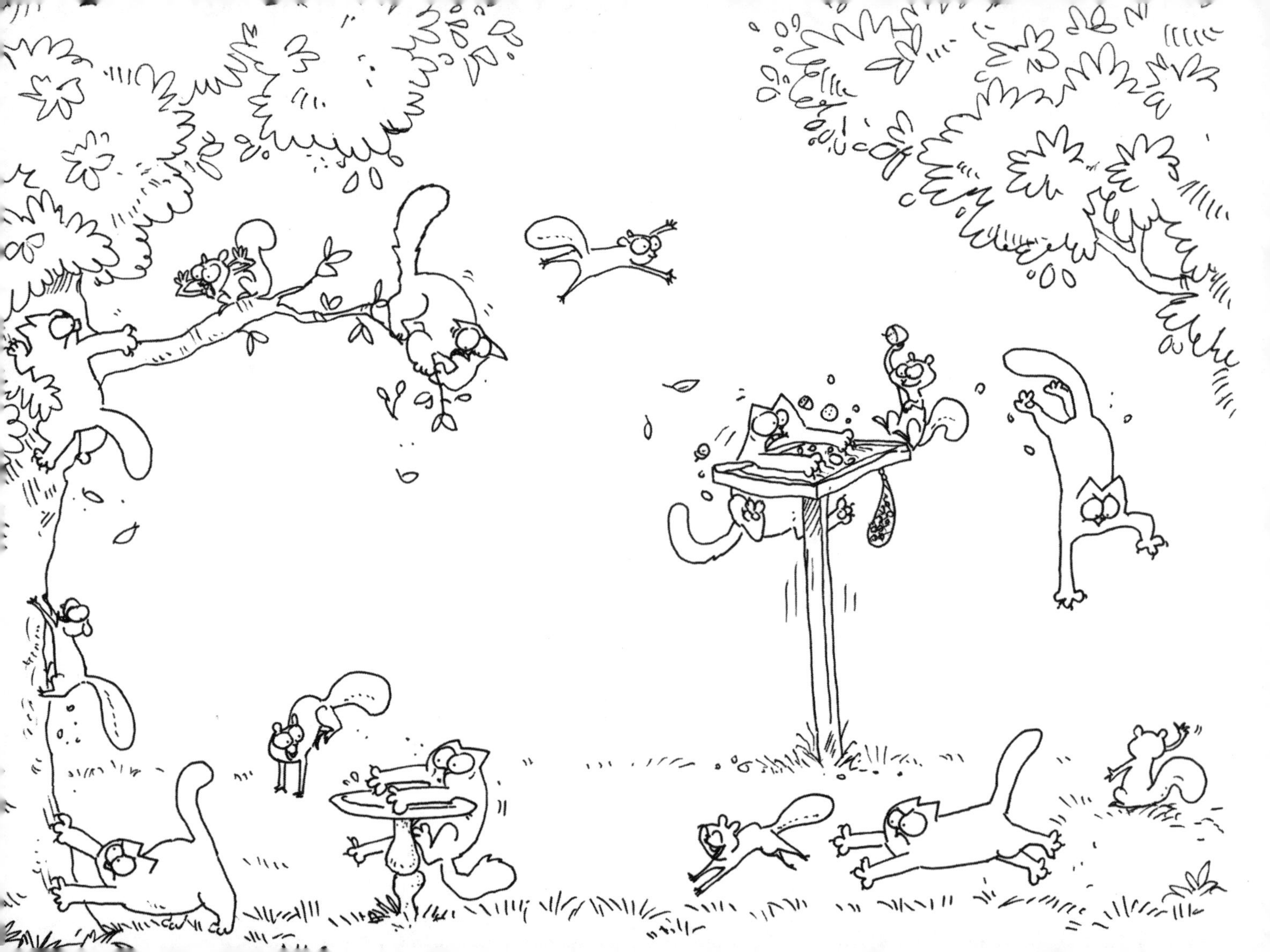

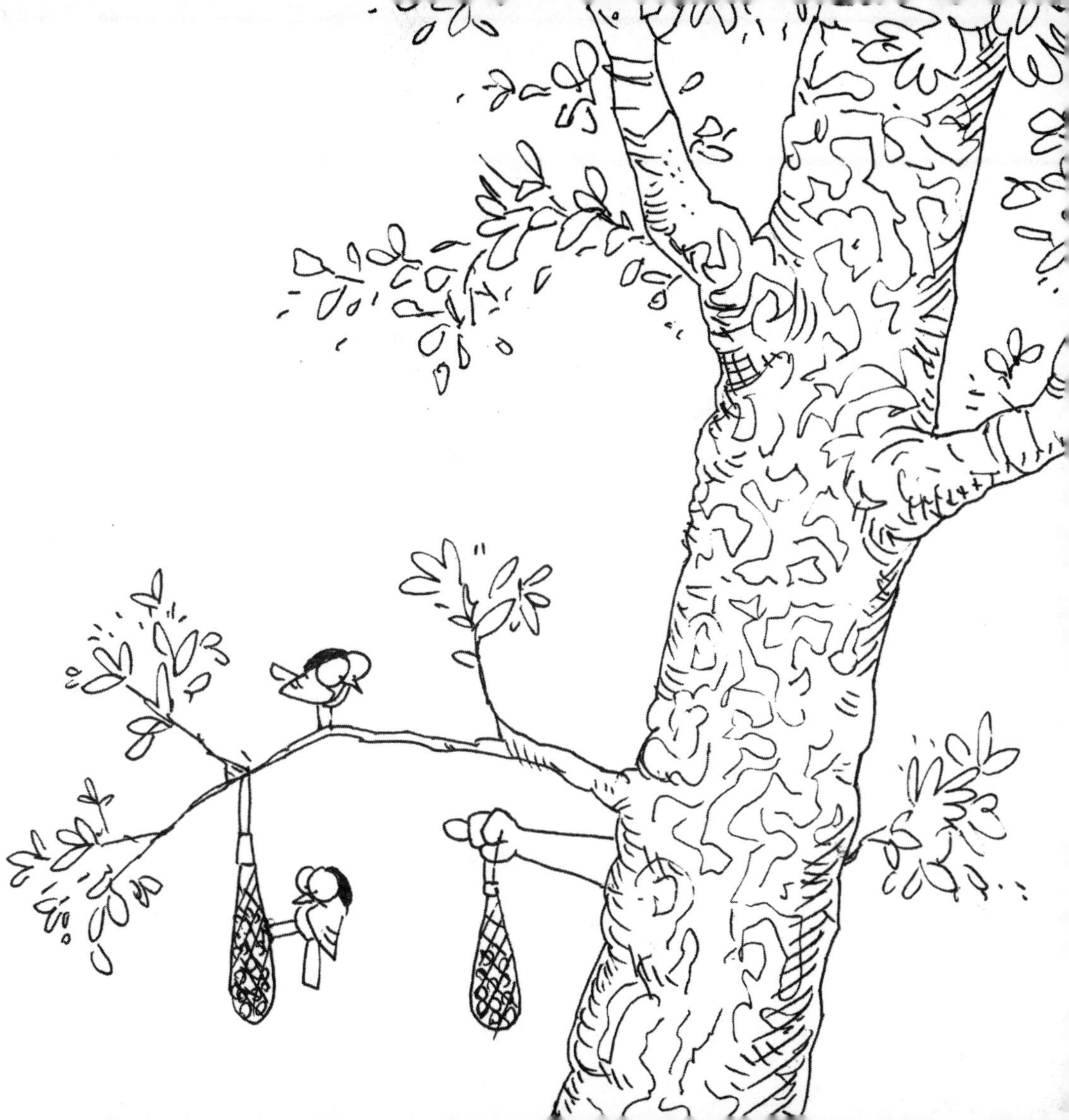

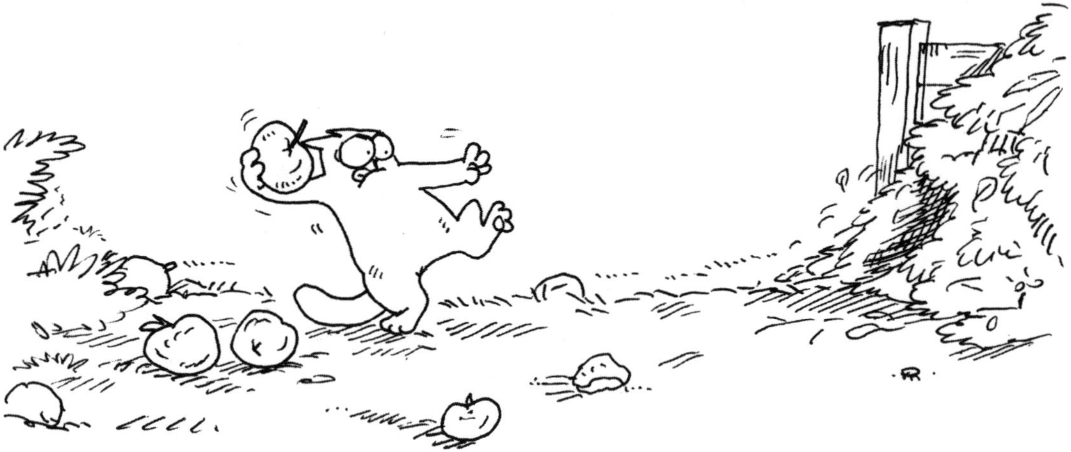

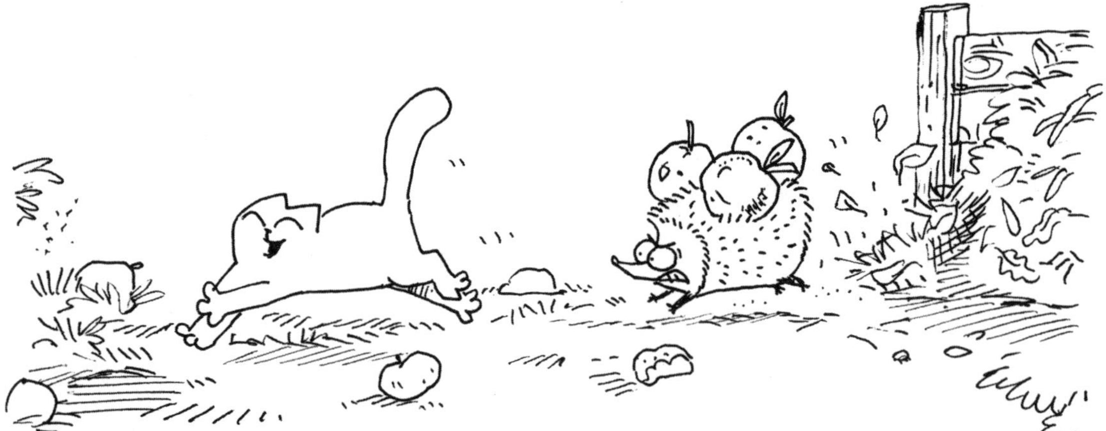

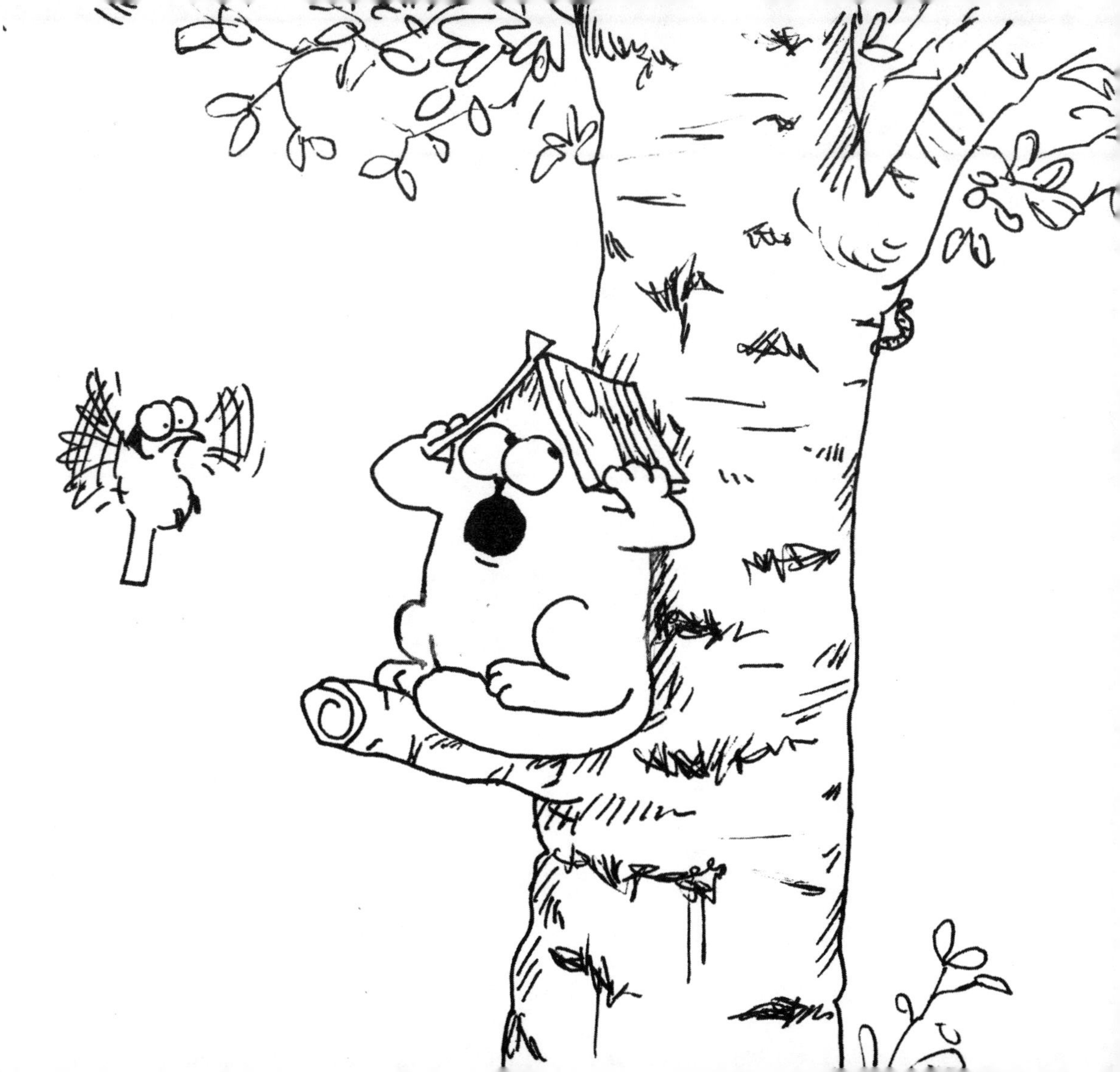

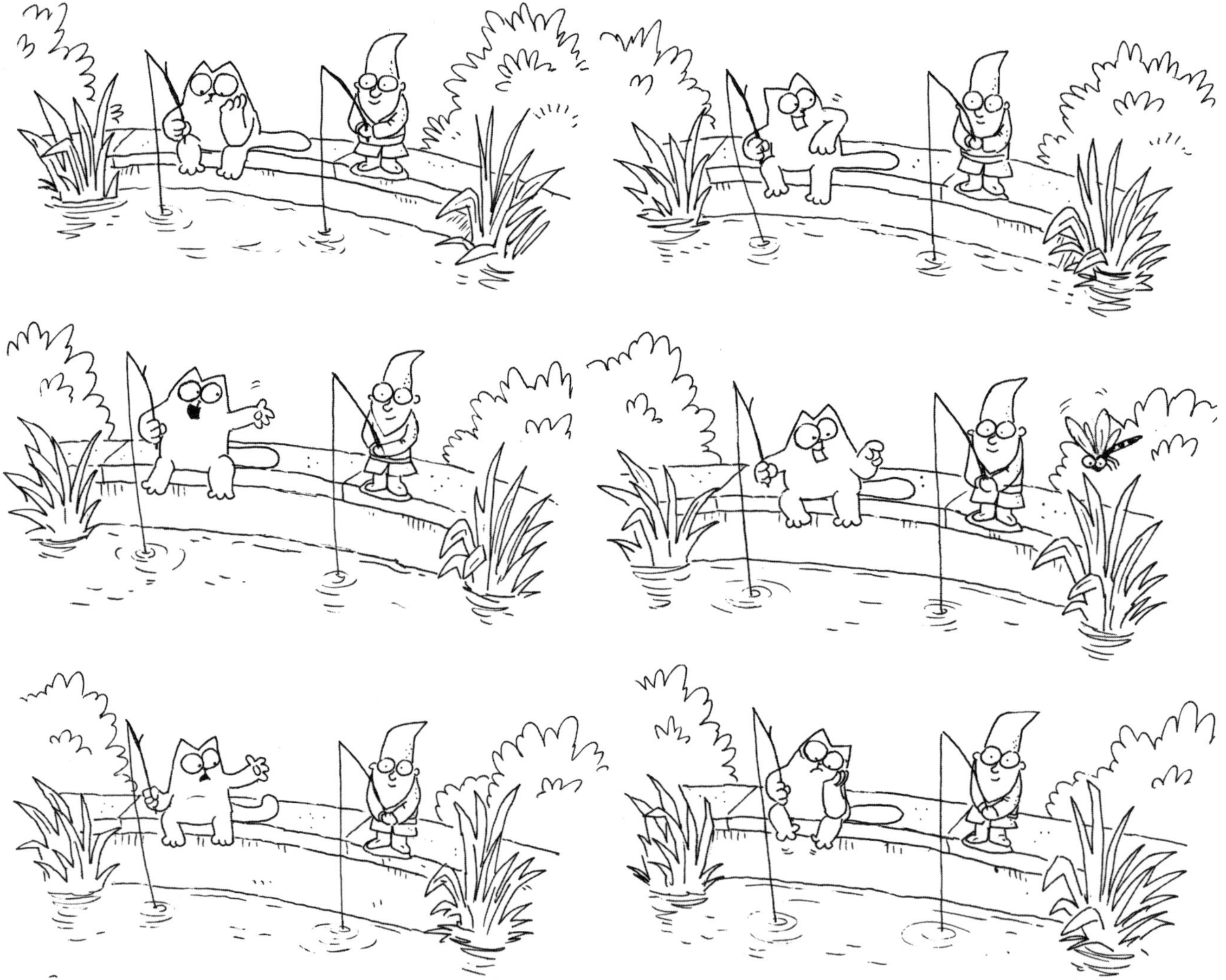

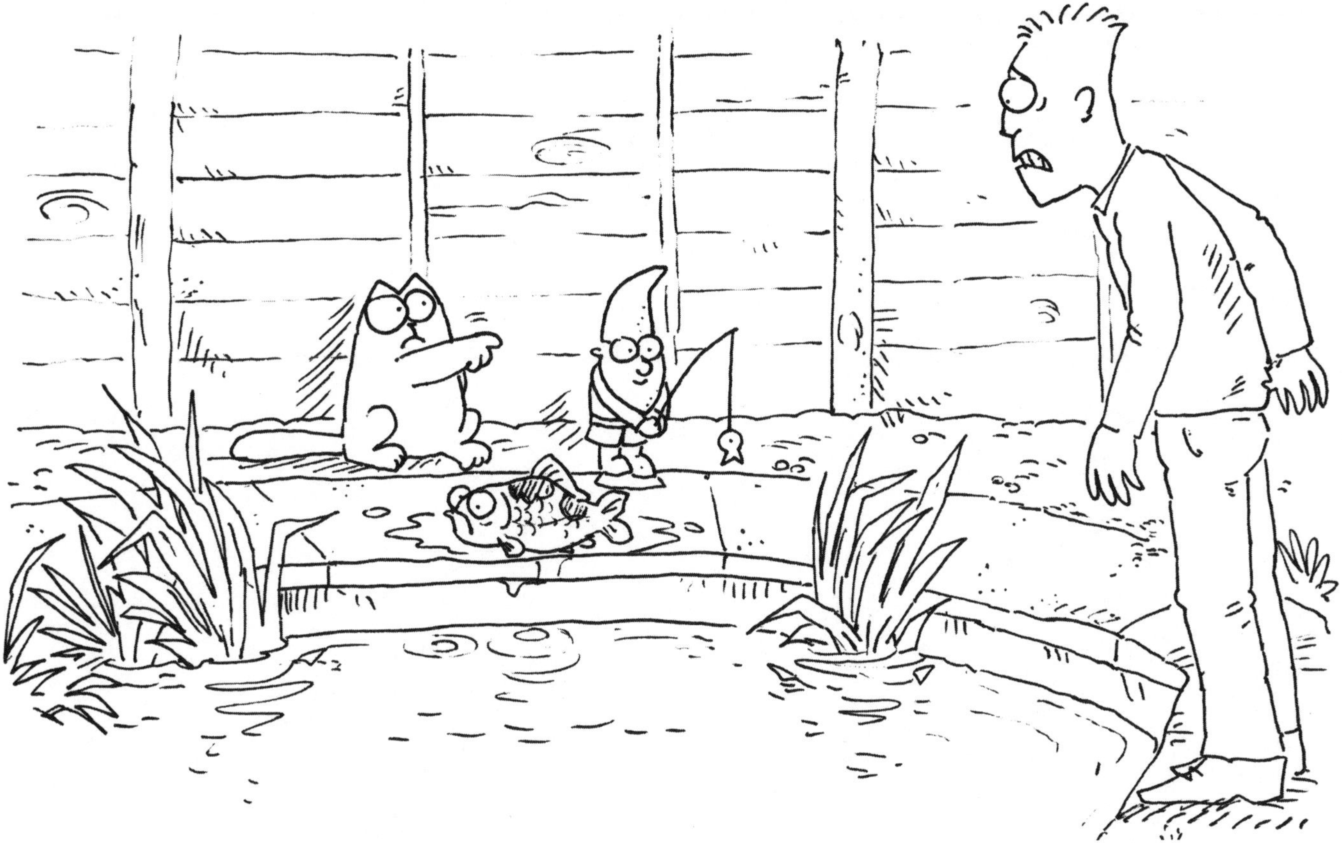

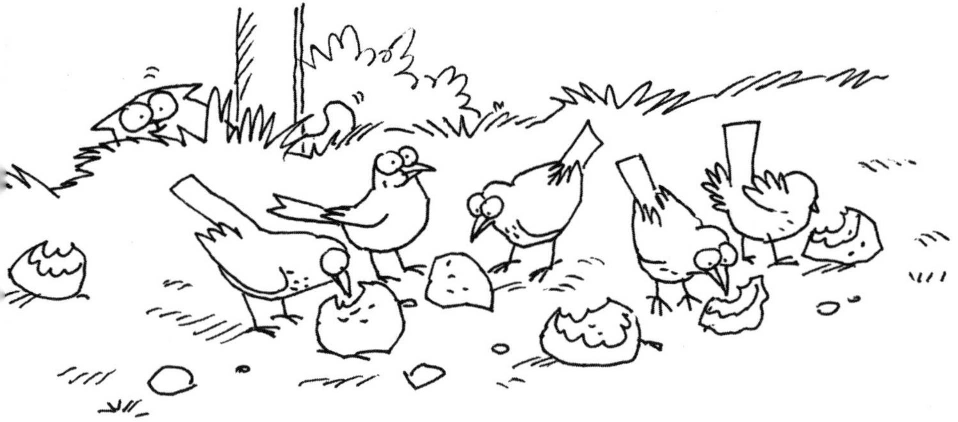

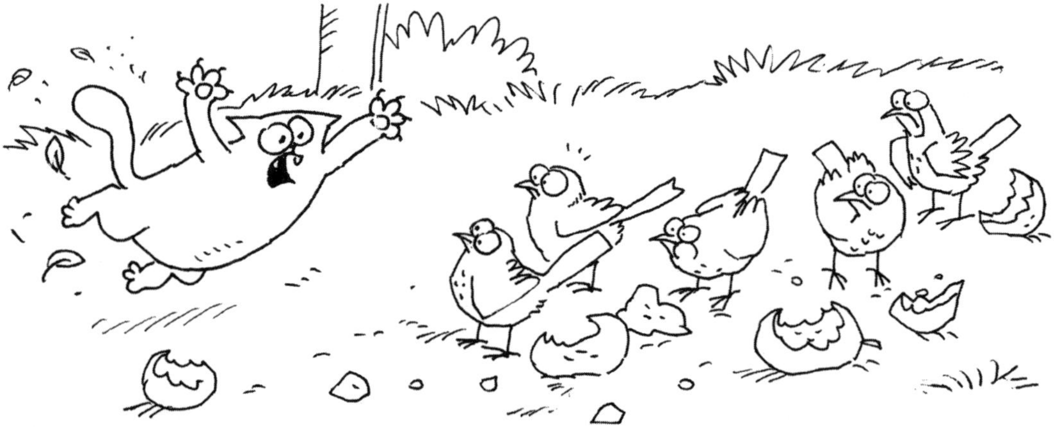

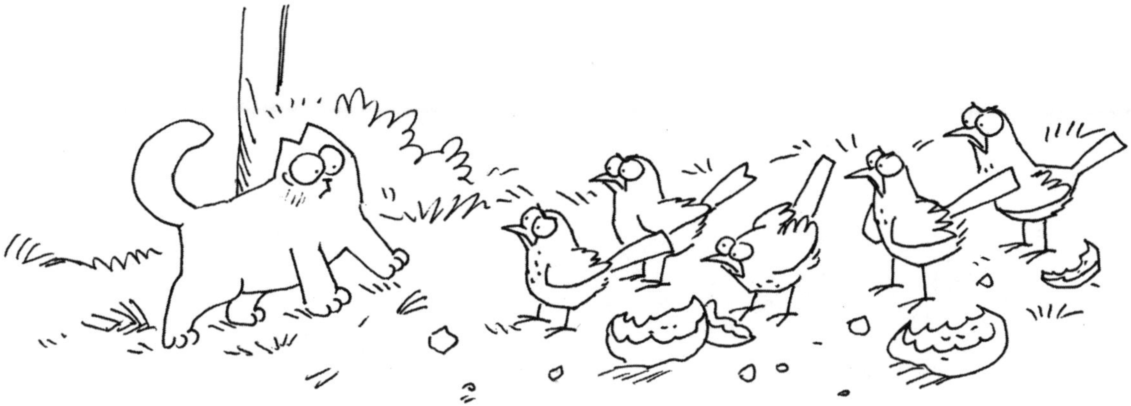

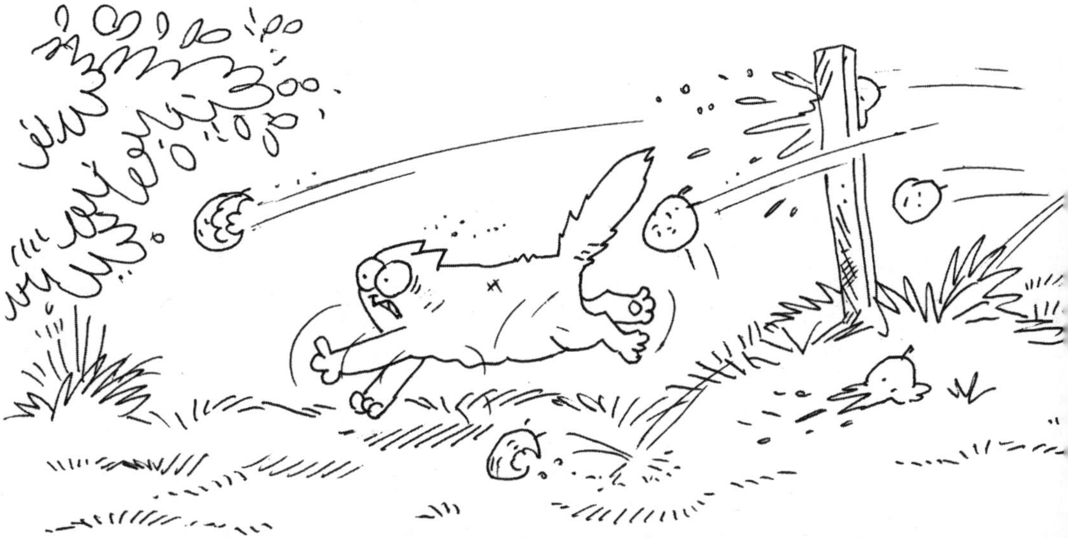

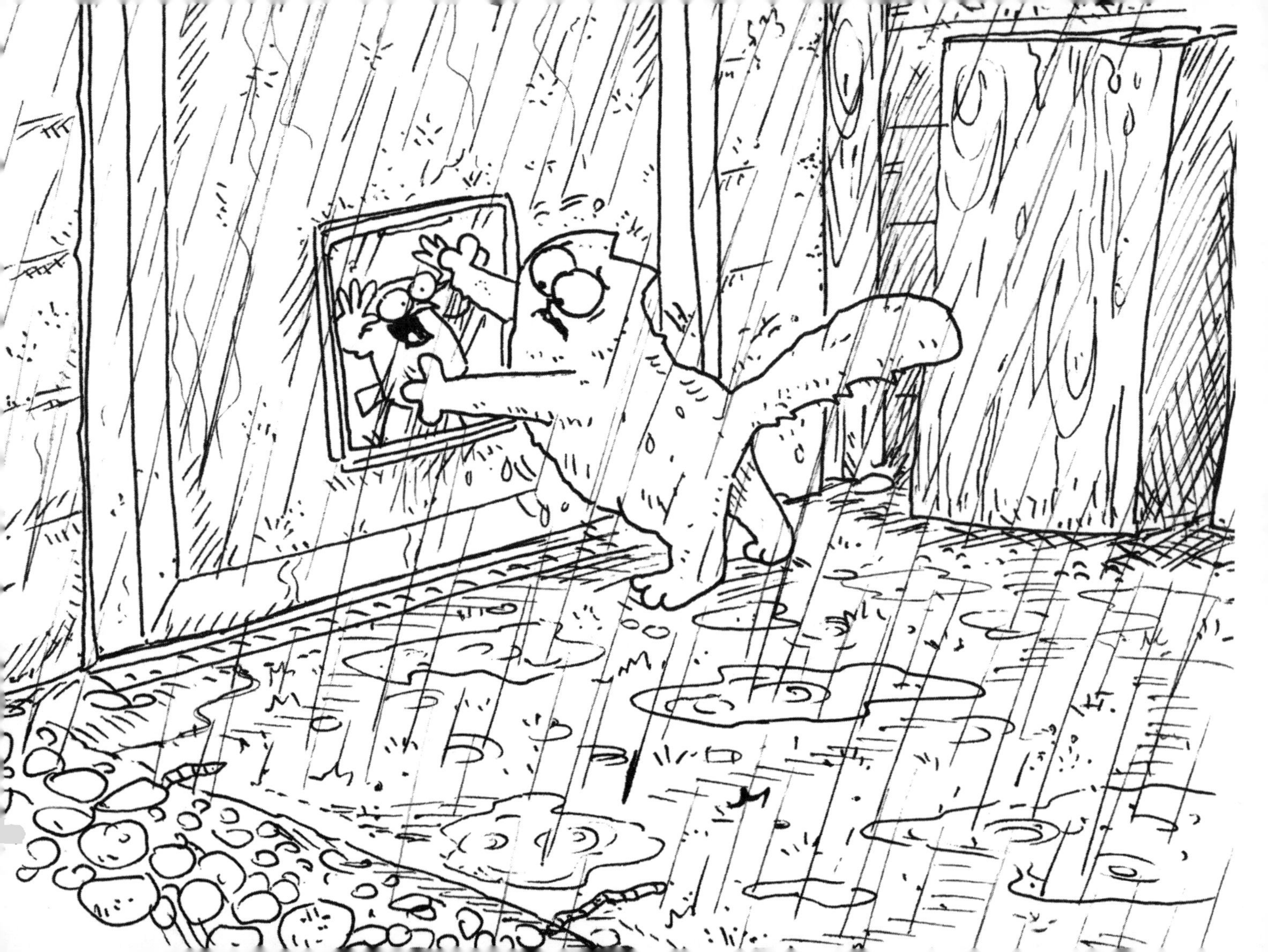

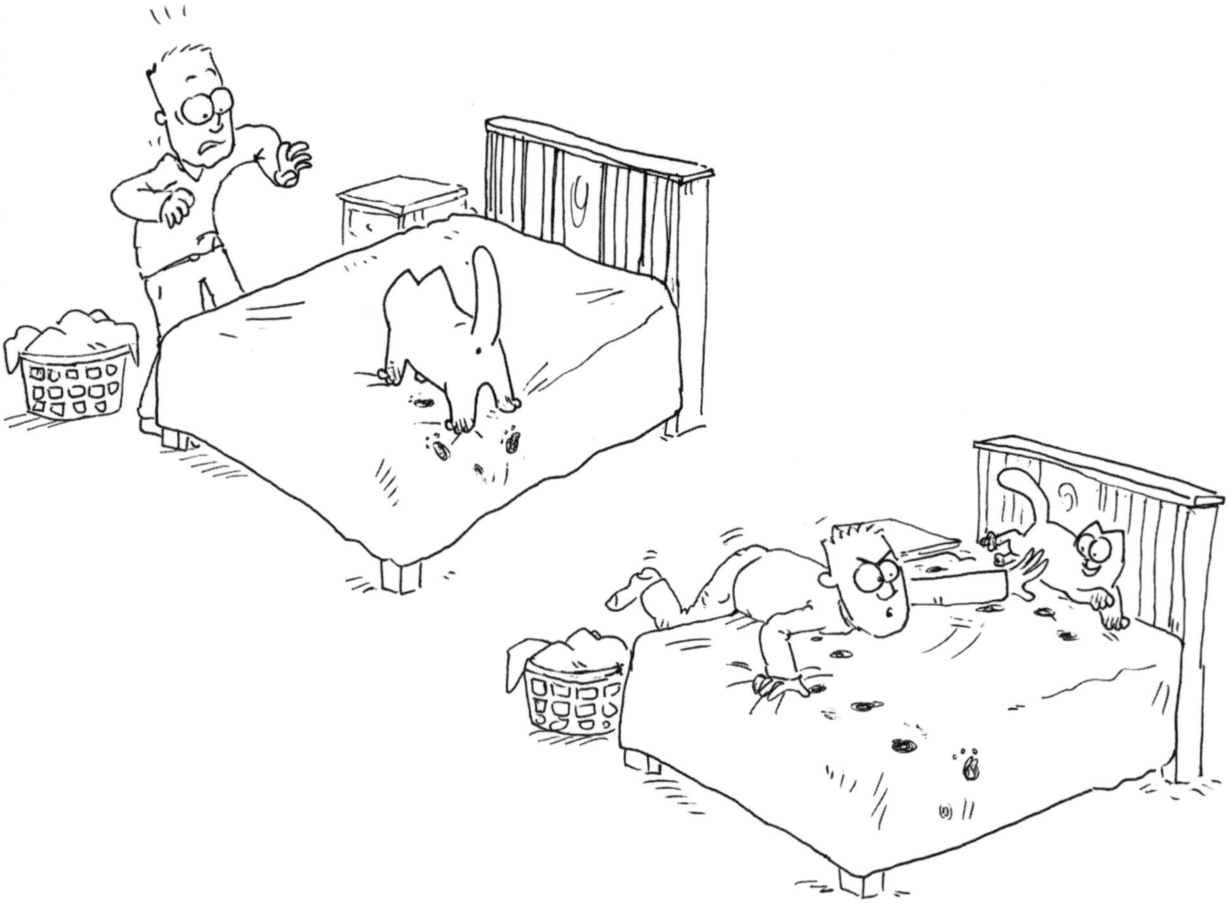

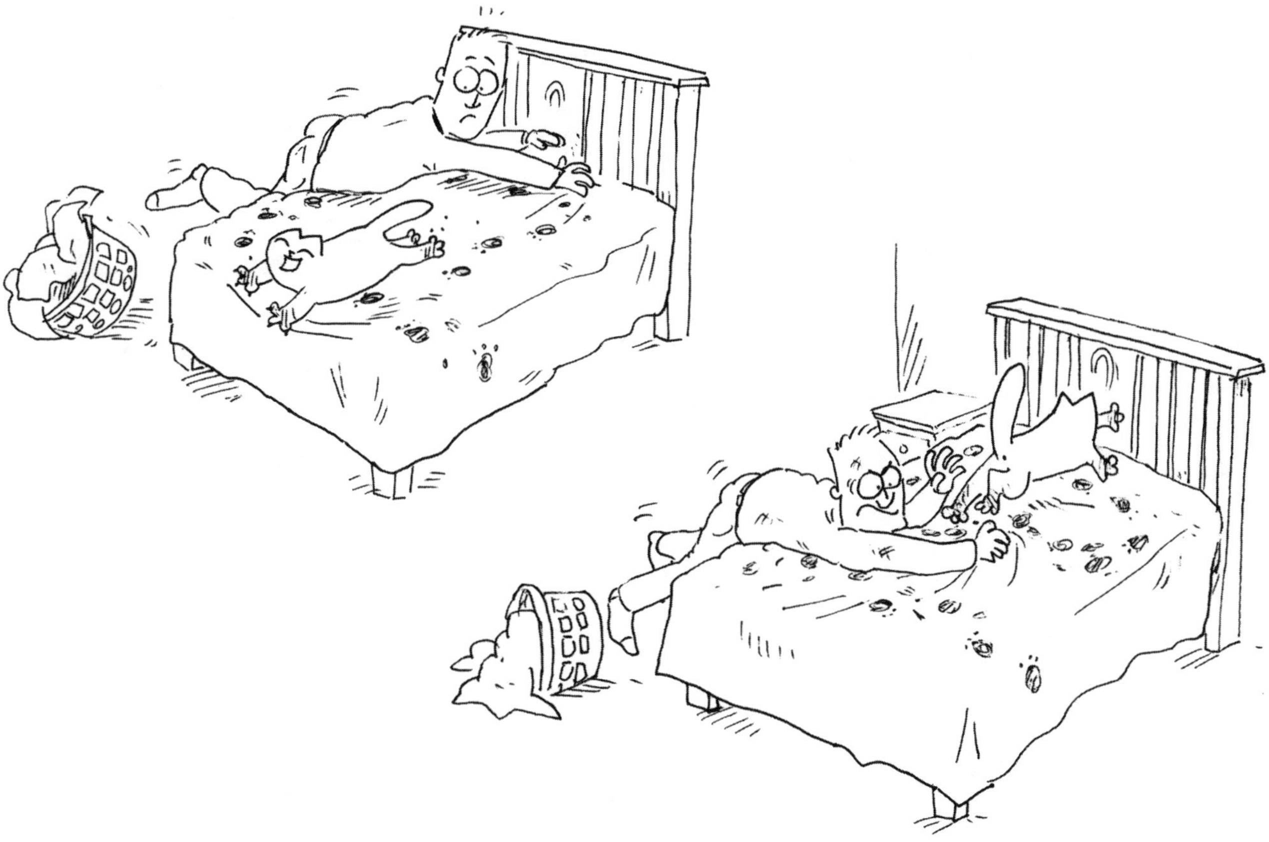

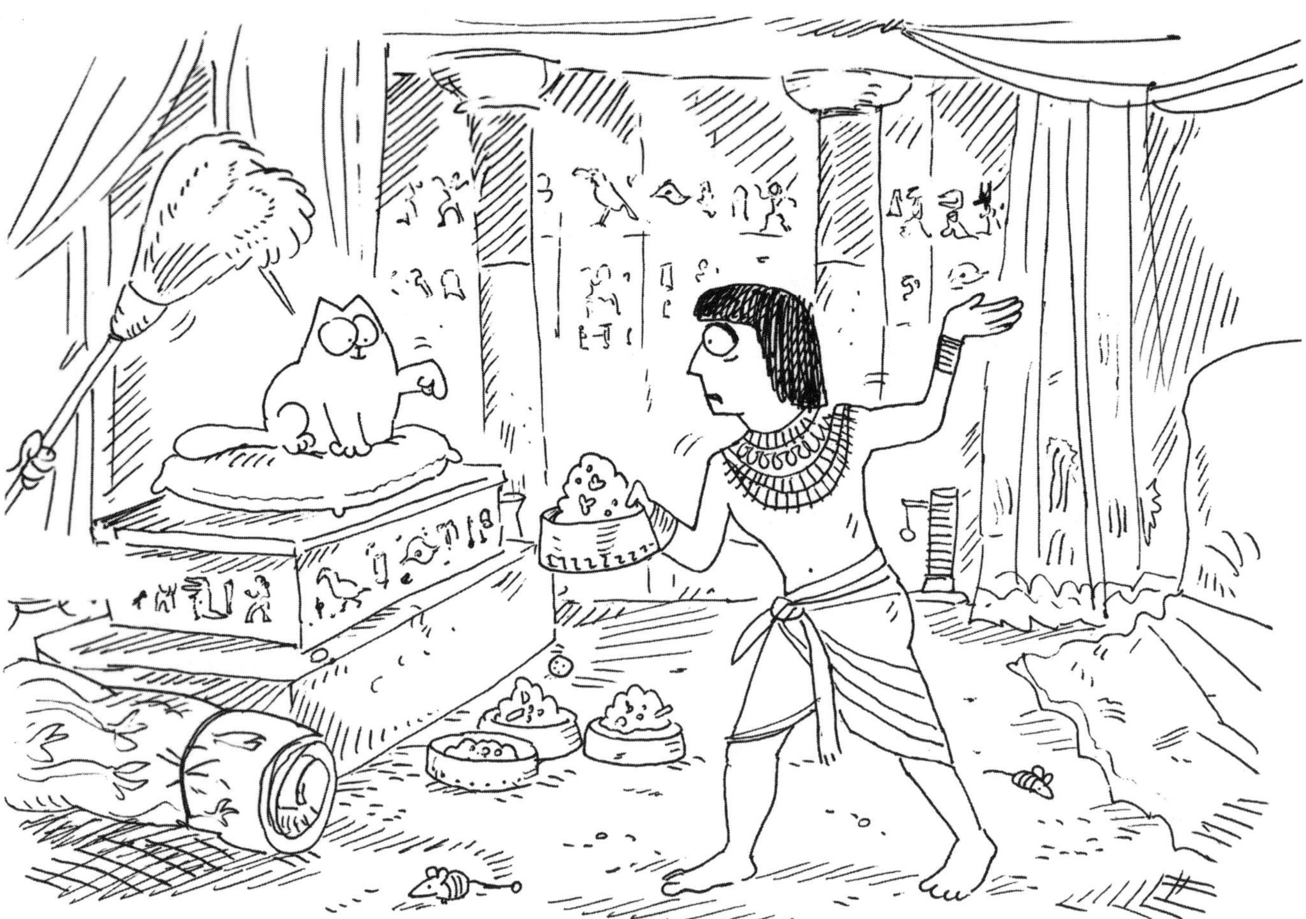

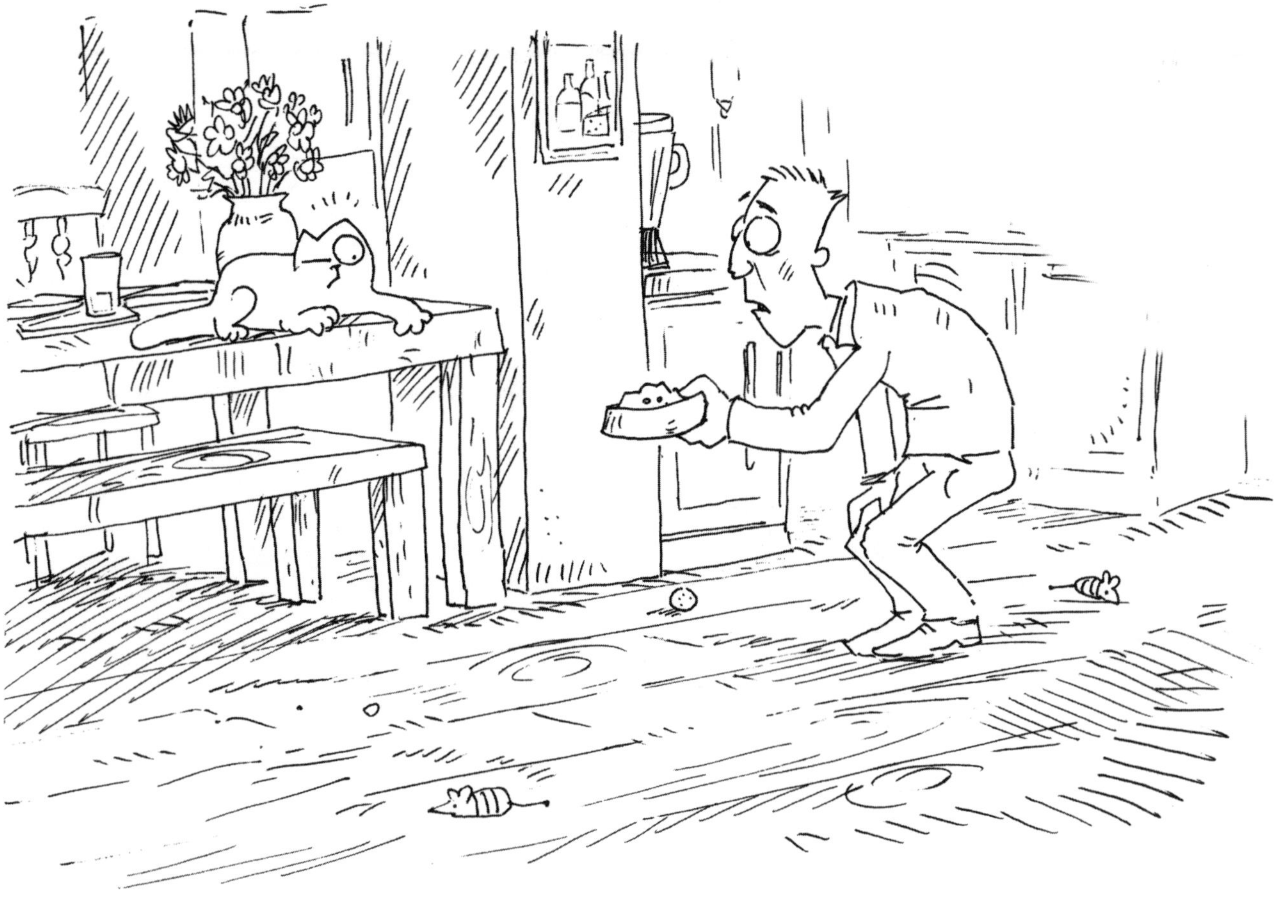

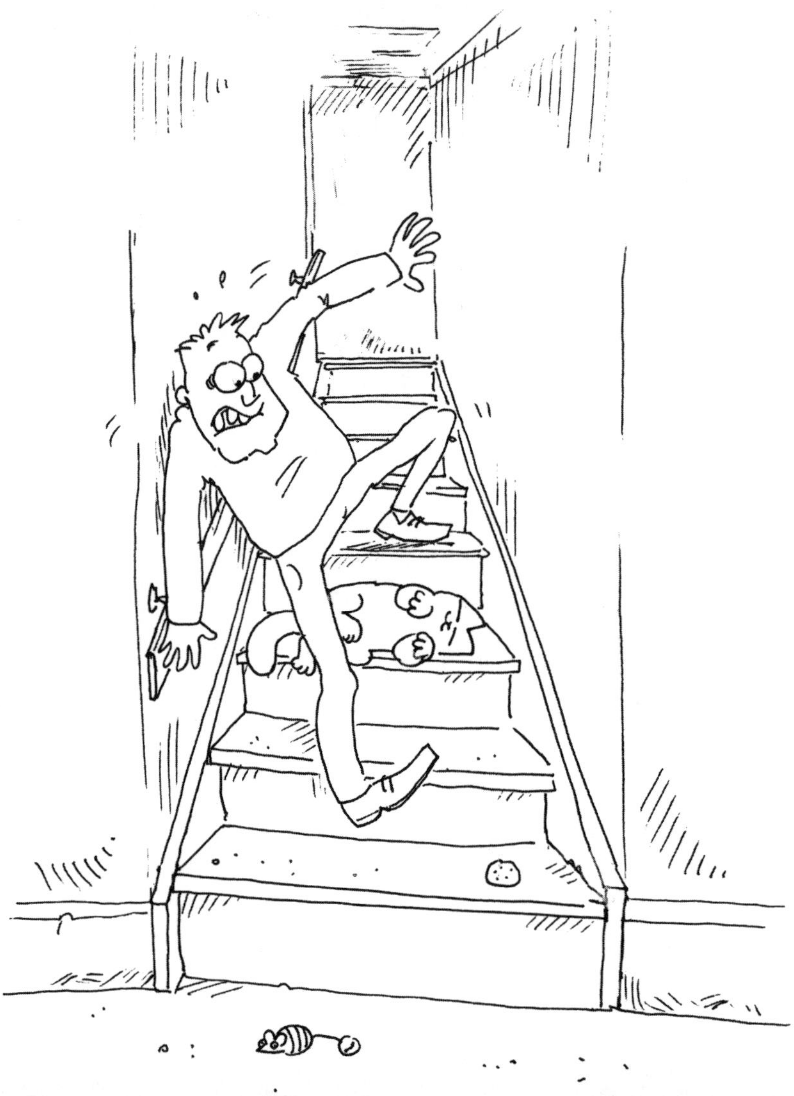

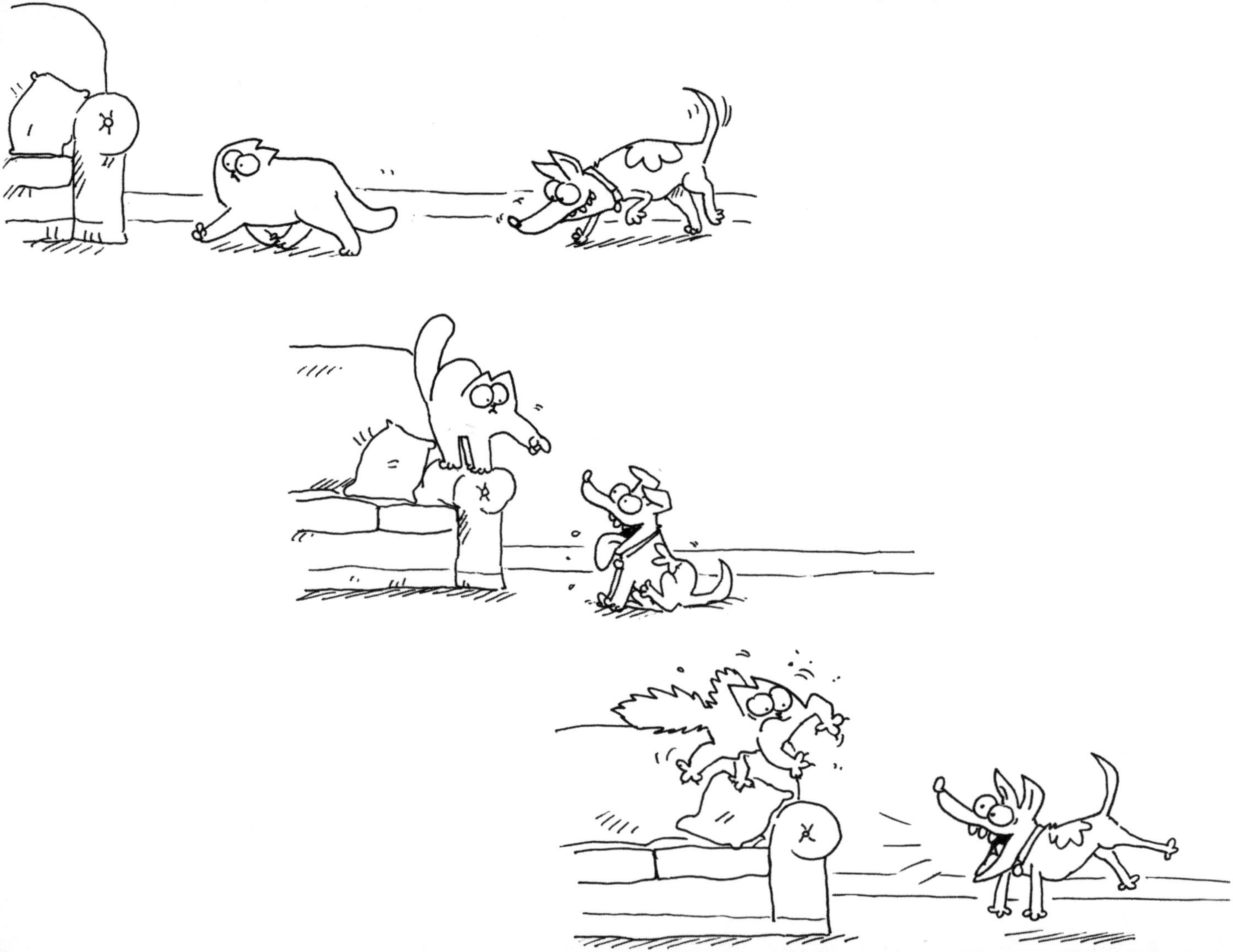

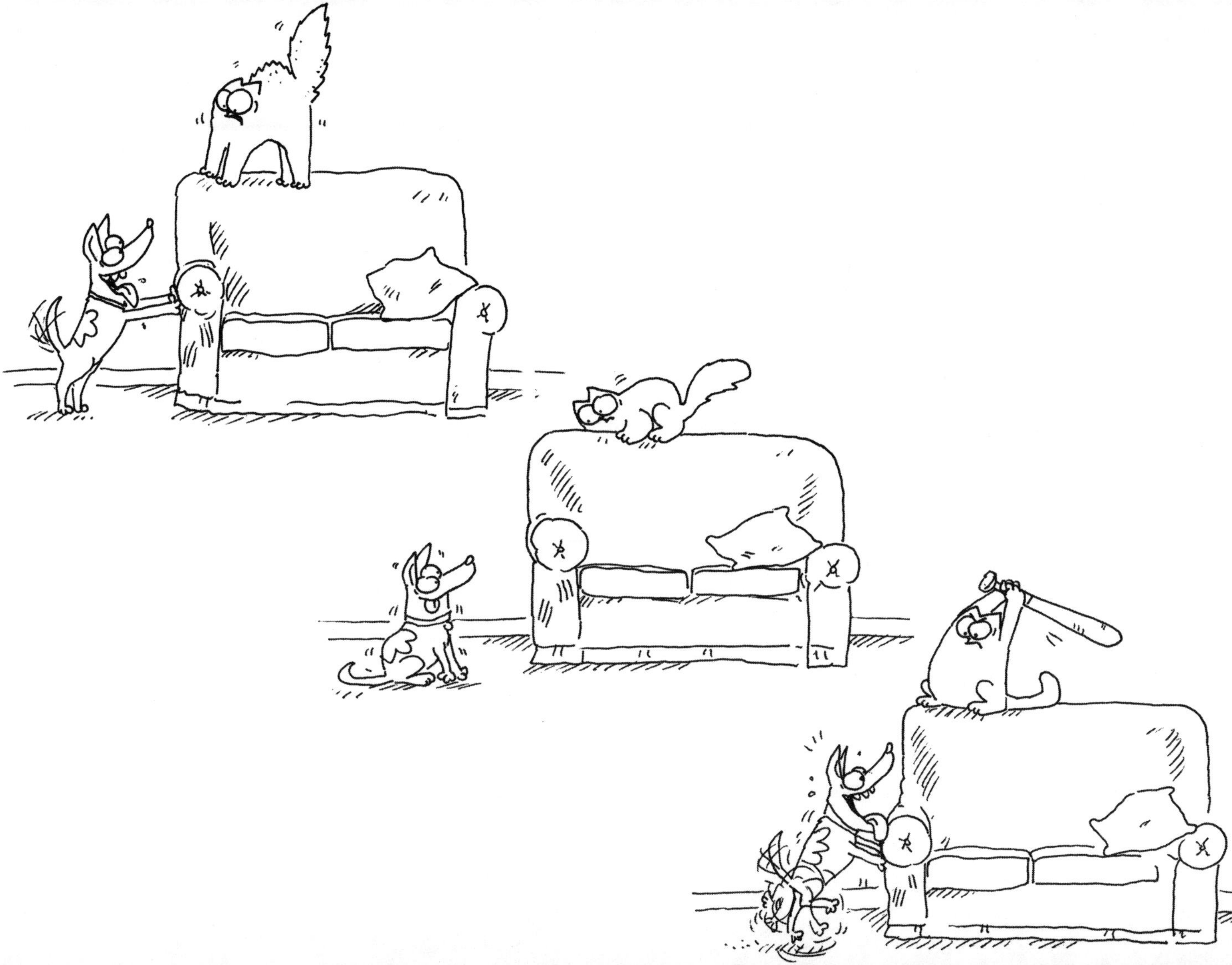

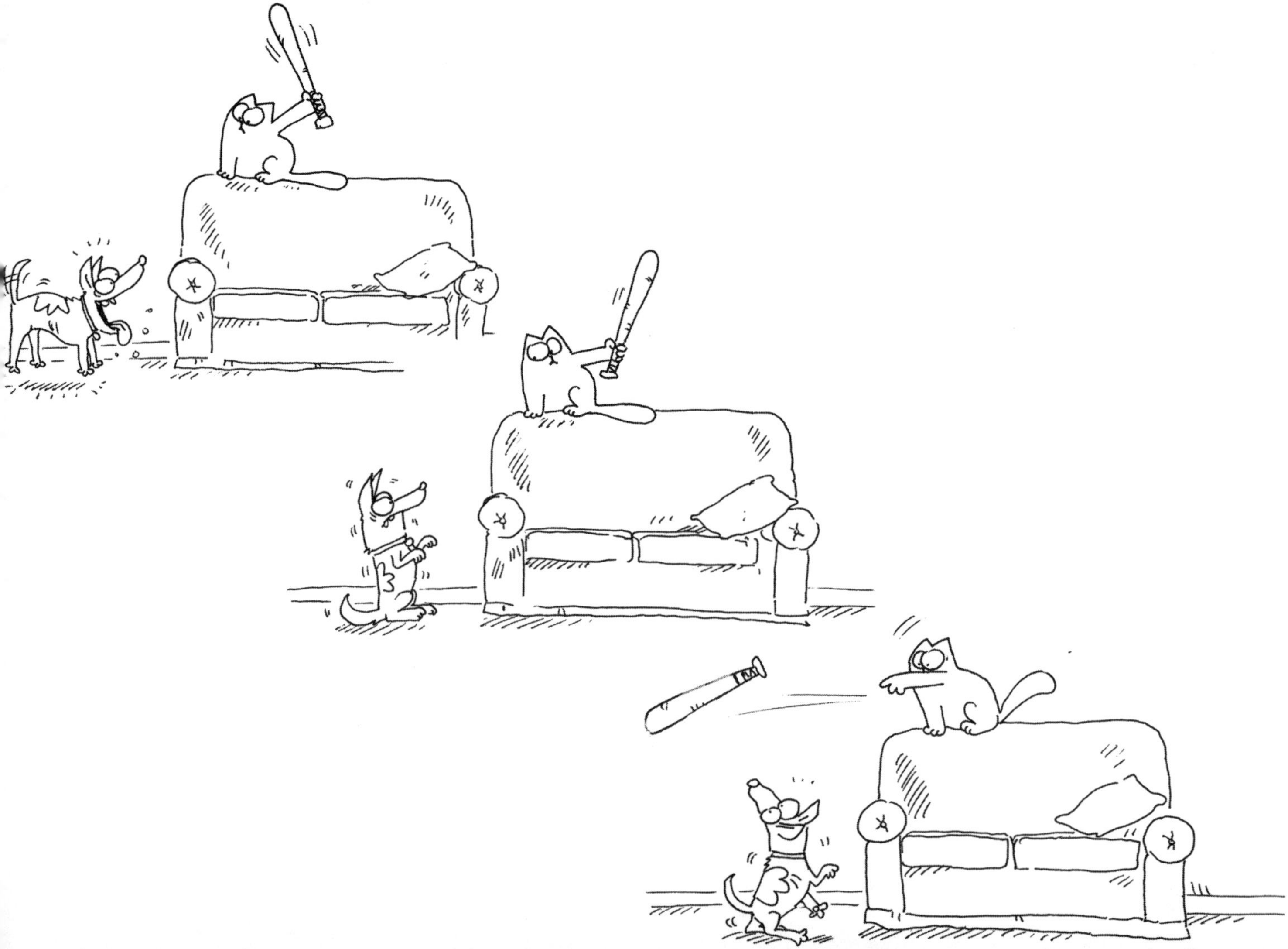

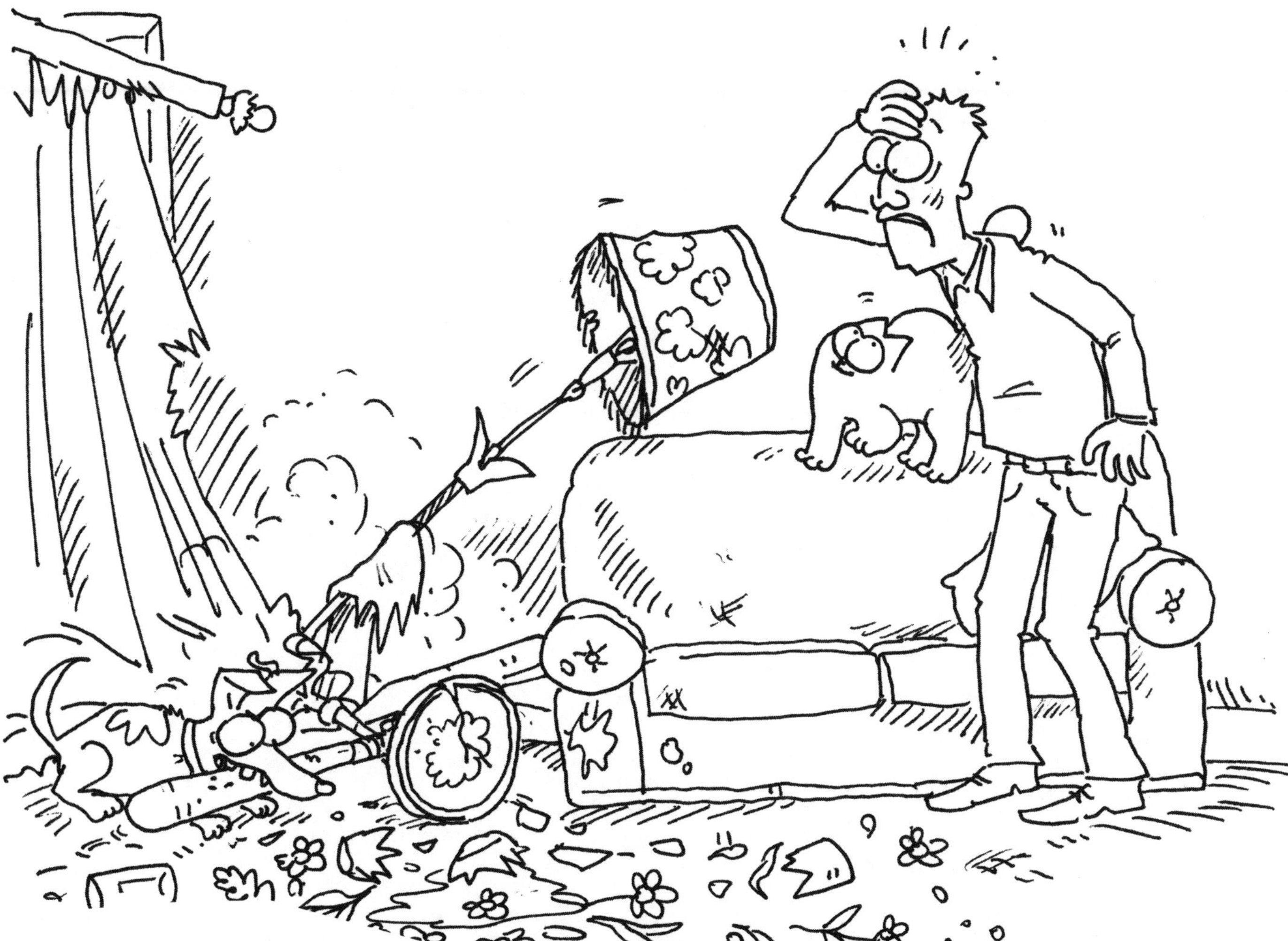

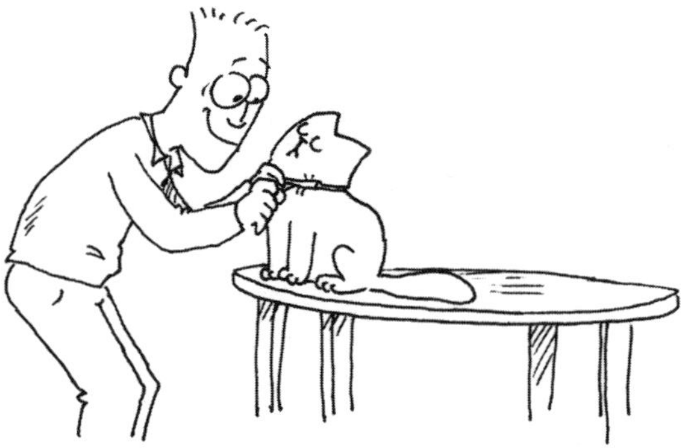

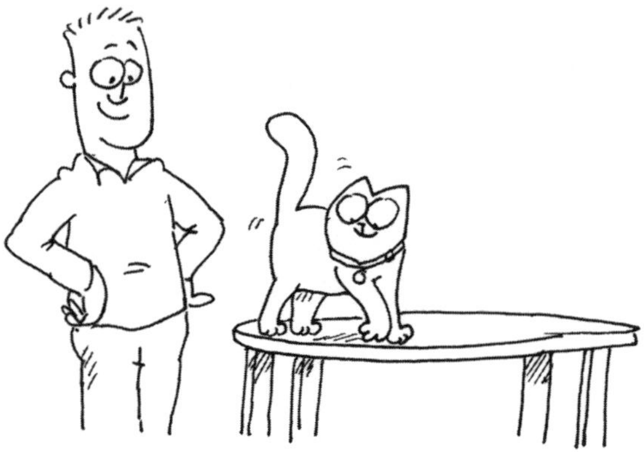

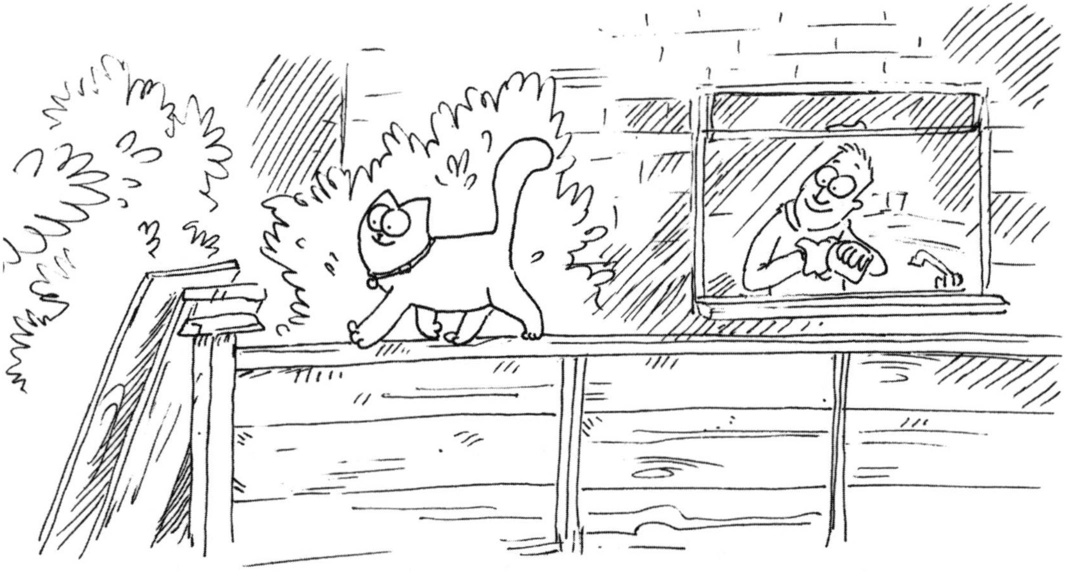

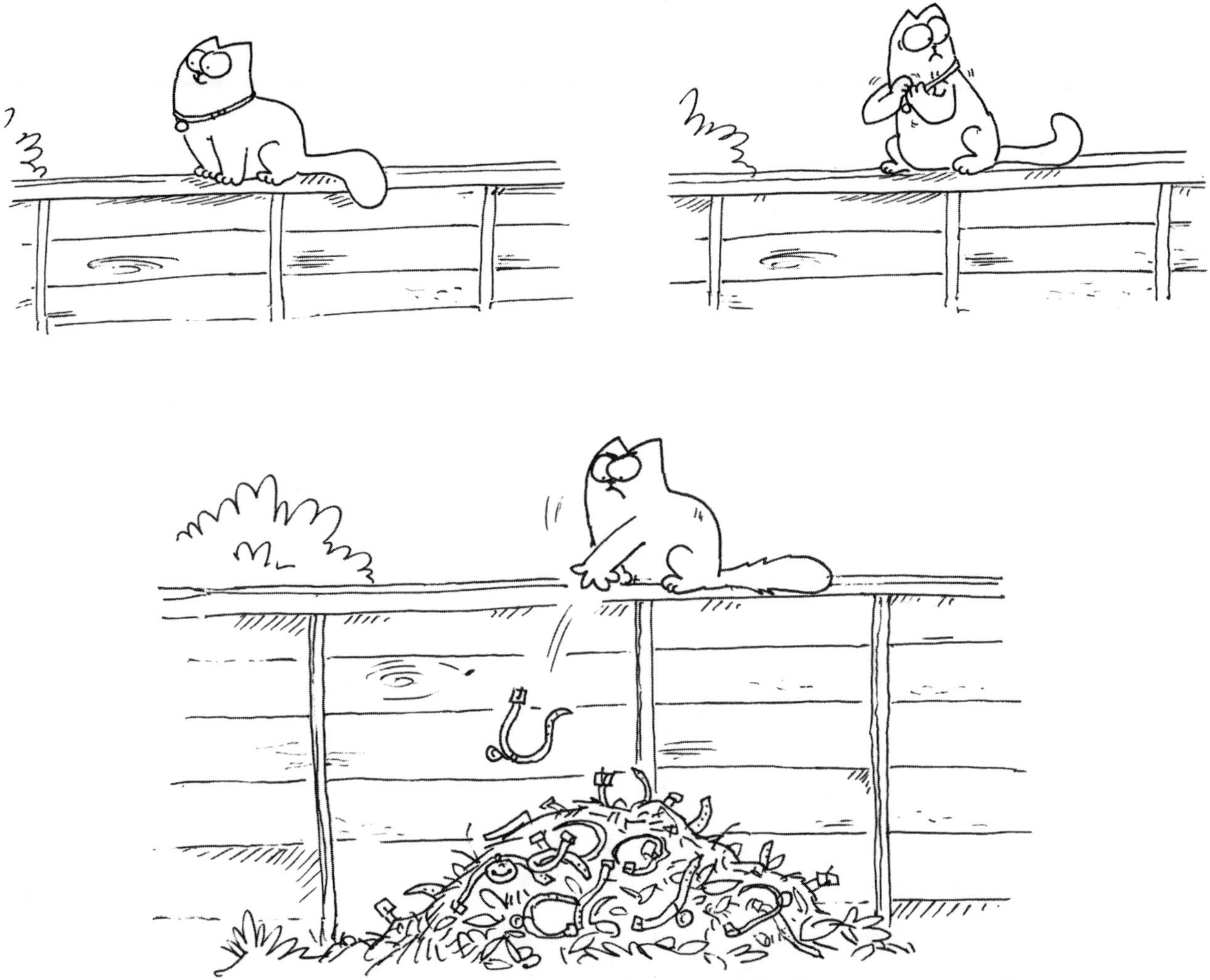

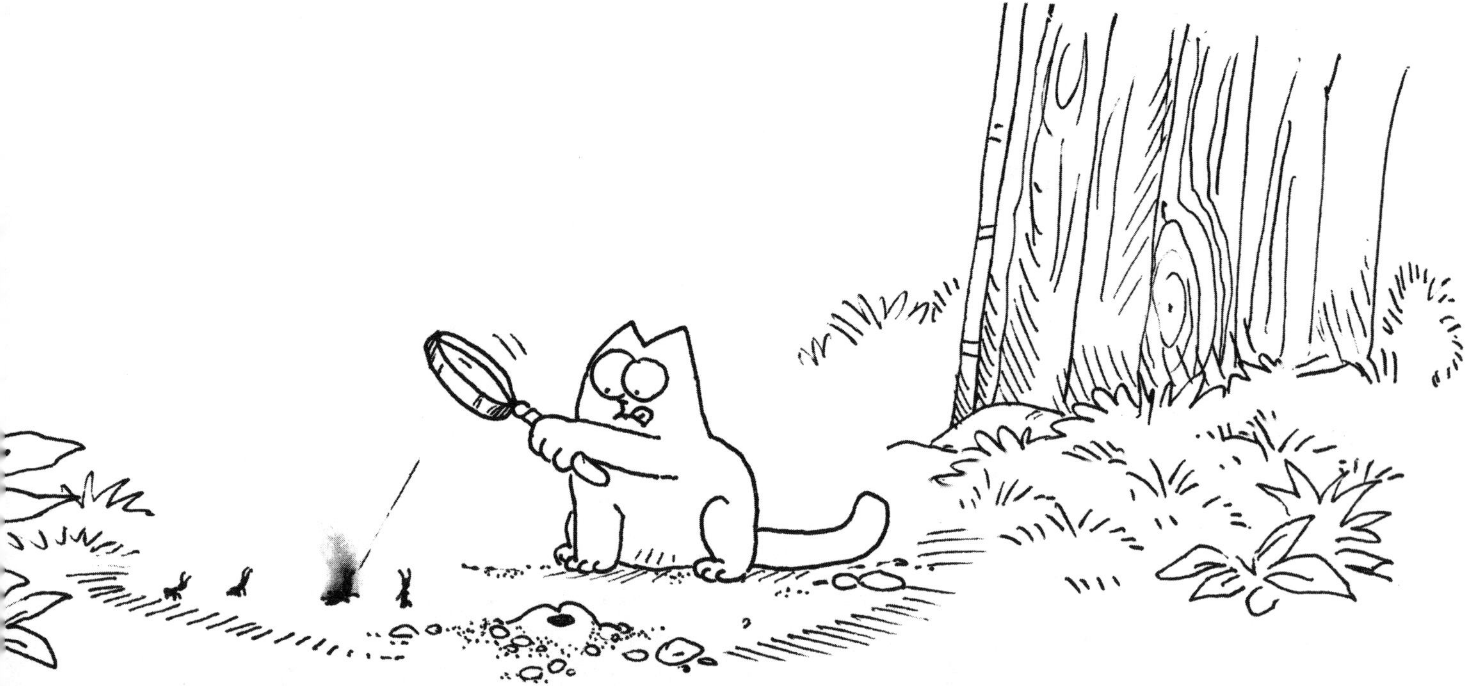

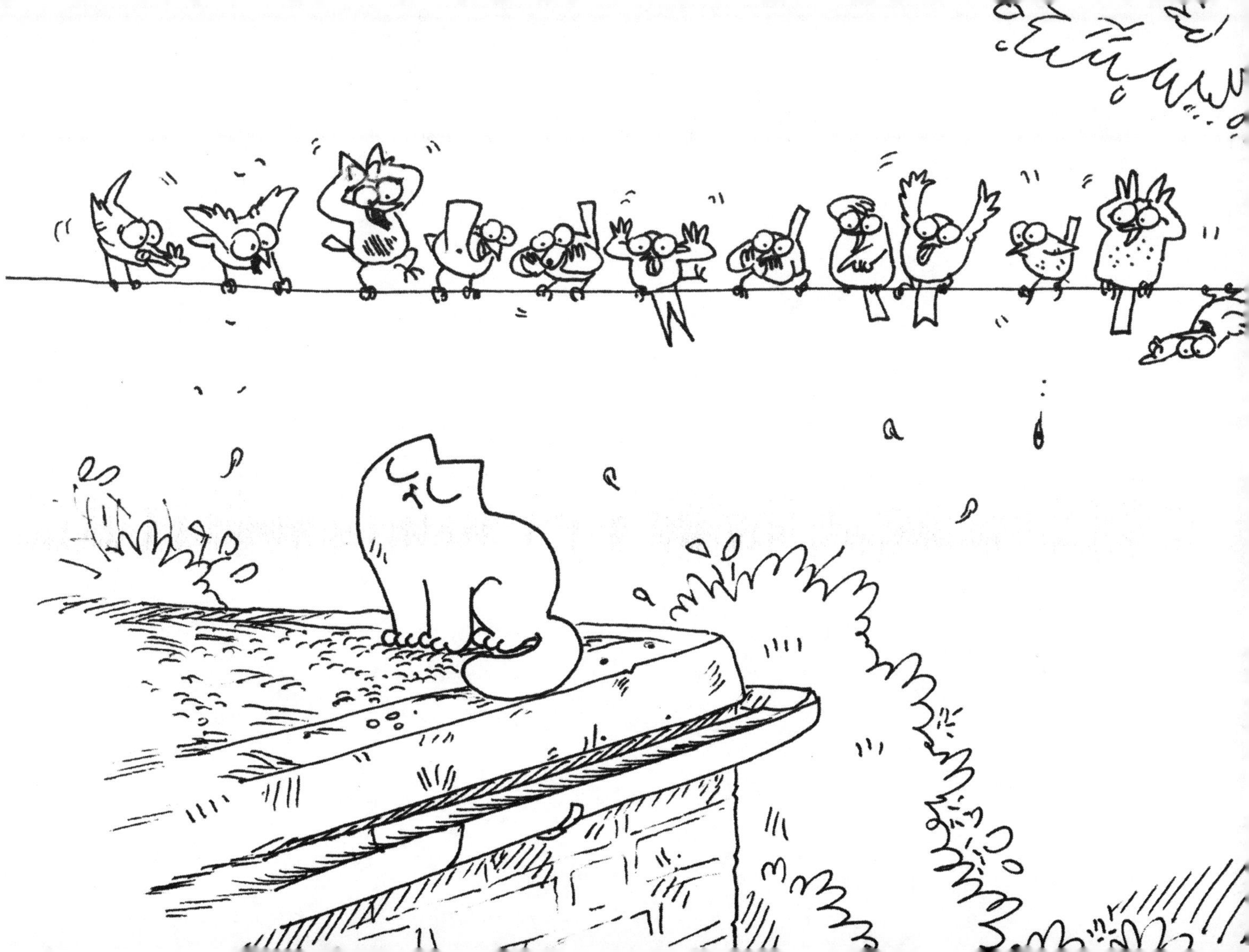

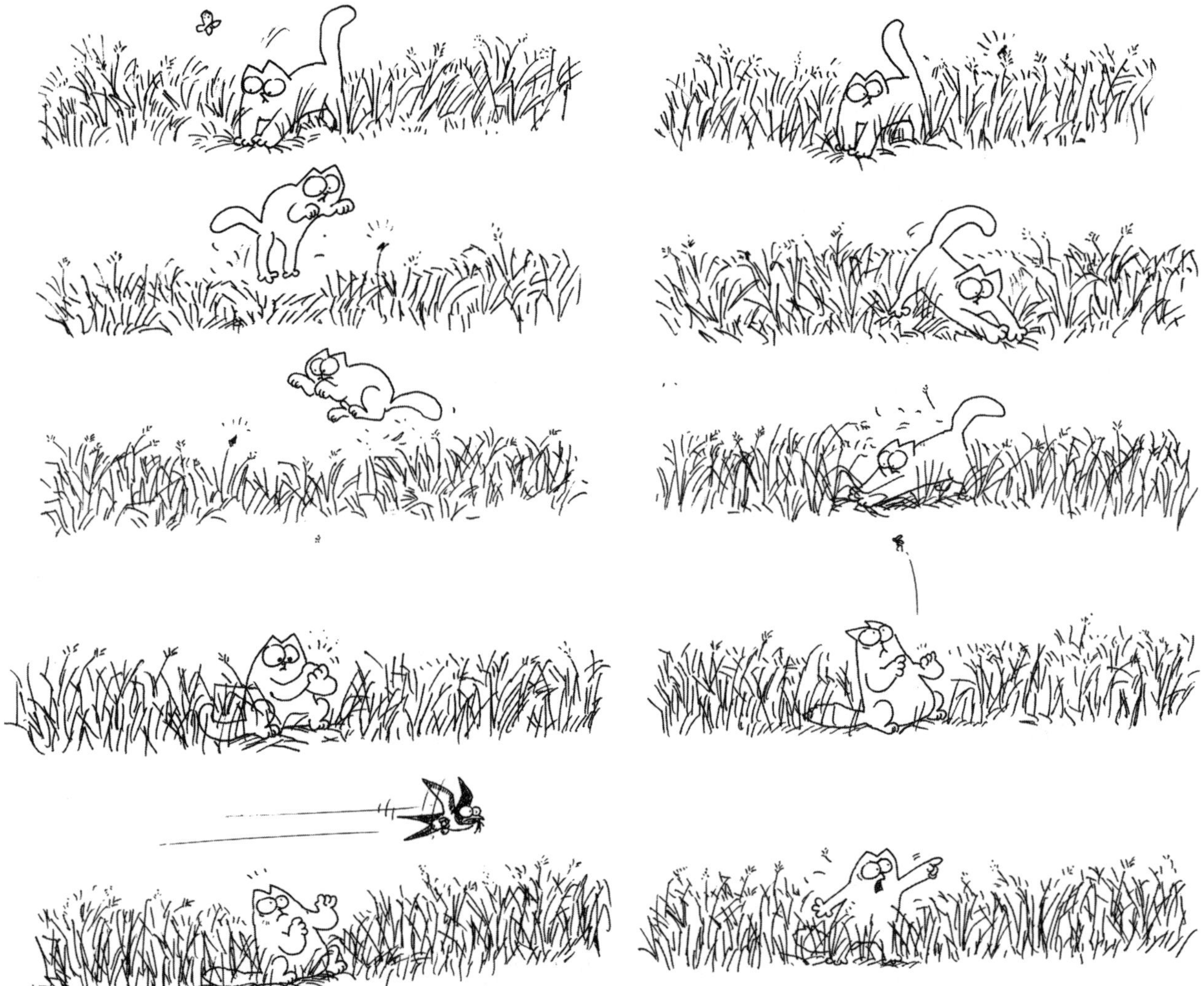

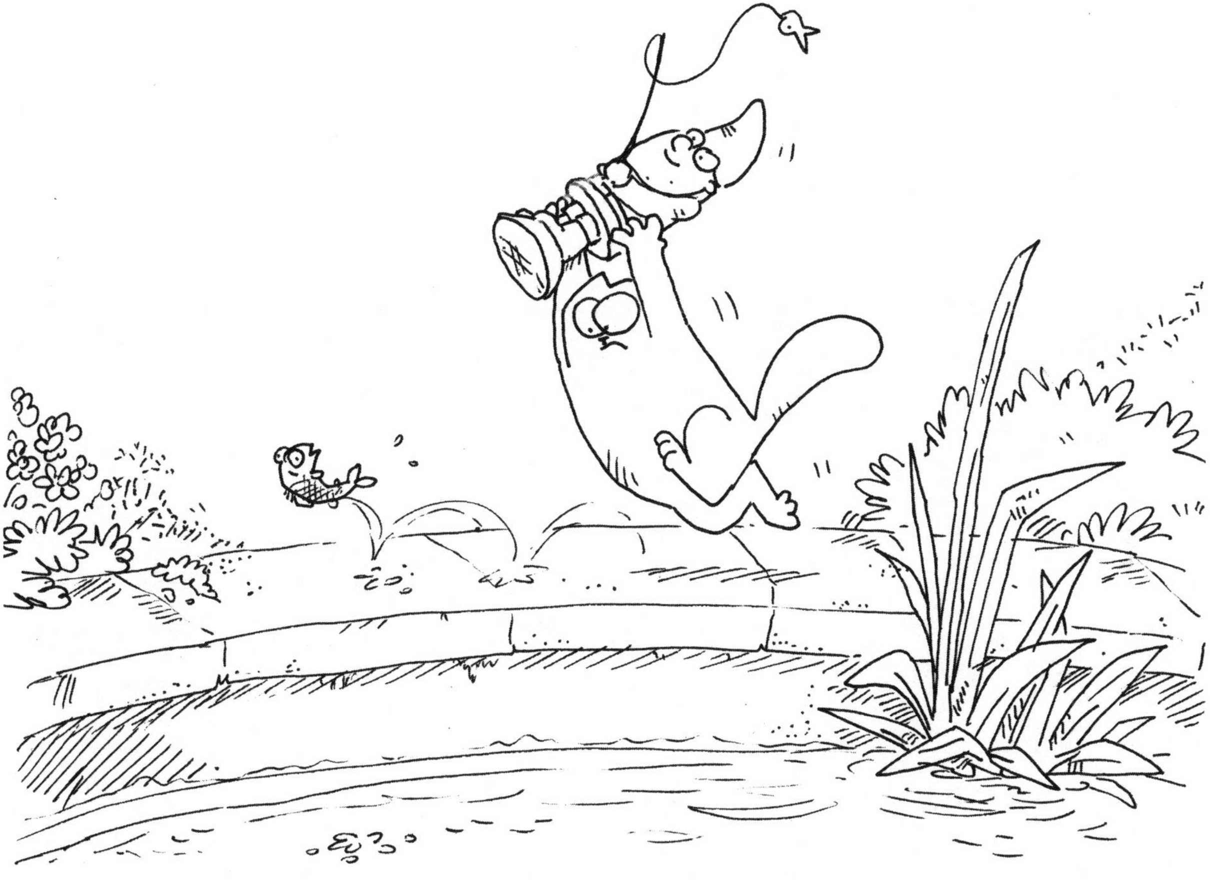

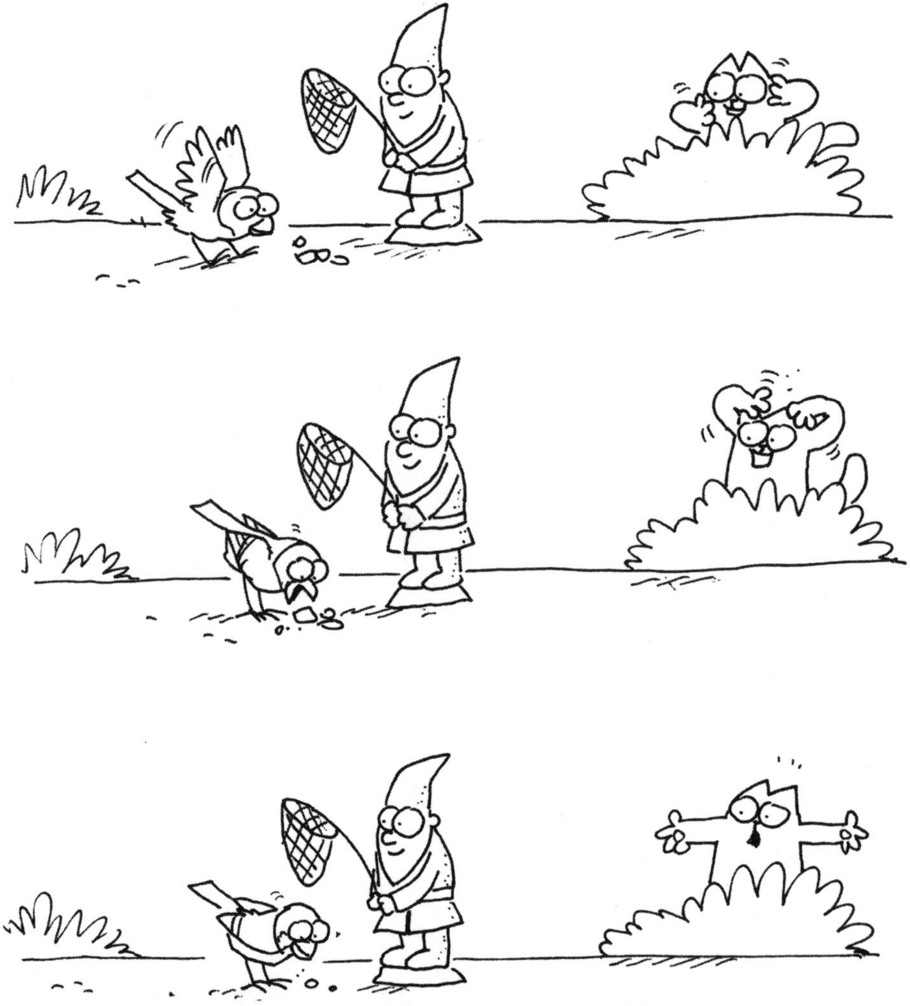

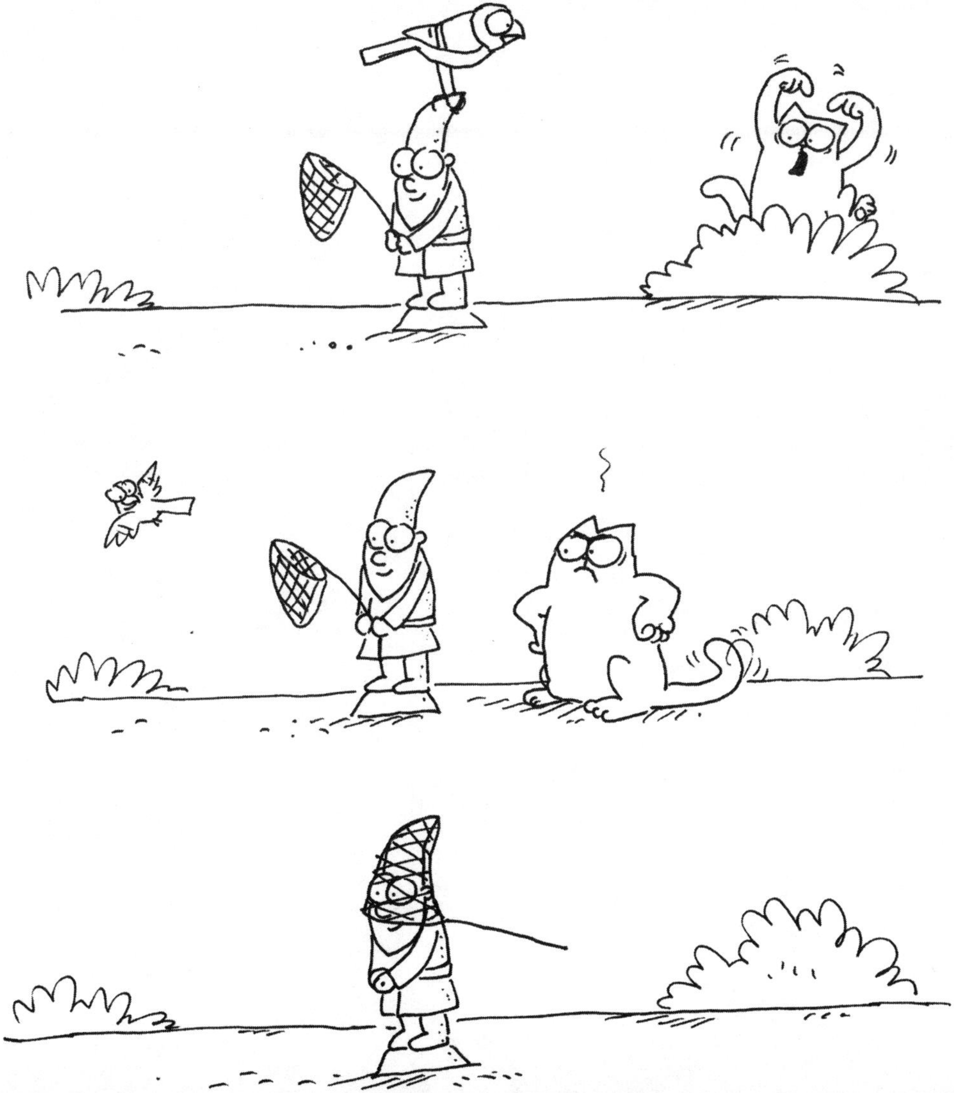

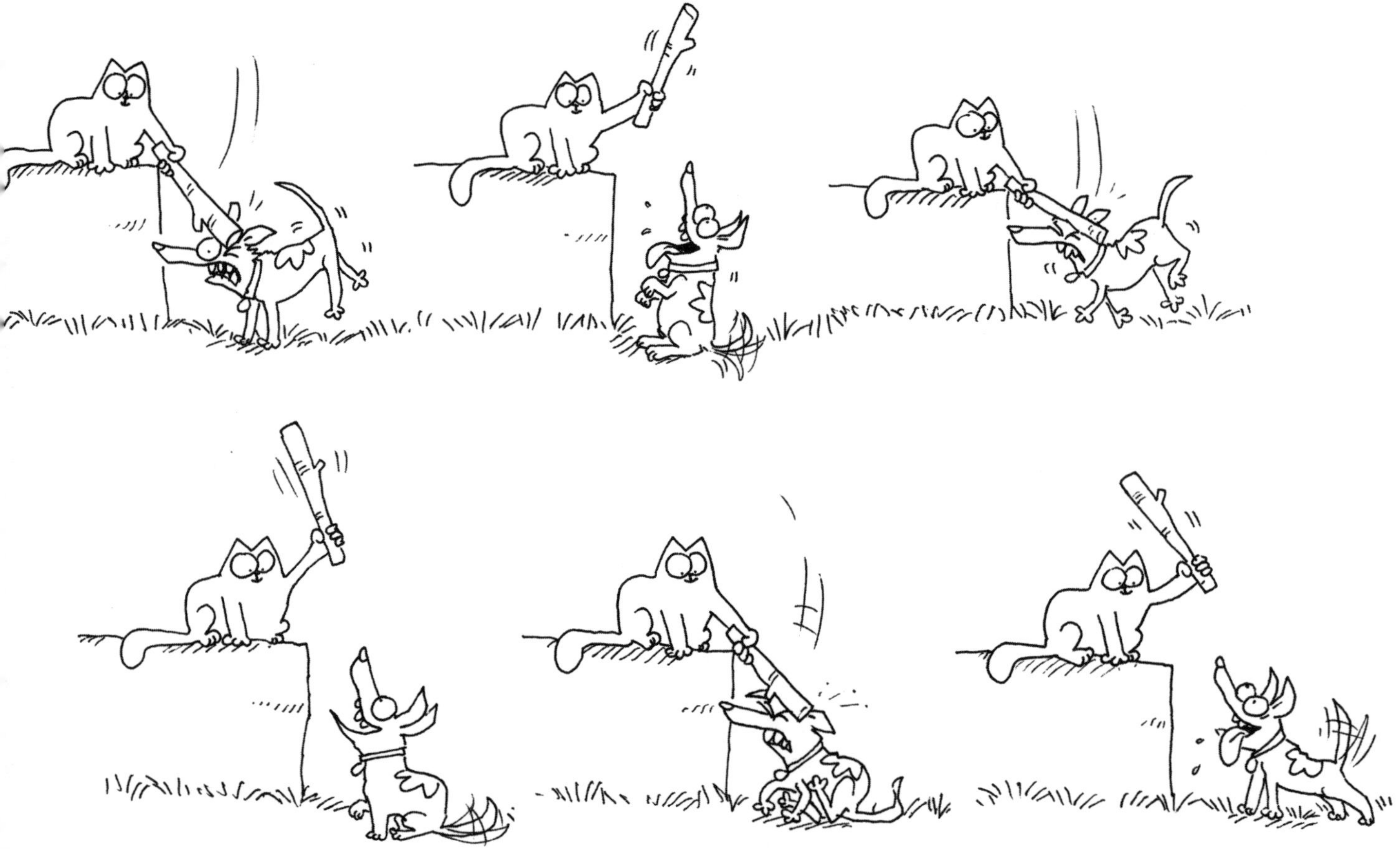

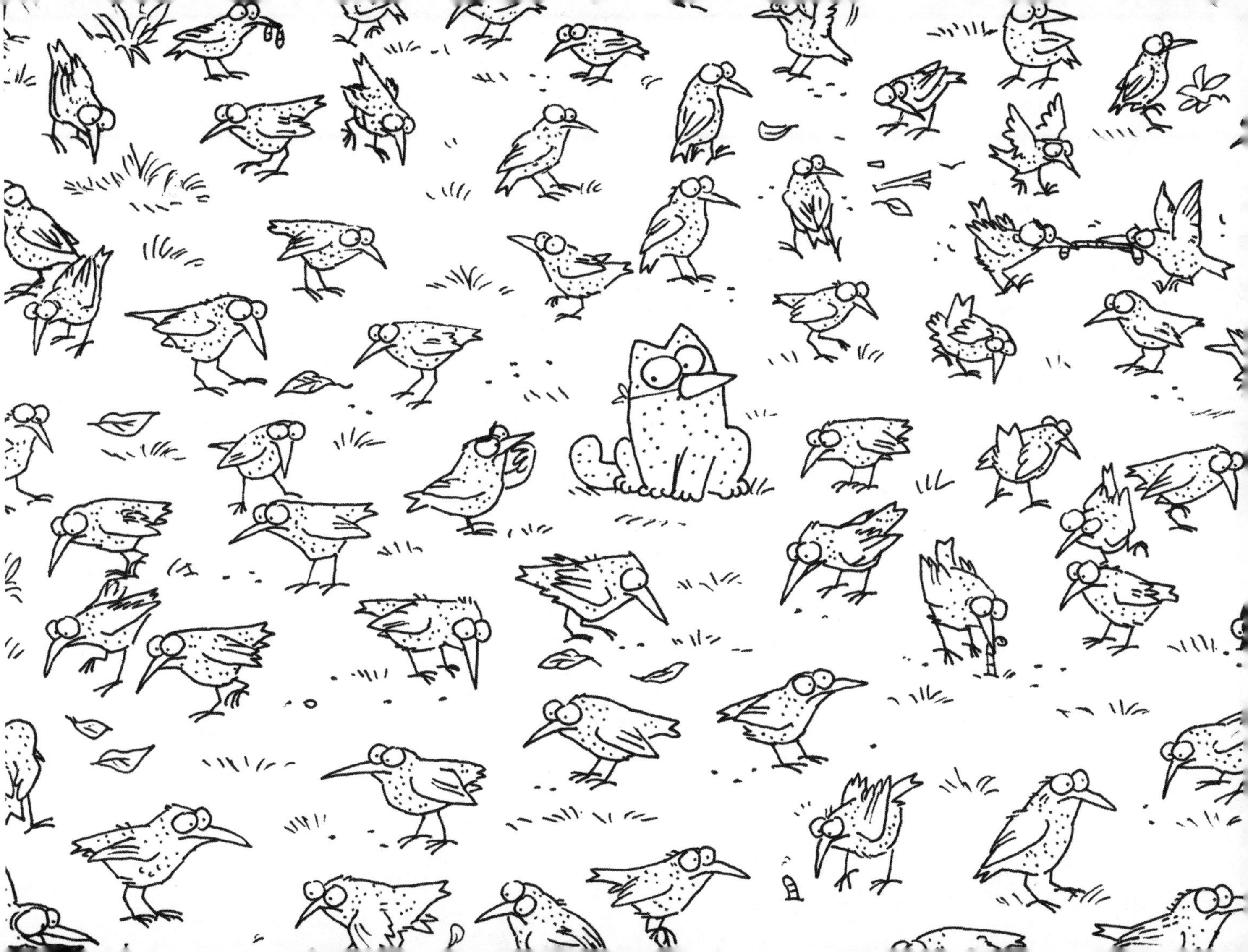

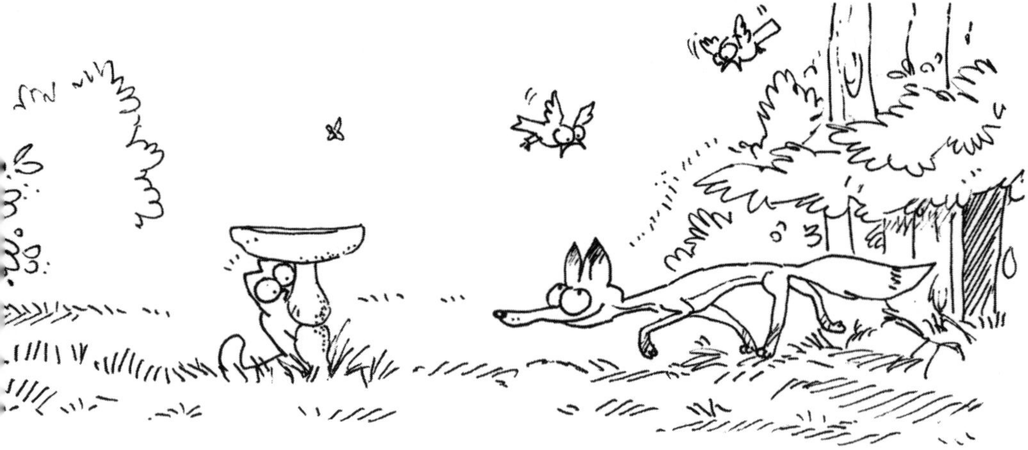

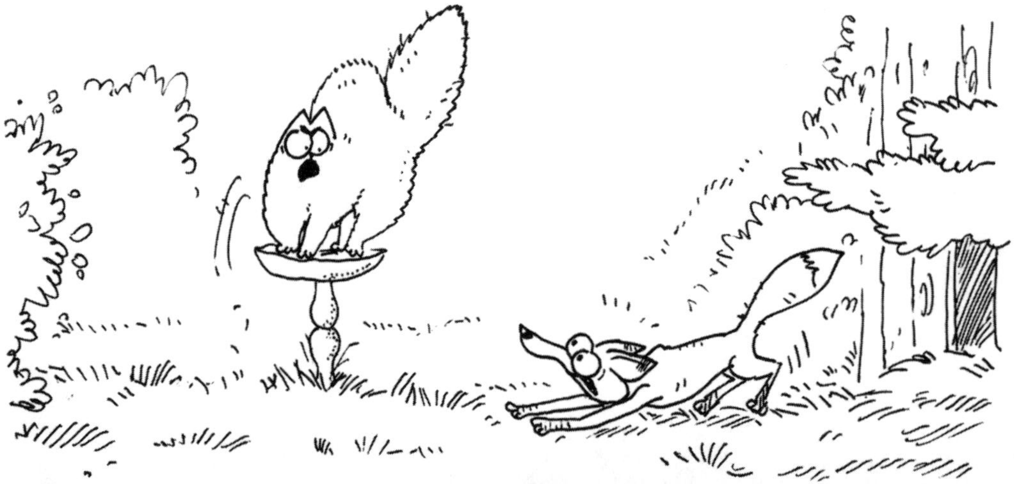

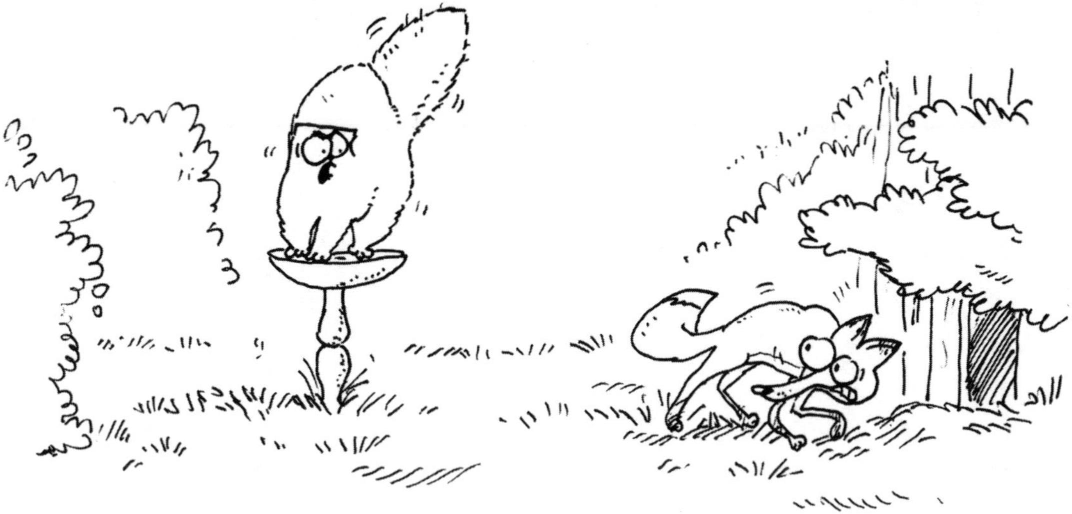

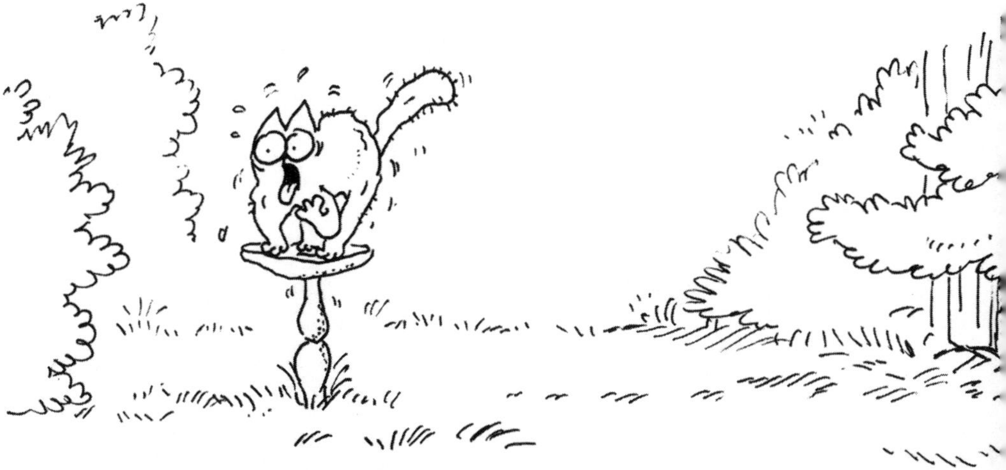

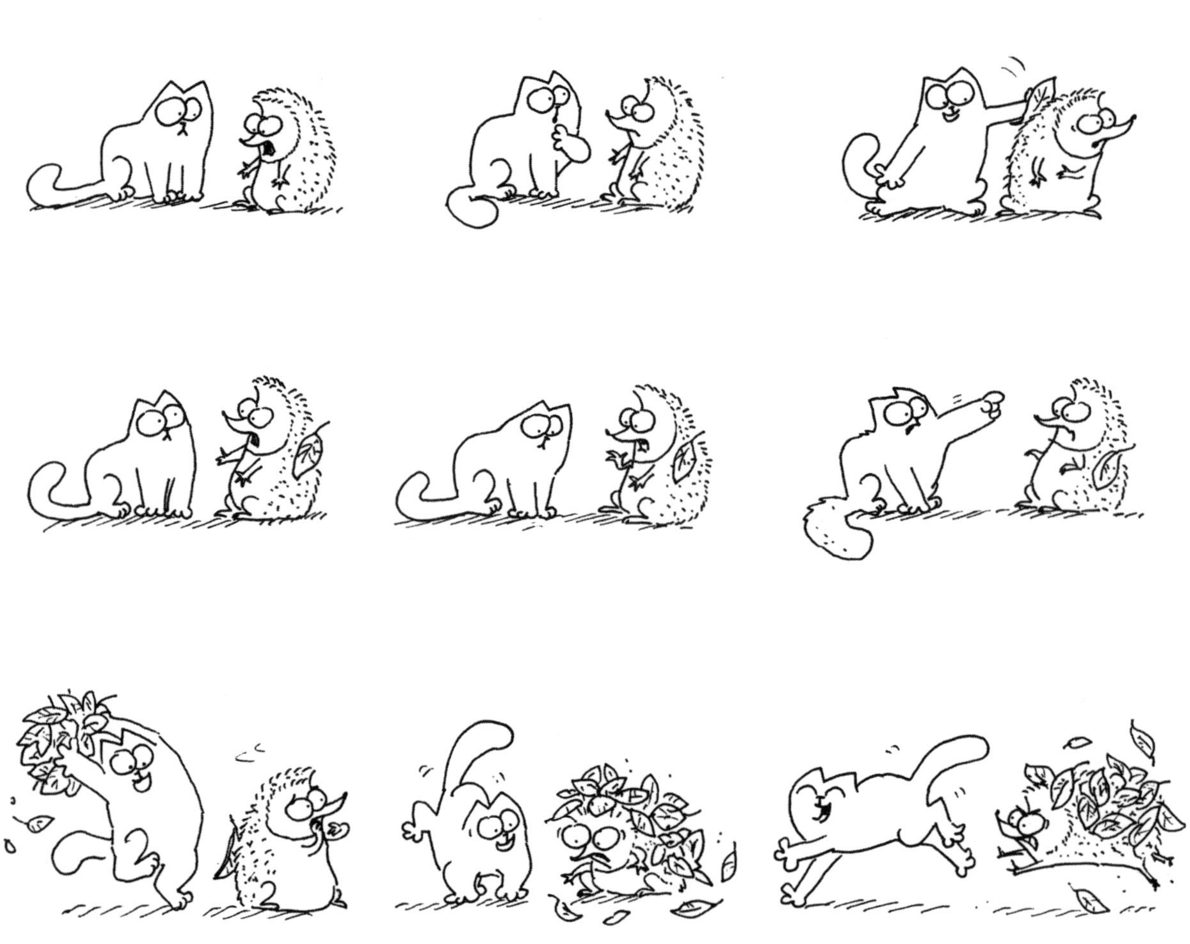

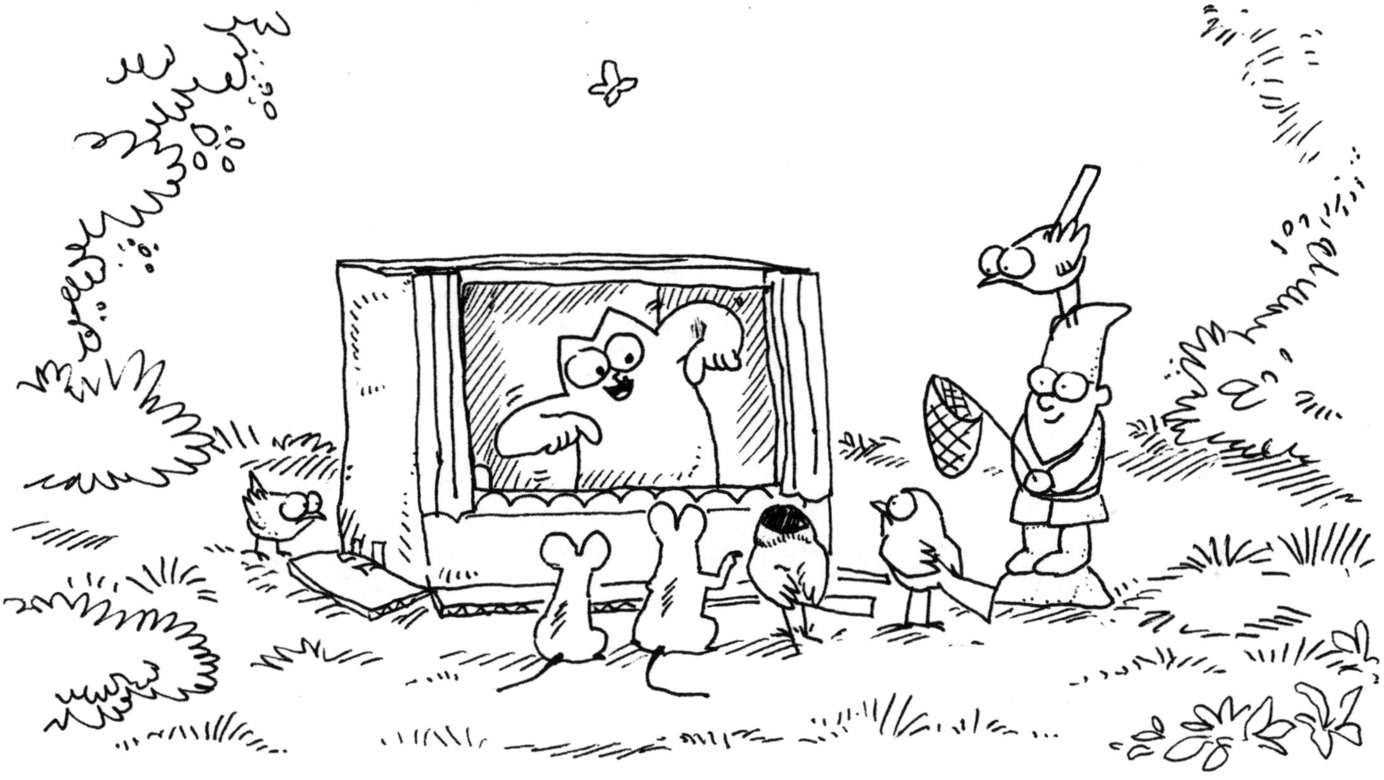

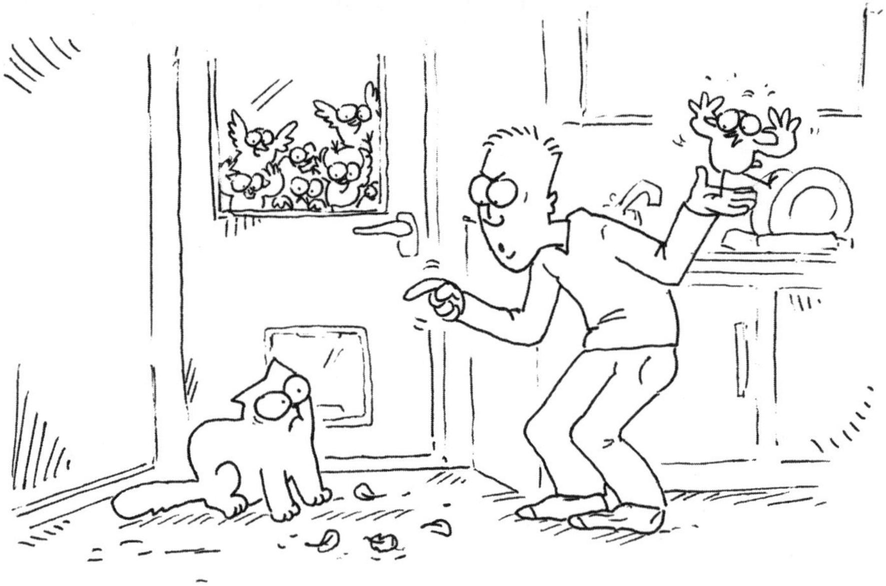

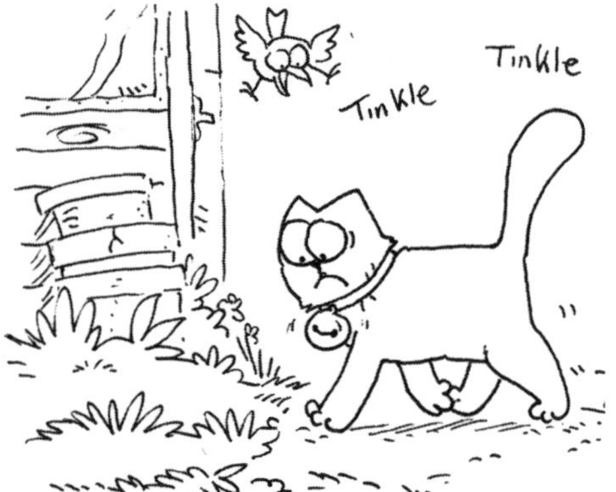
Tinkle
Tinkle

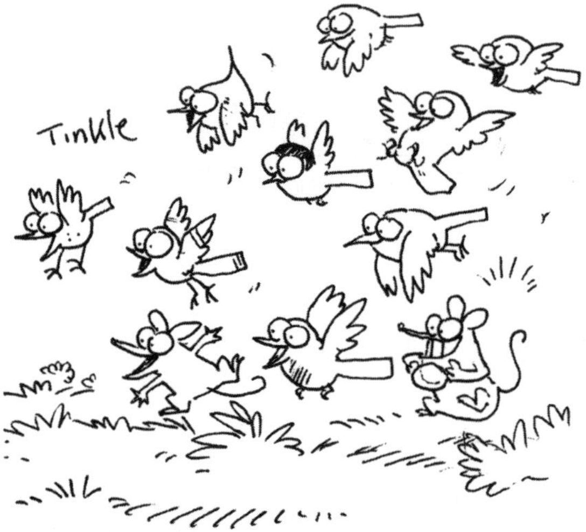
Tinkle

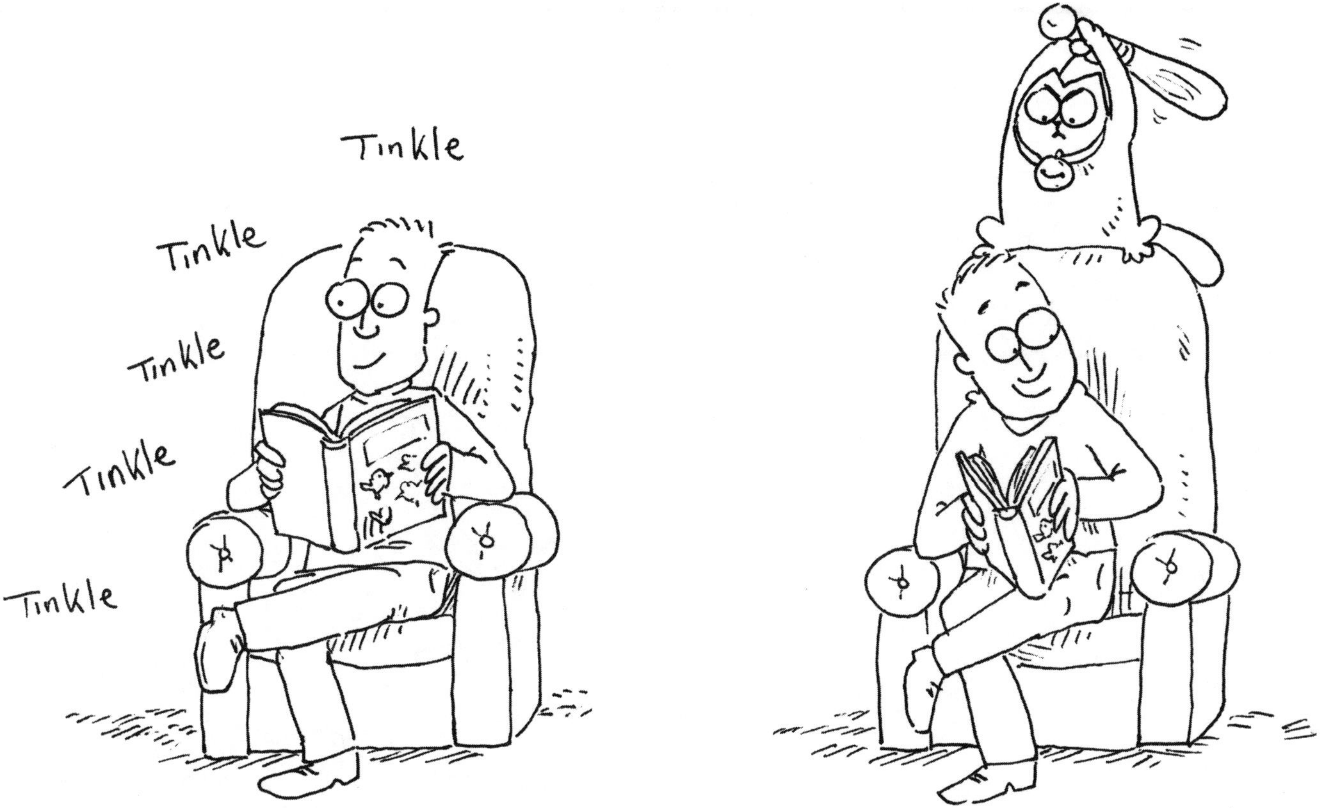
Tinkle
Tinkle
Tinkle
Tinkle
Tinkle

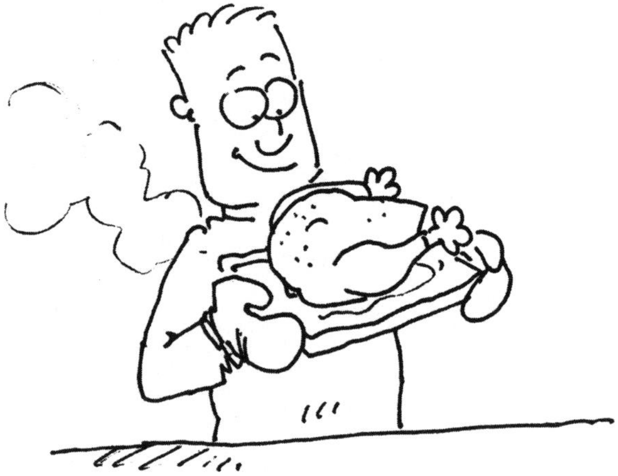

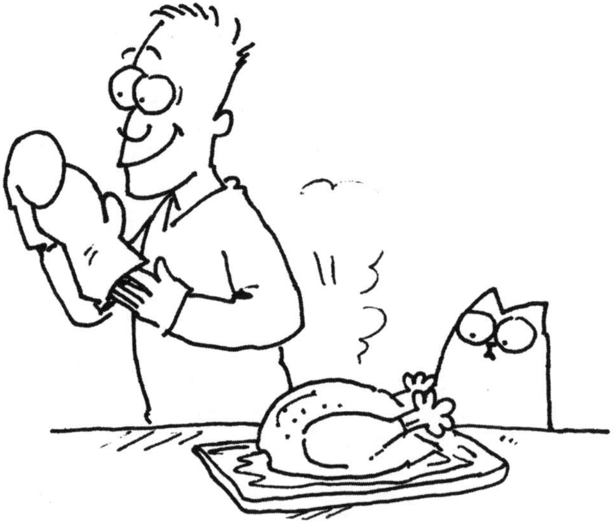

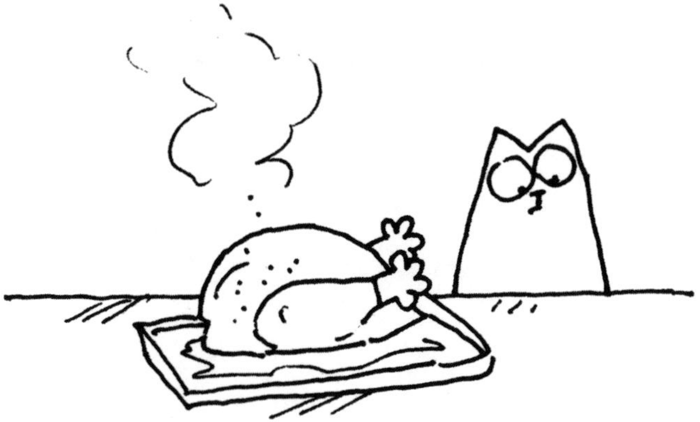

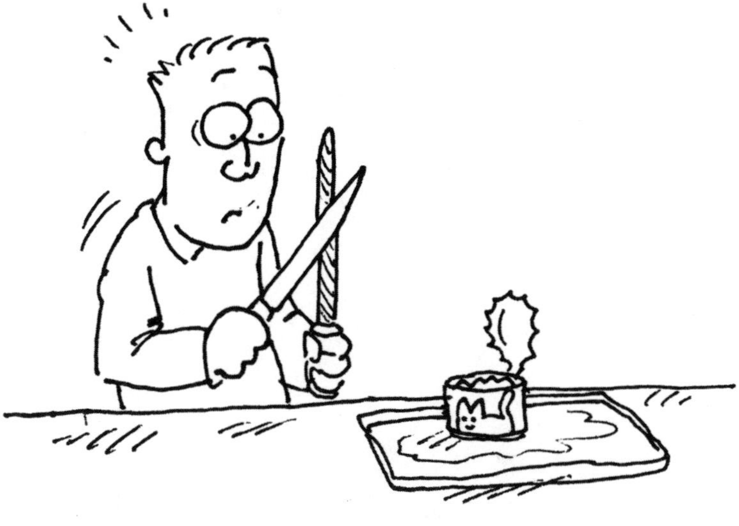

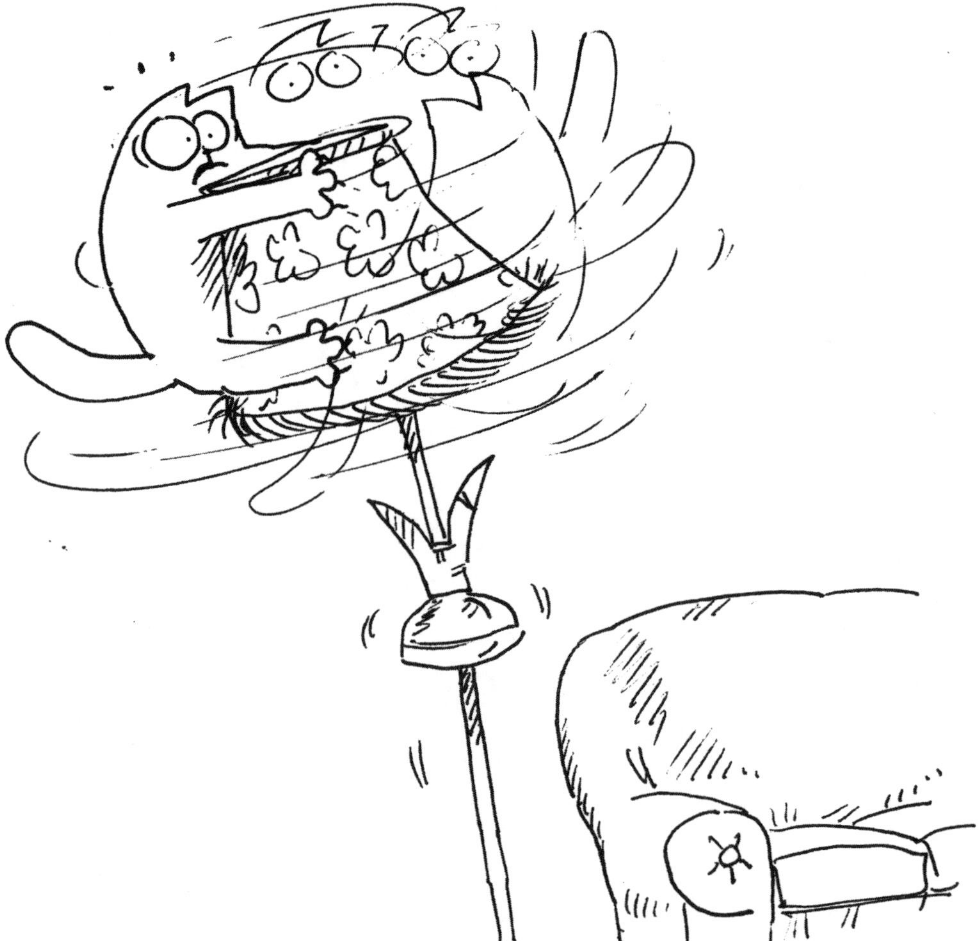

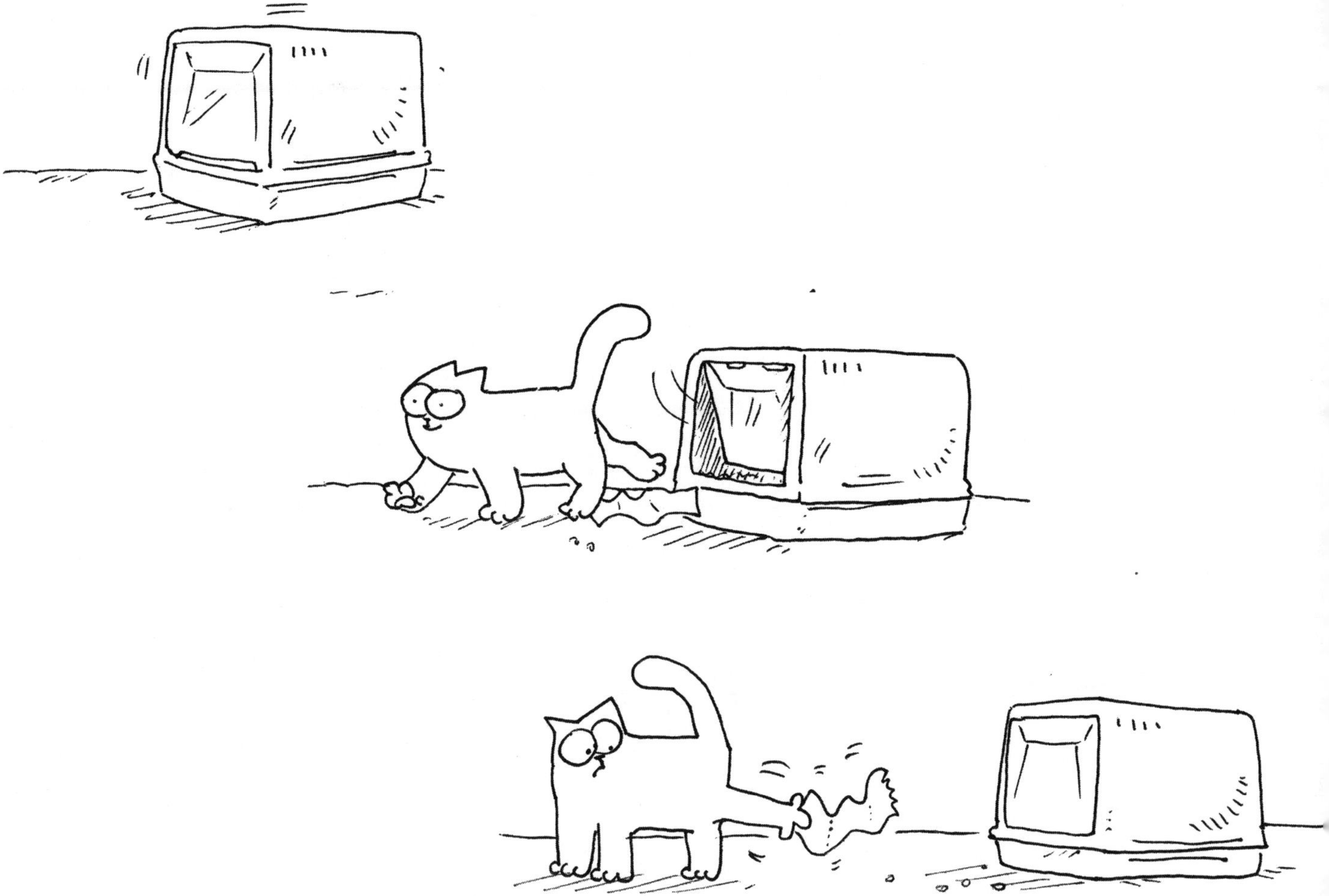

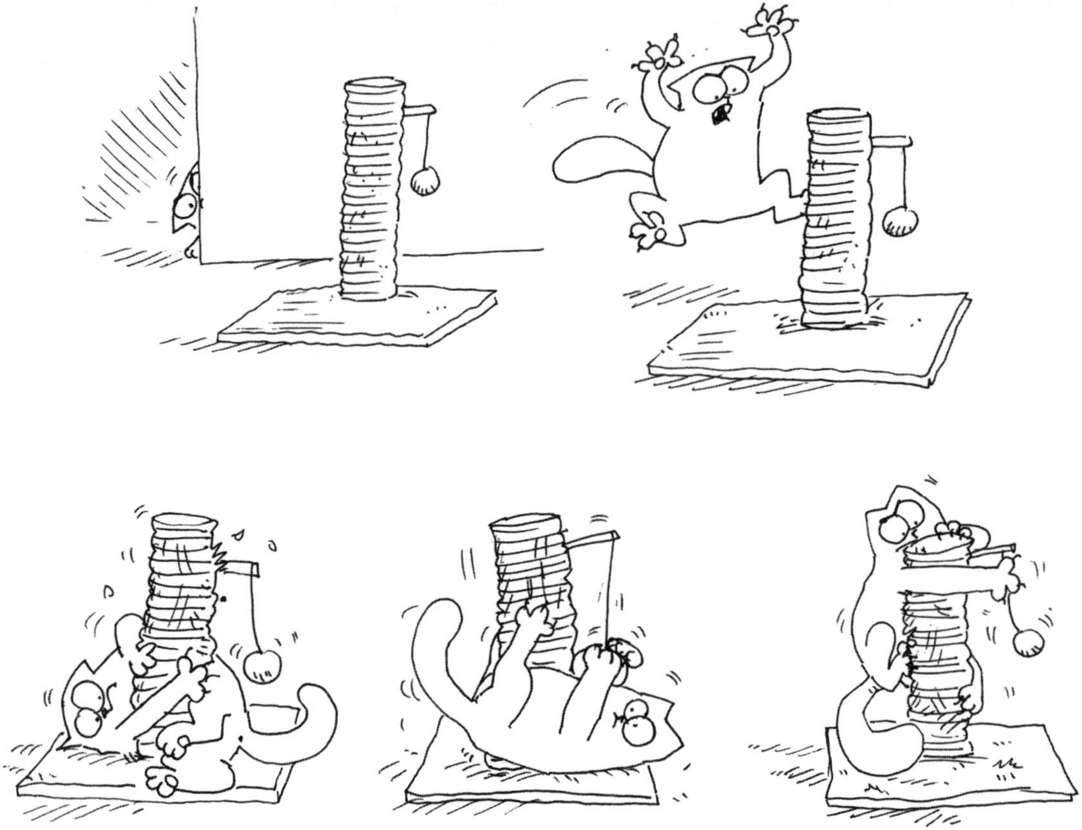

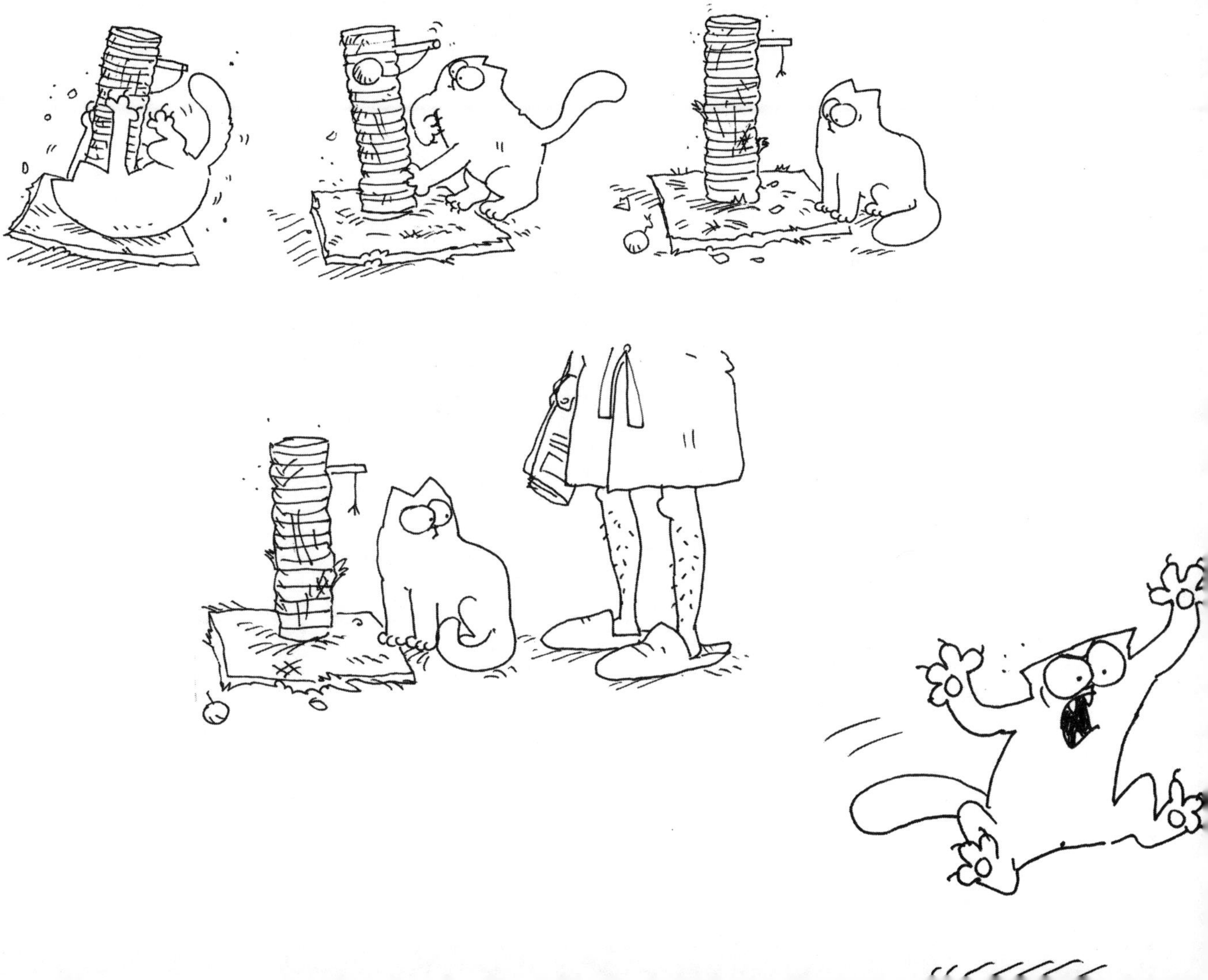

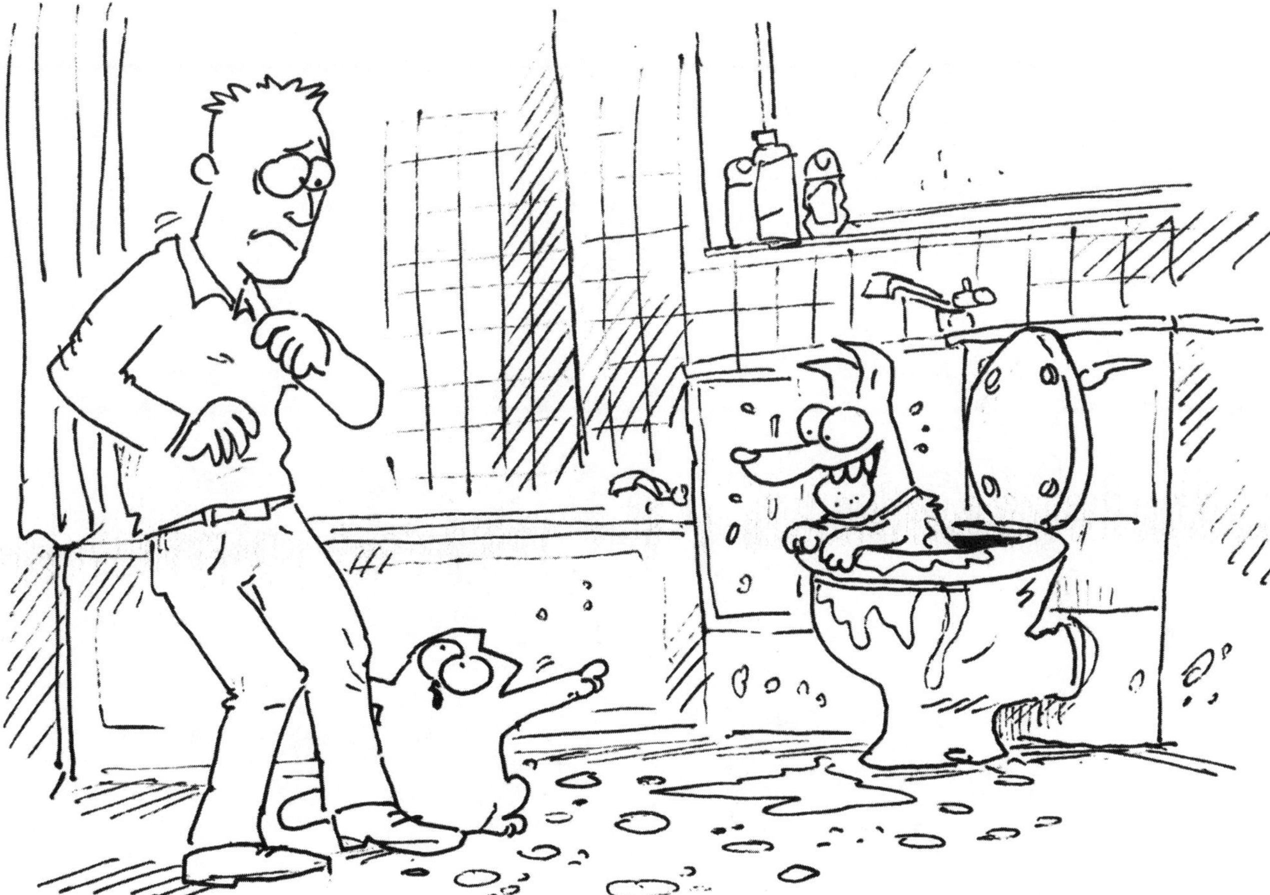

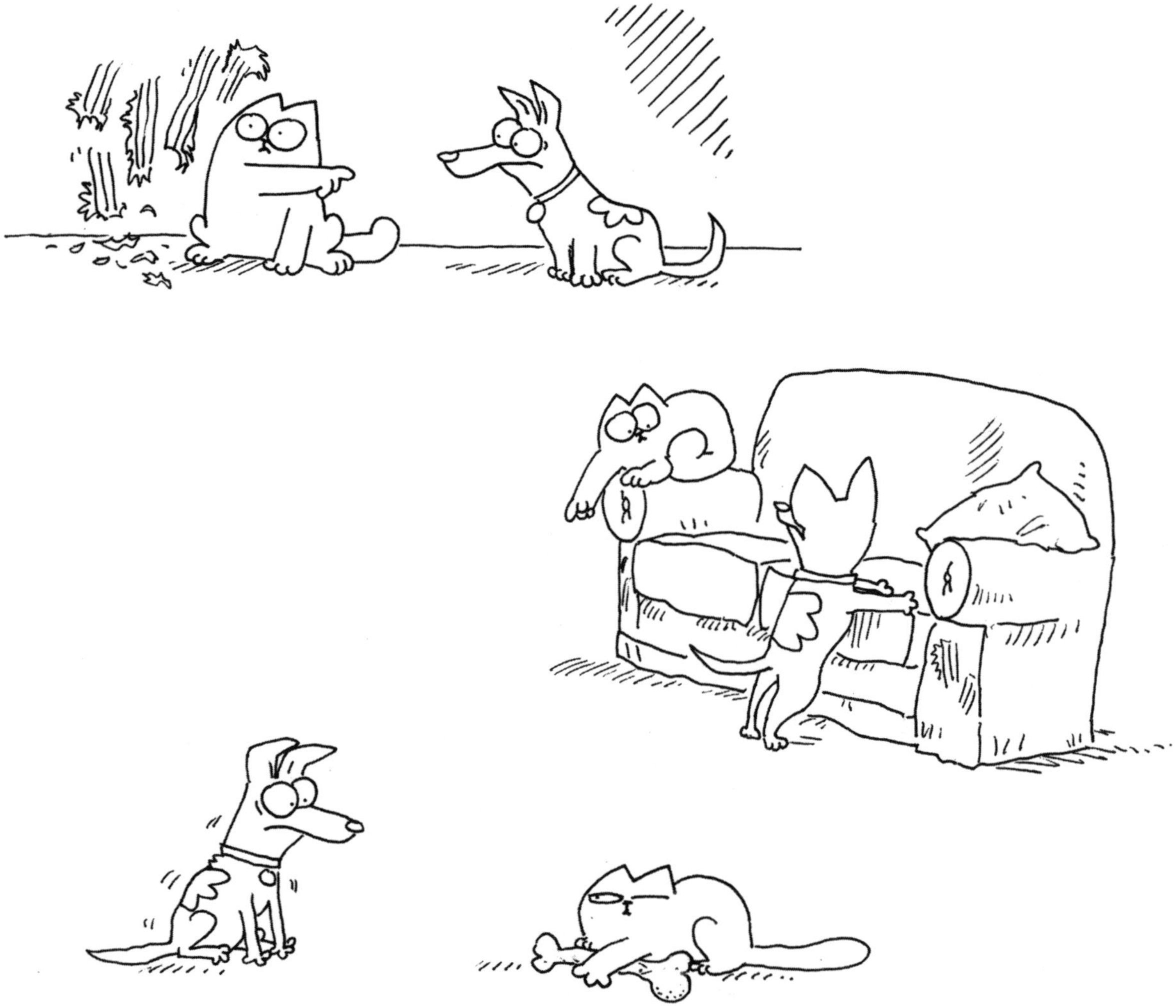

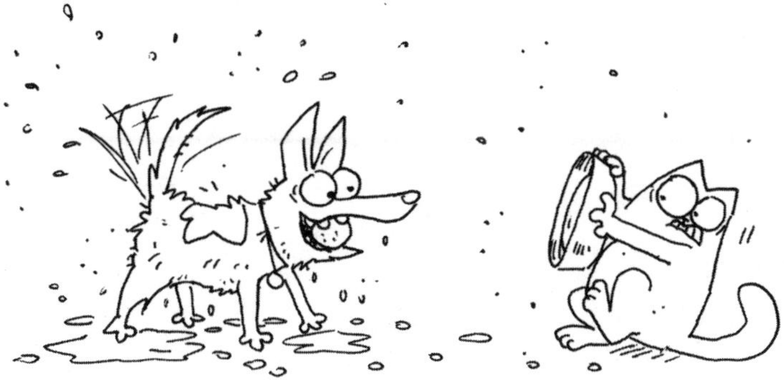

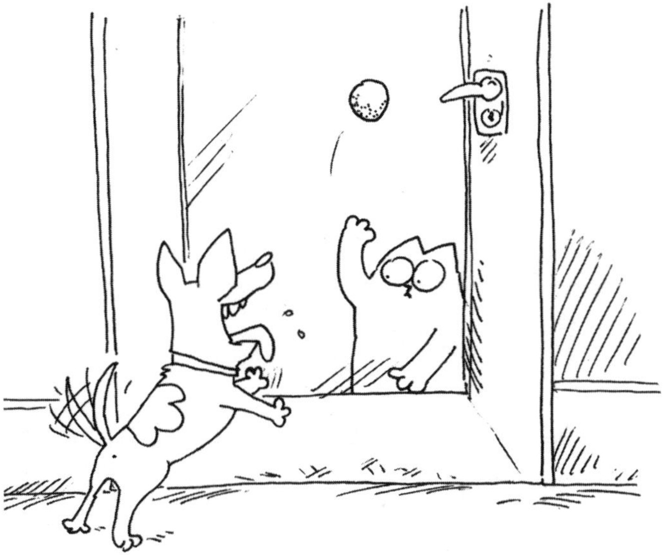

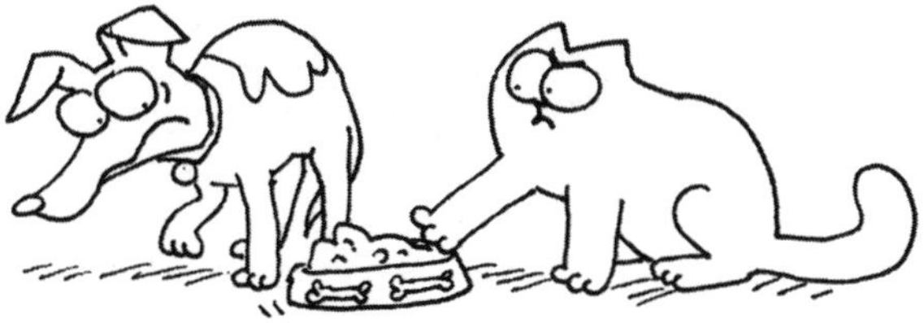

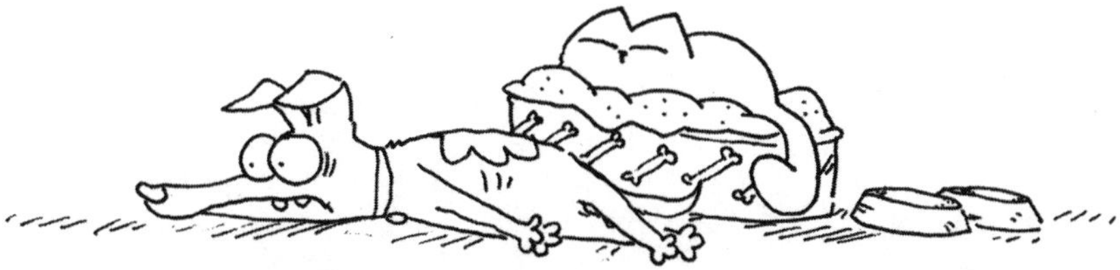

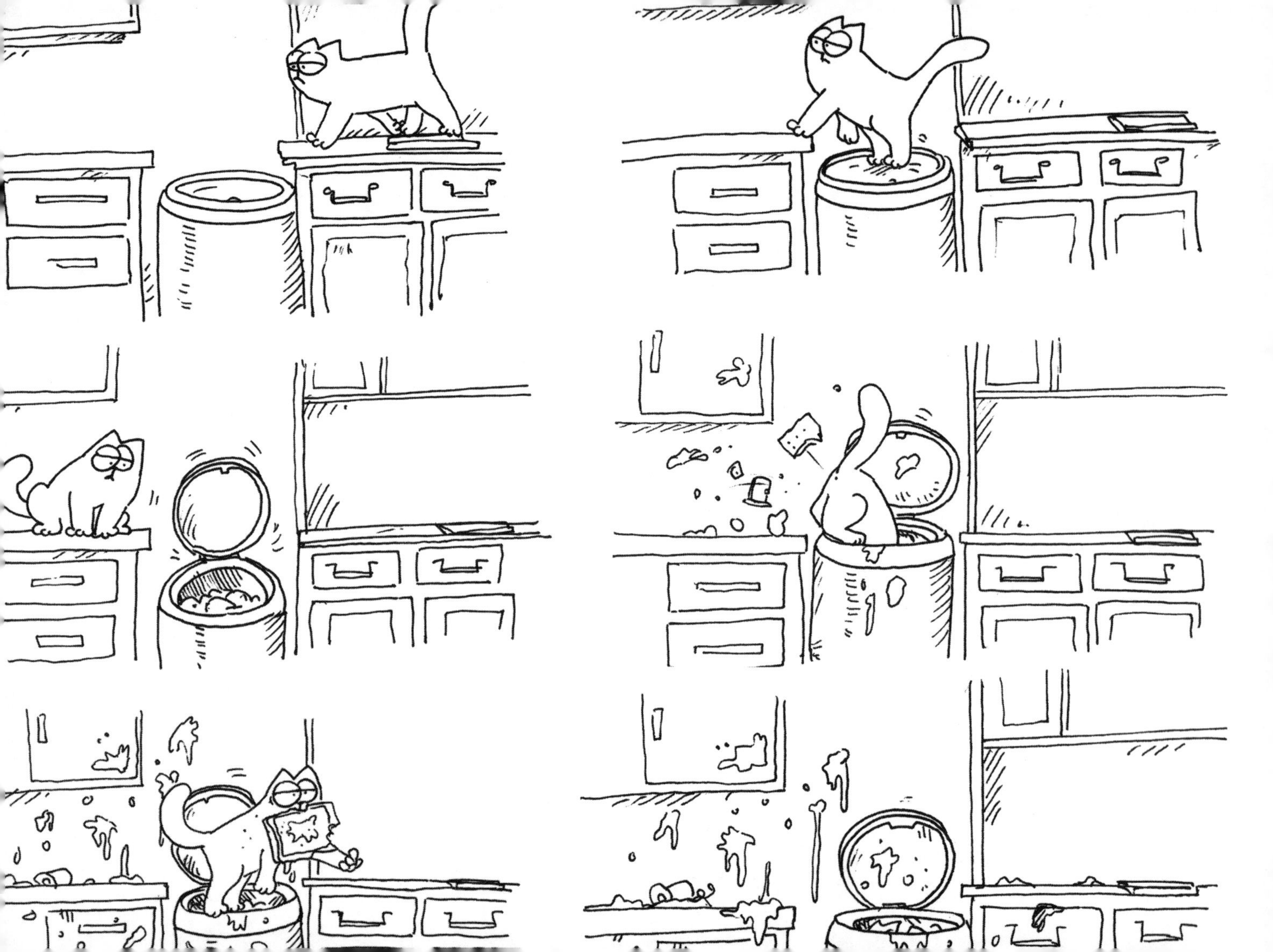

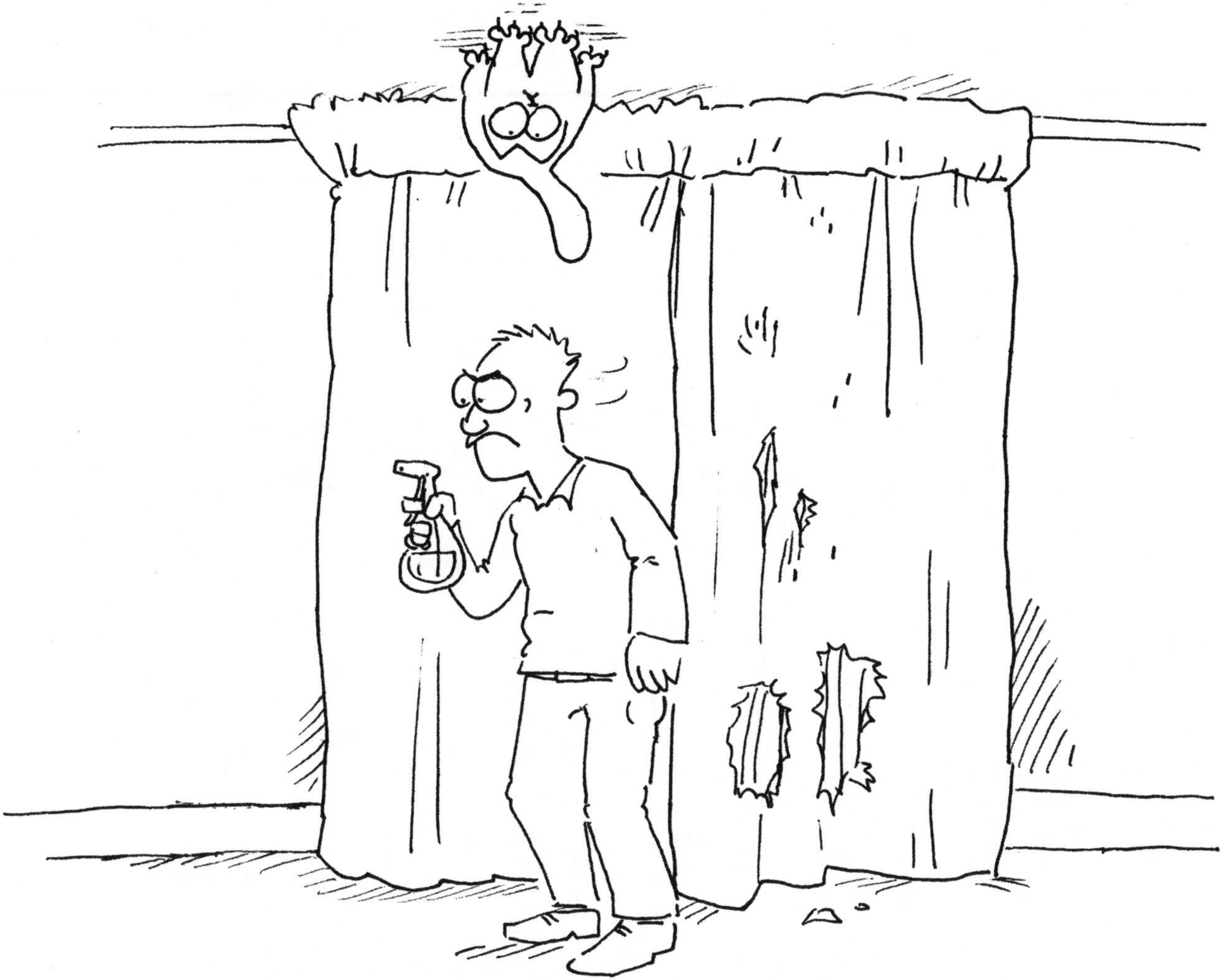

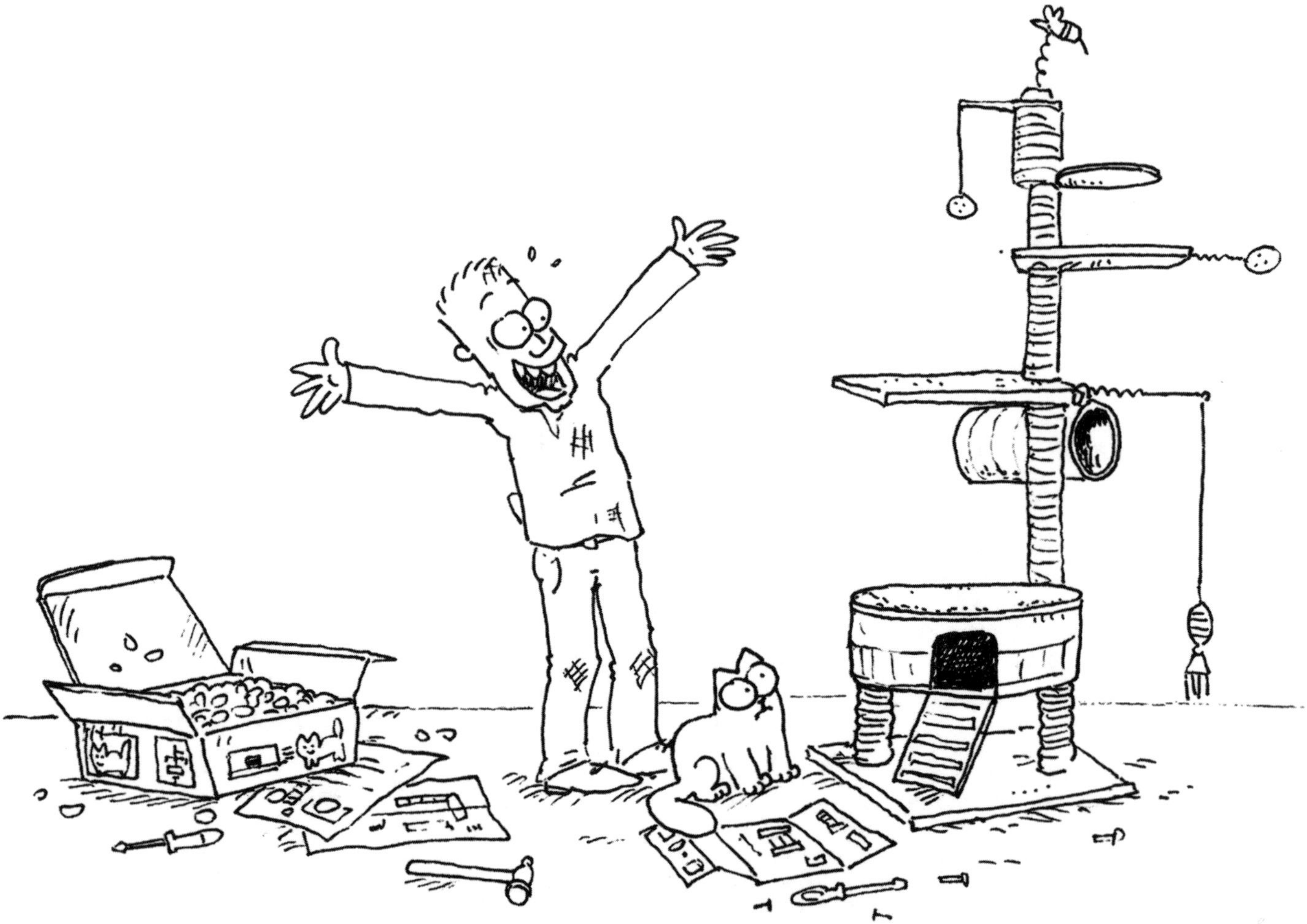

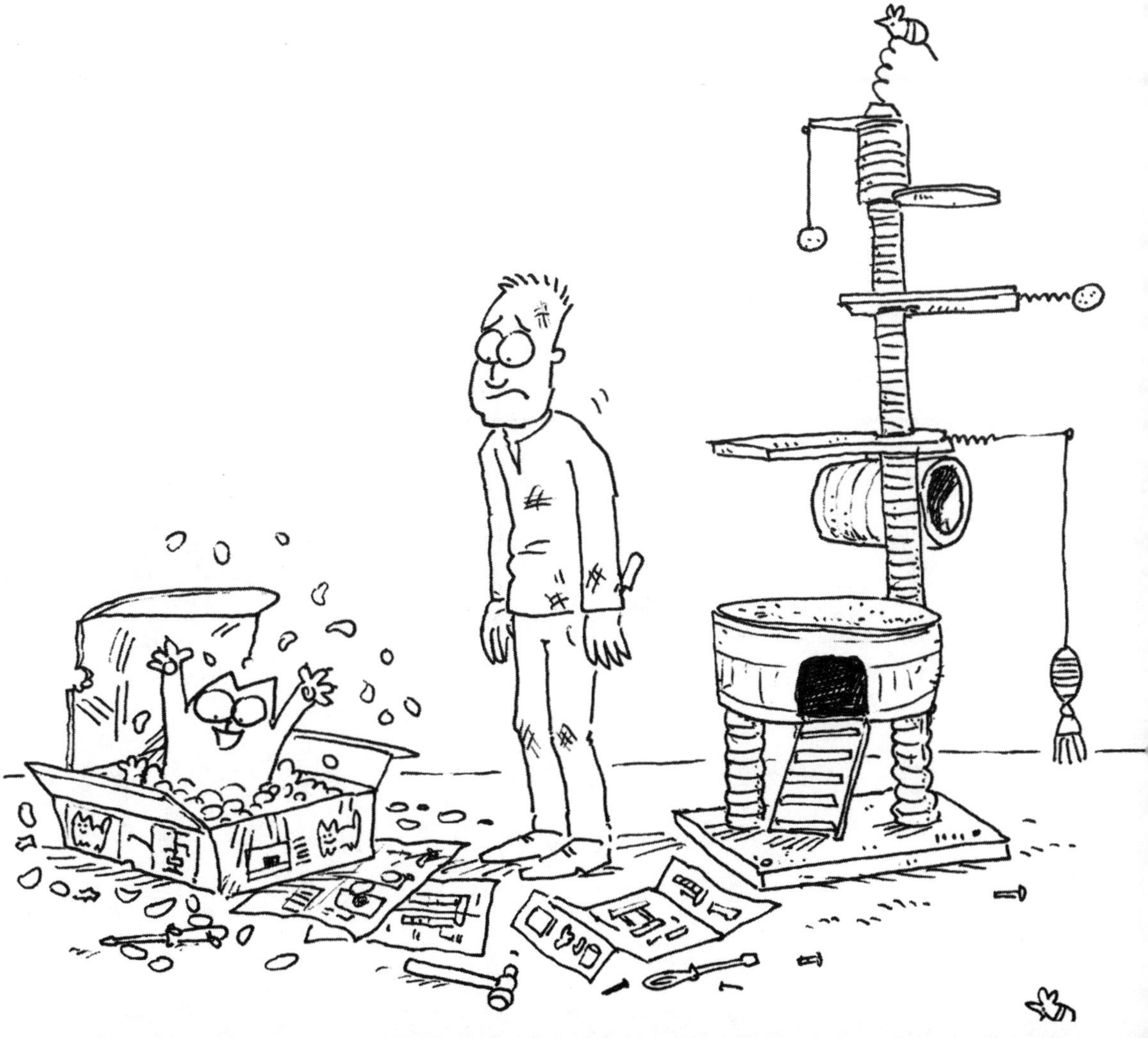

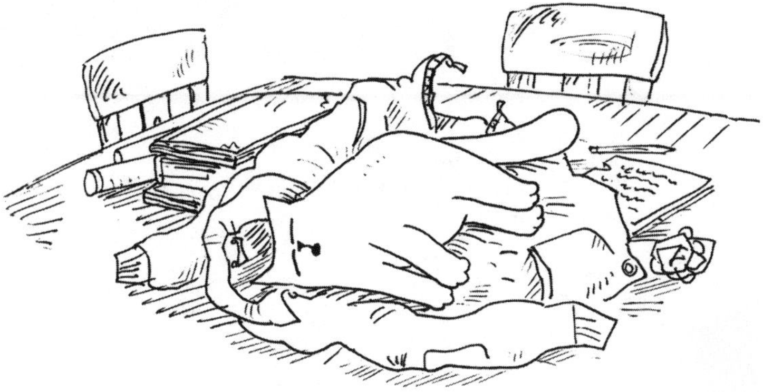

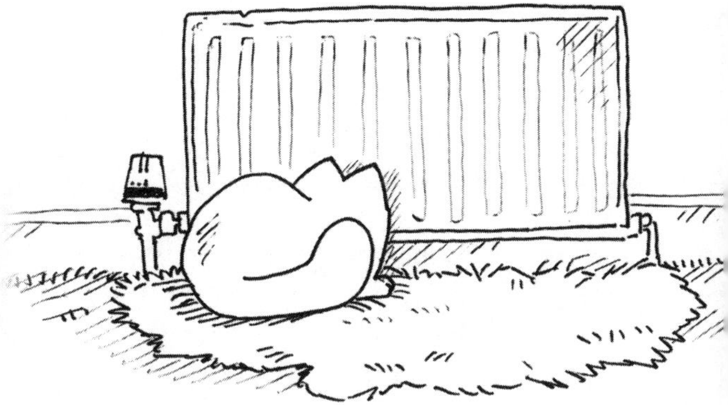

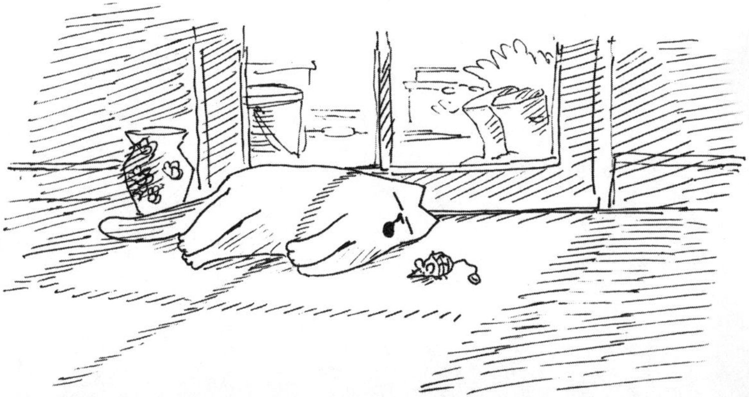

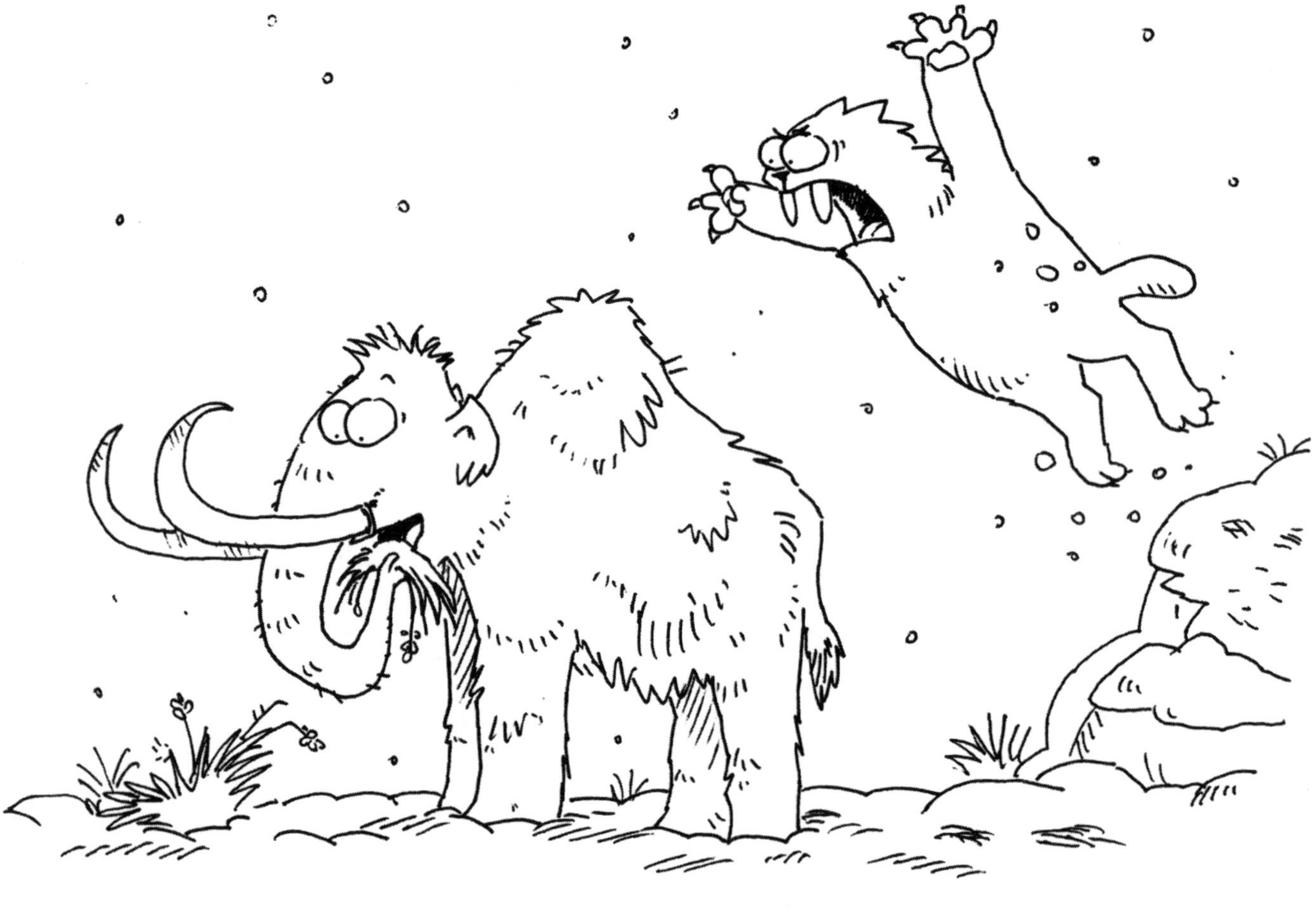

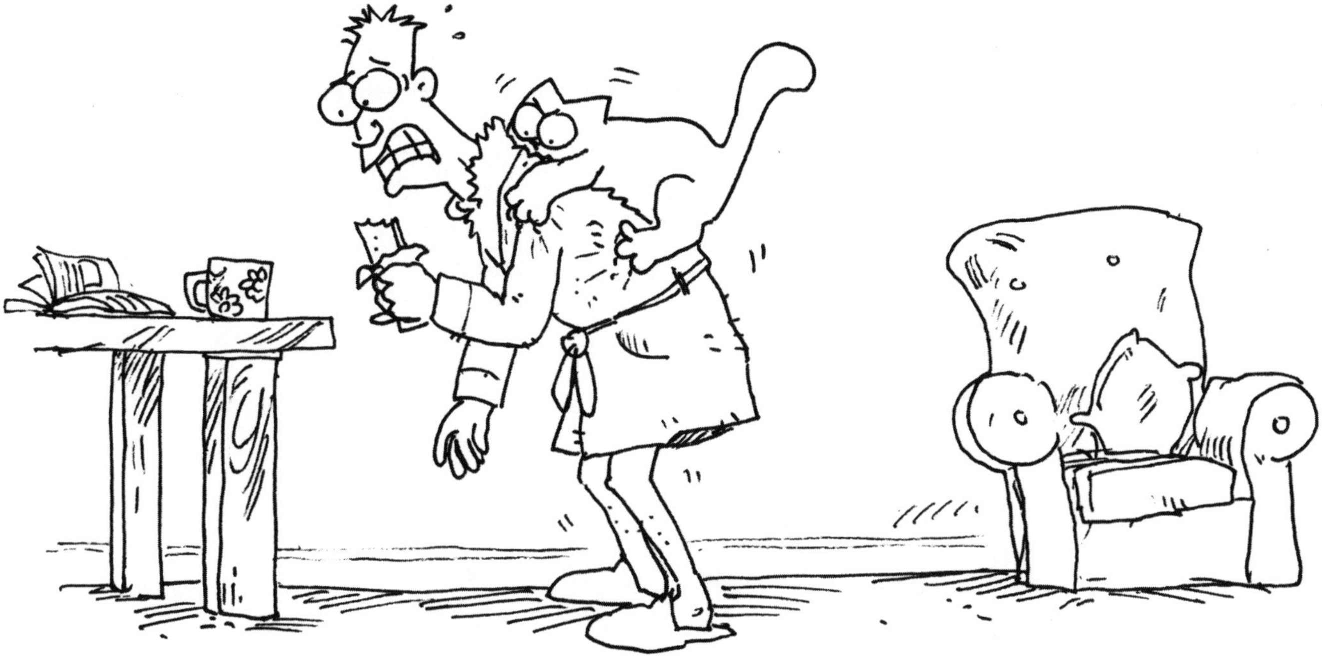

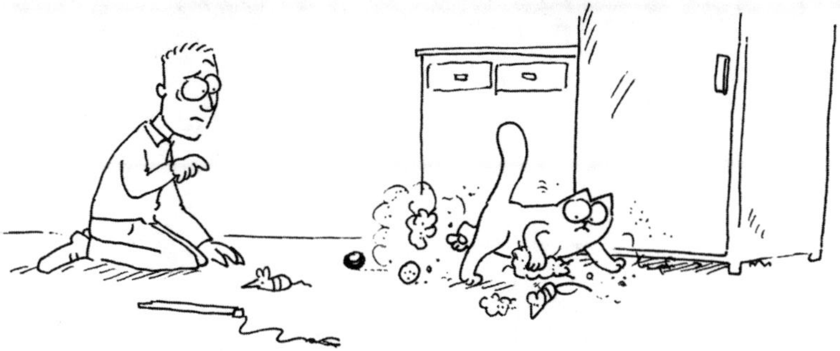
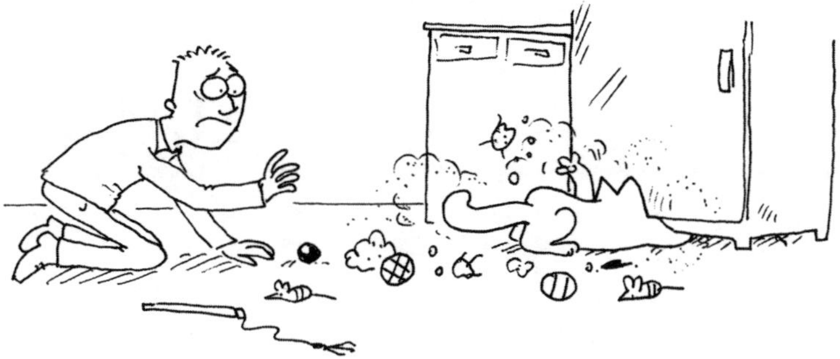
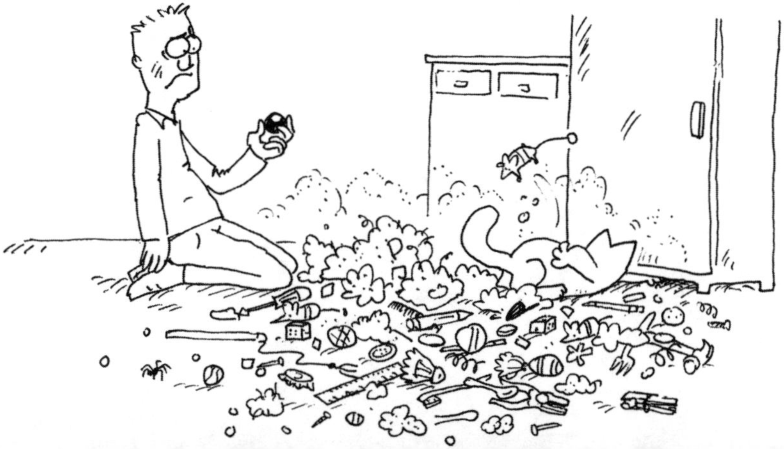

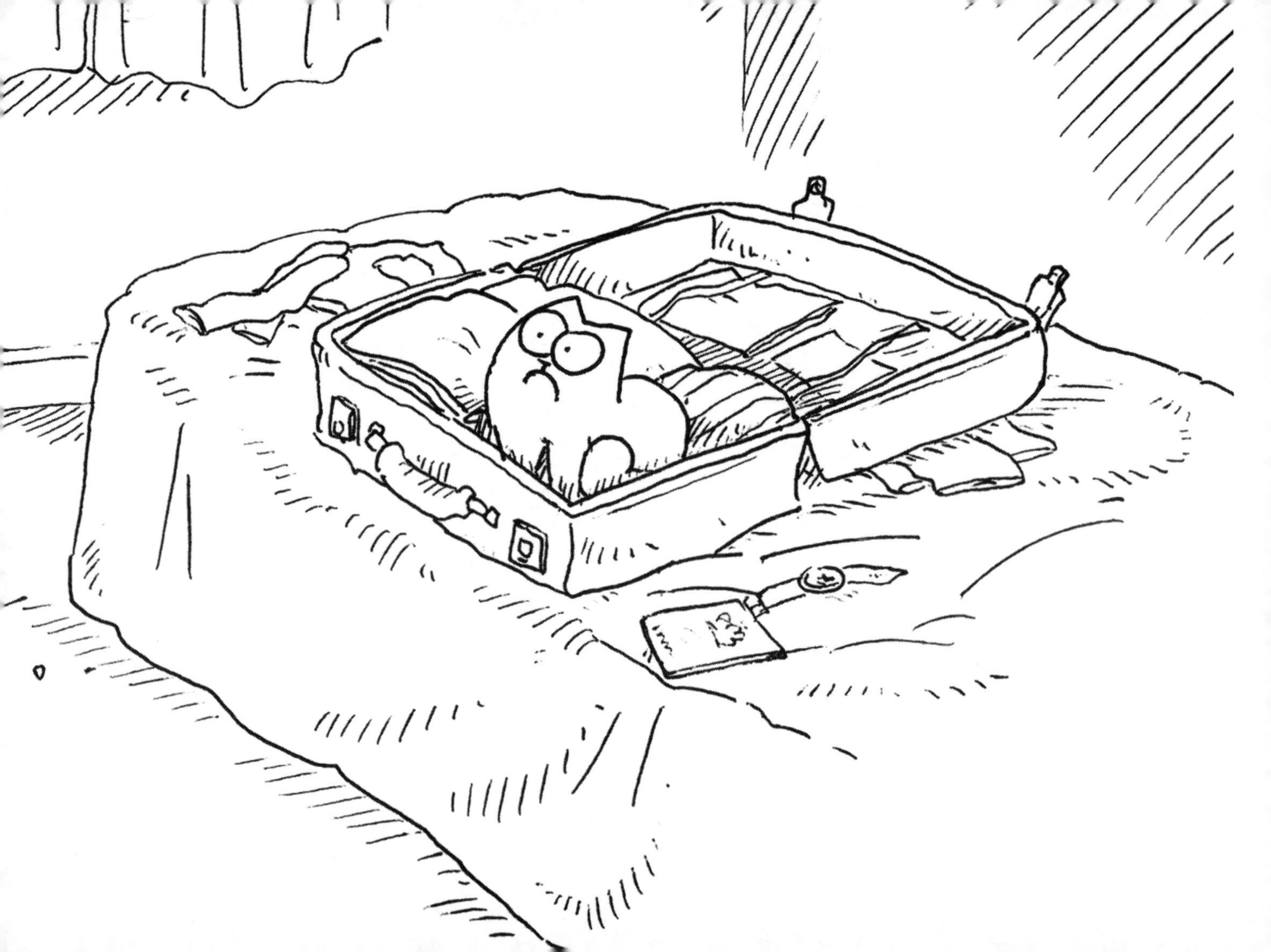

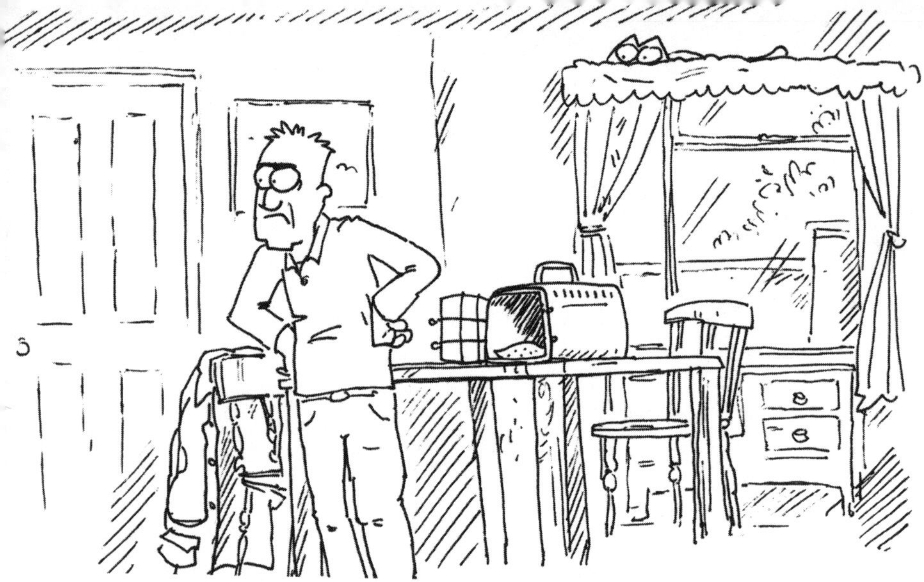

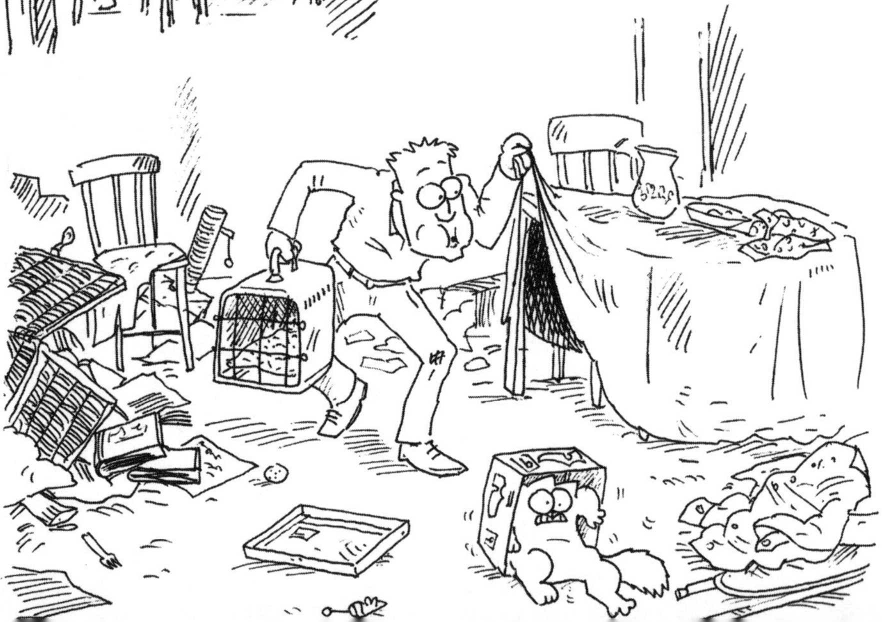

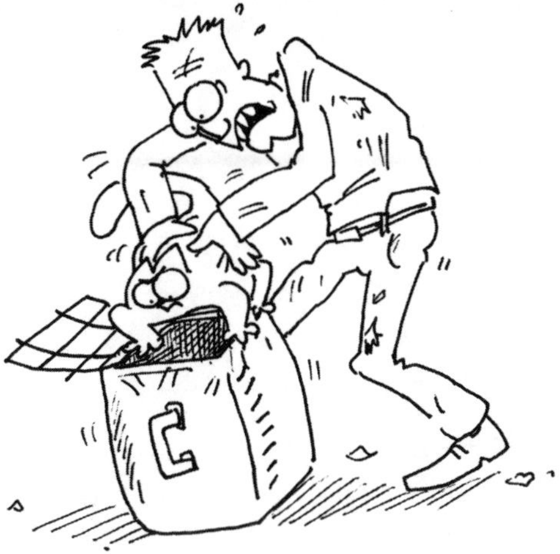

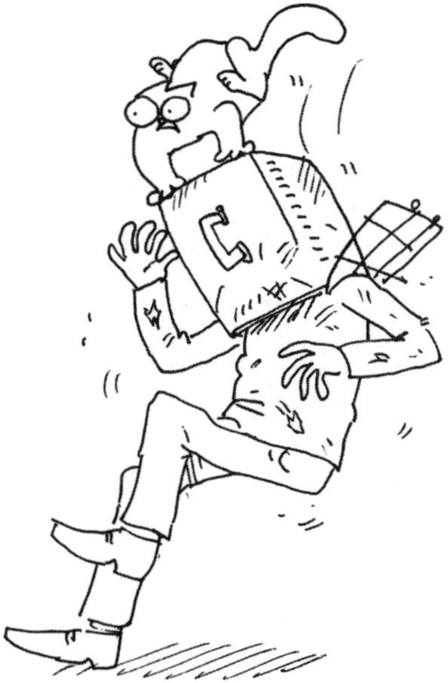

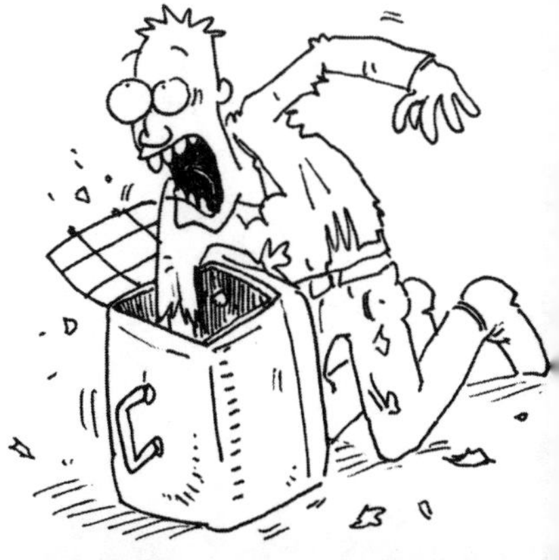

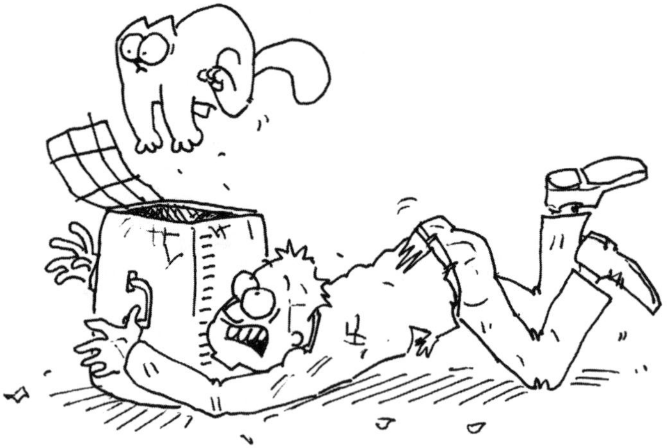

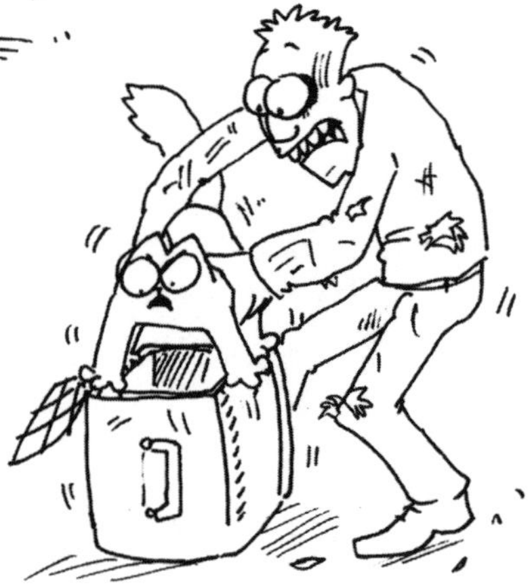

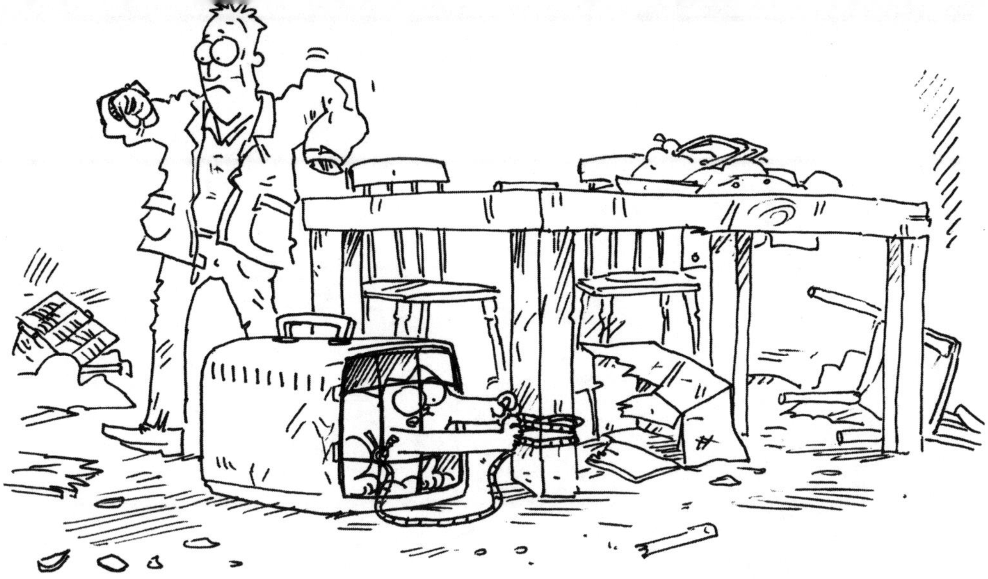

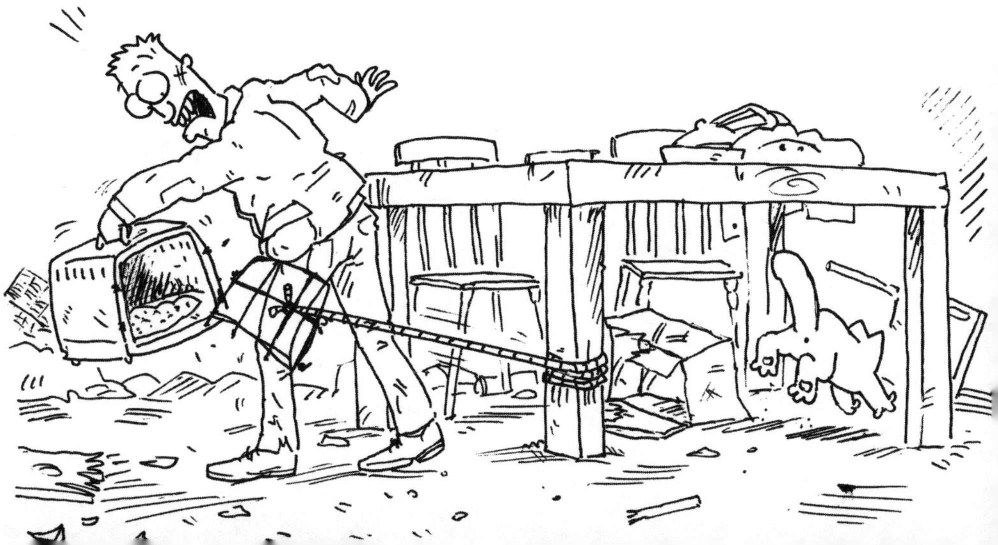

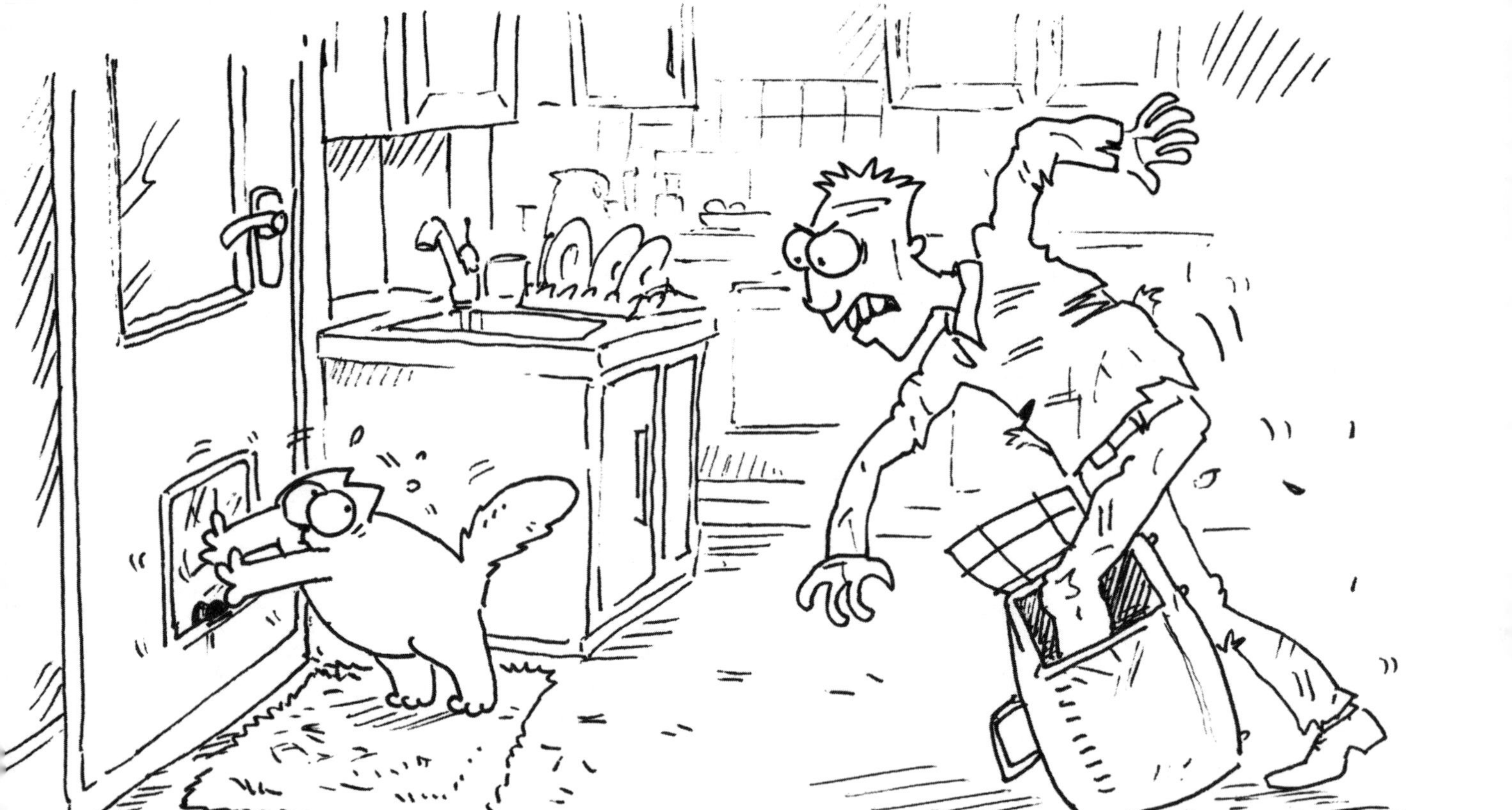

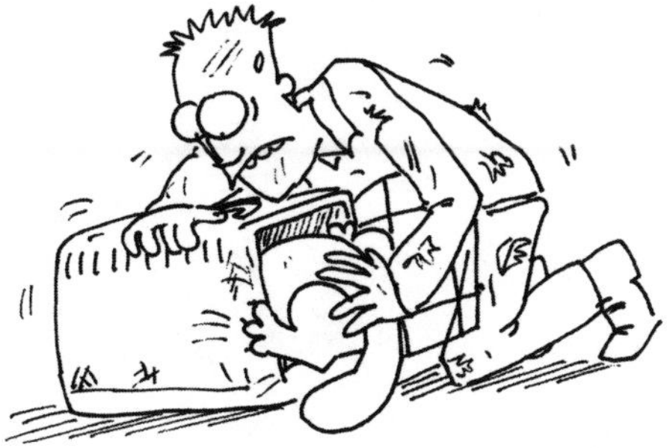

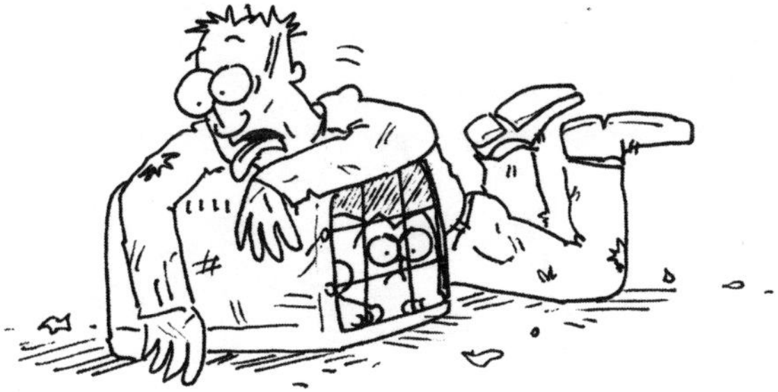

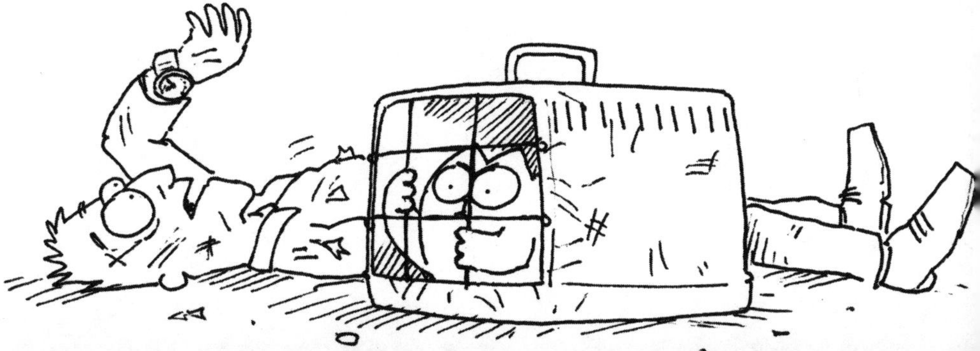

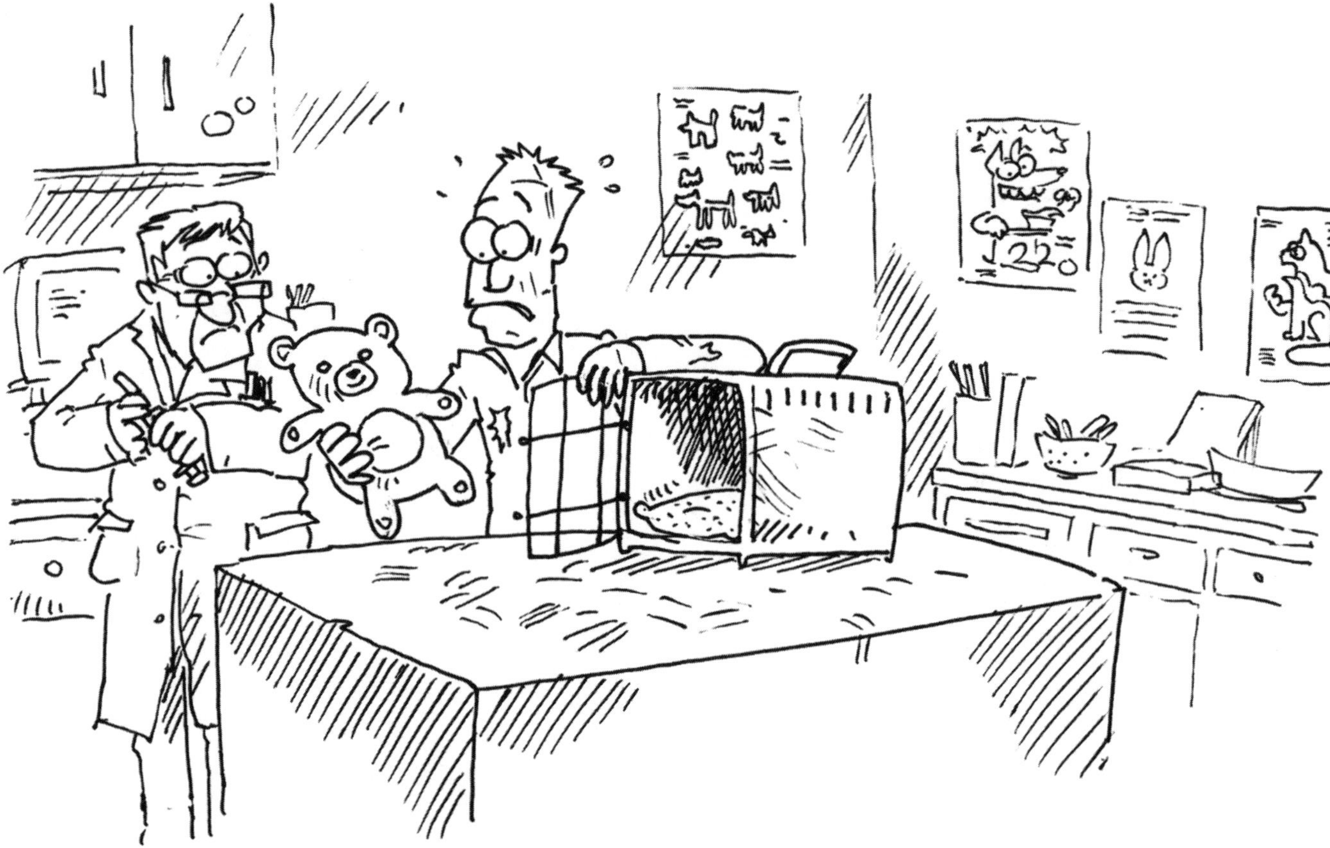

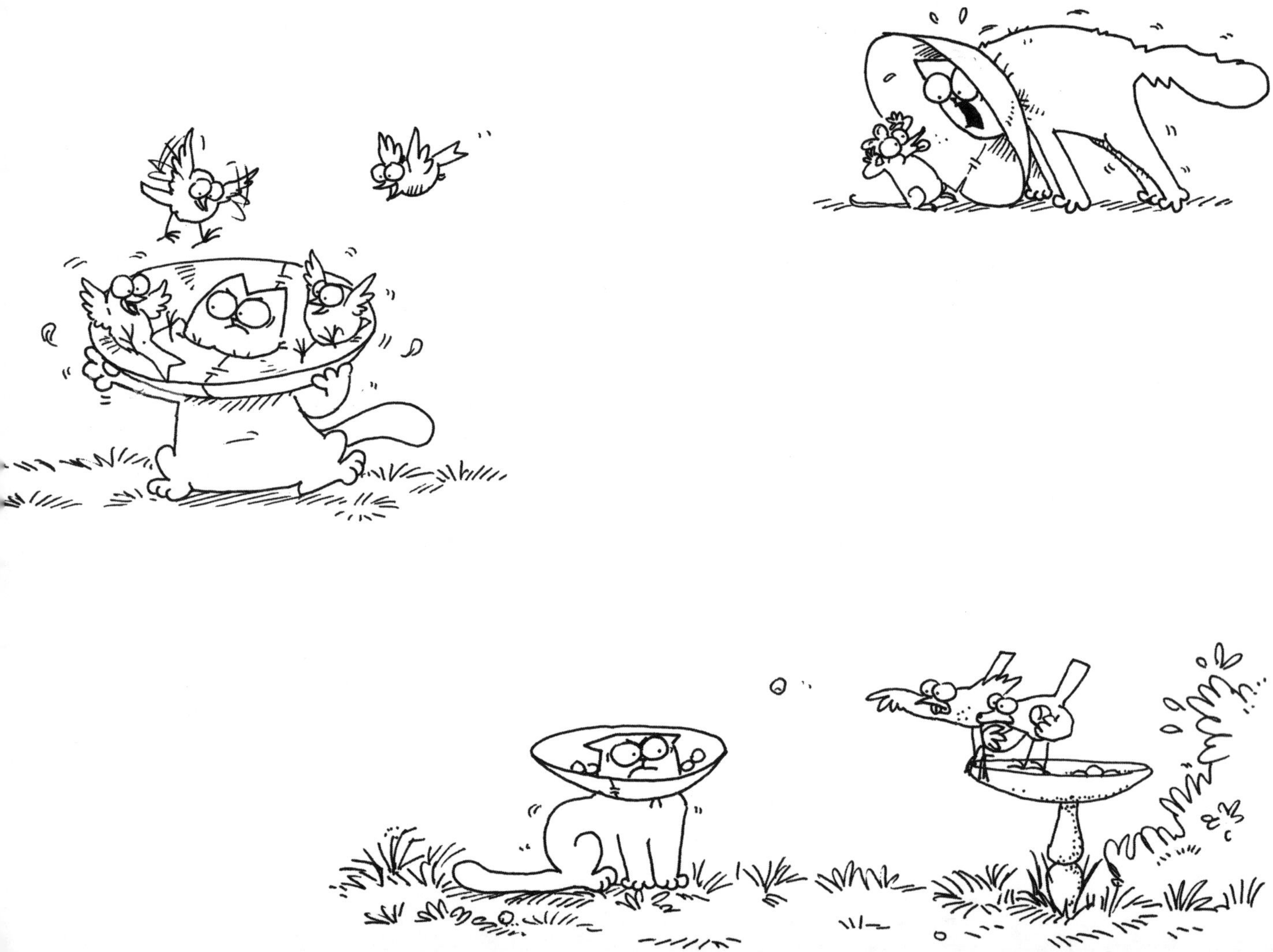

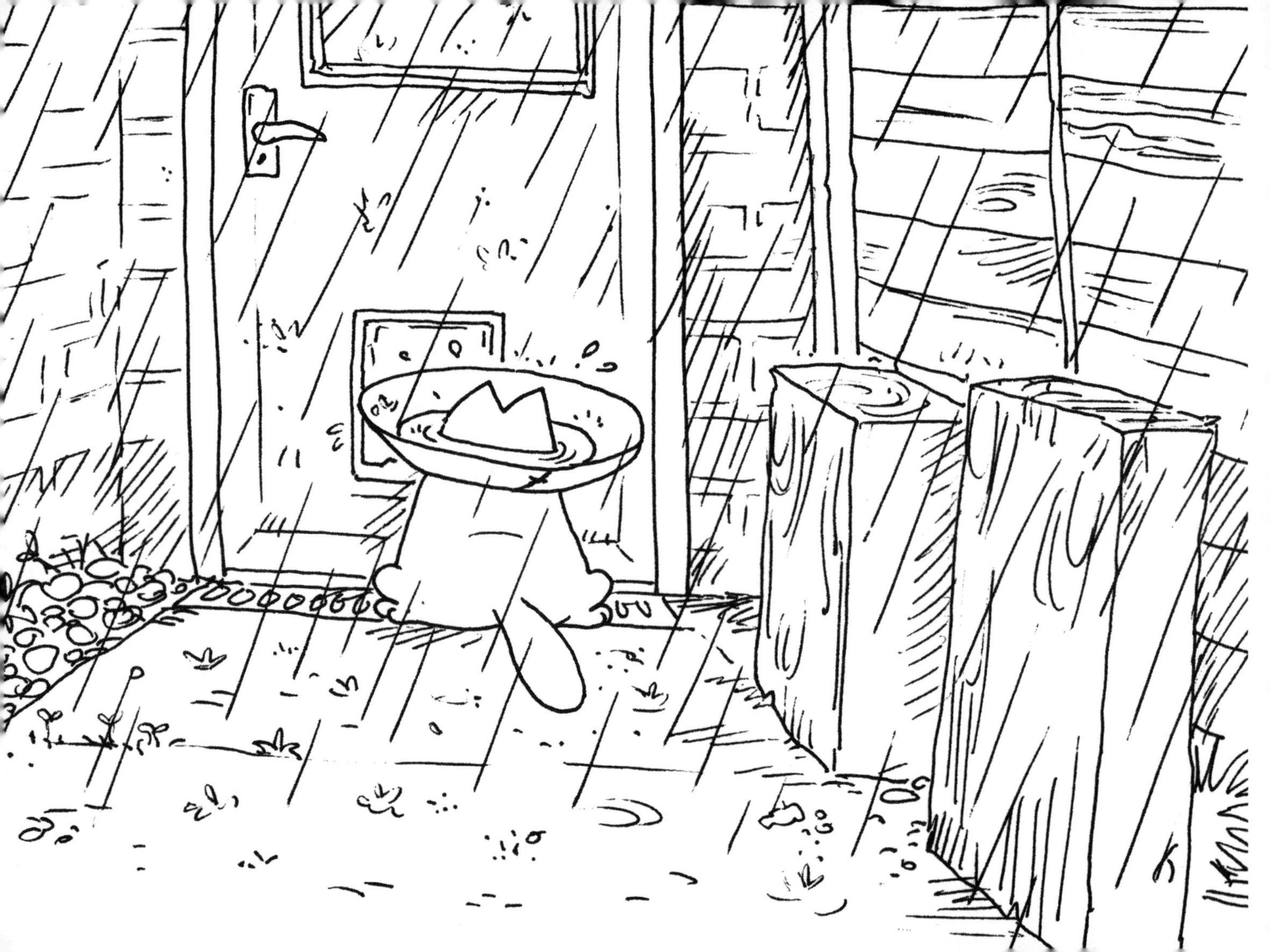

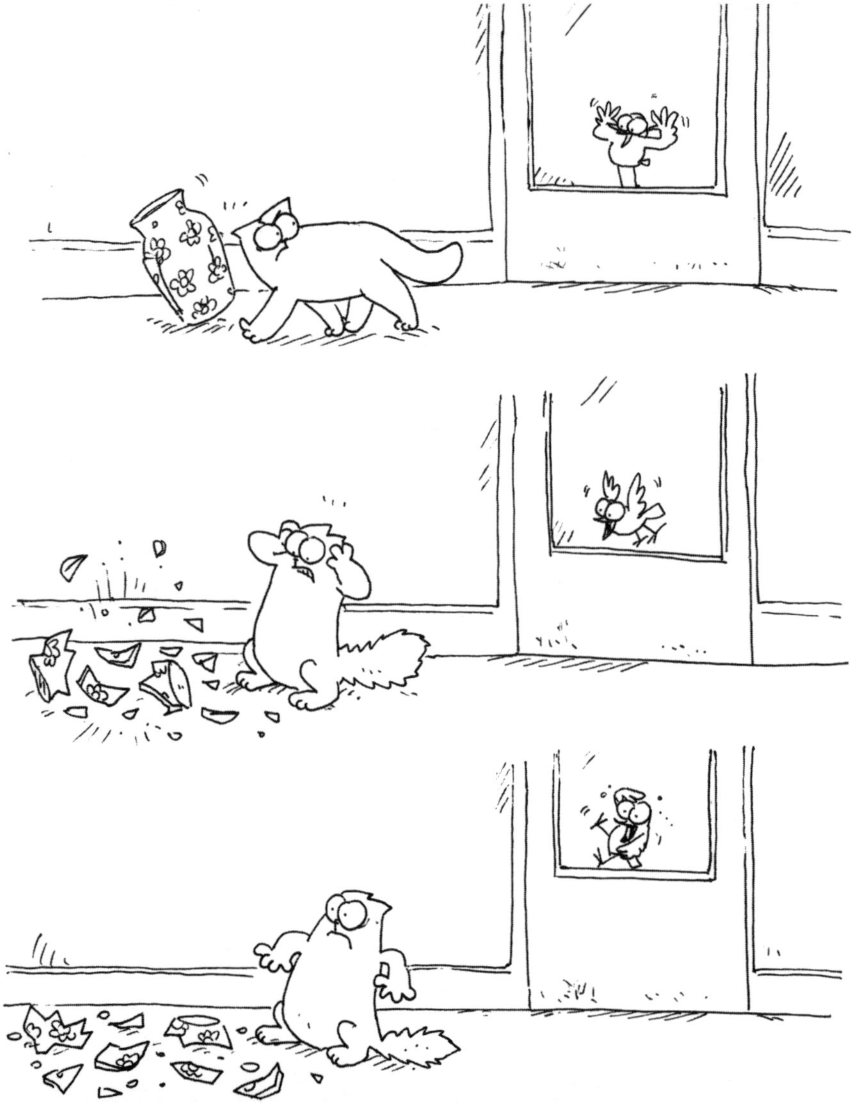

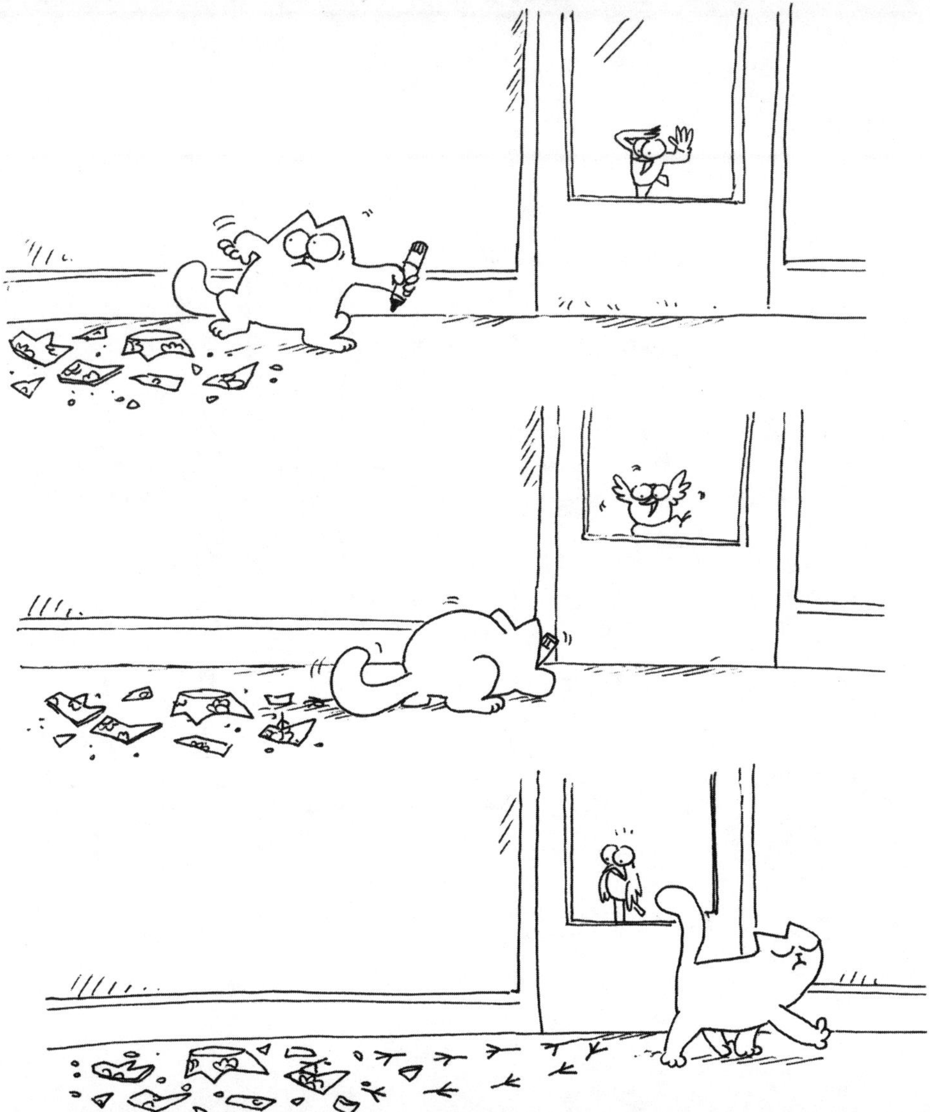

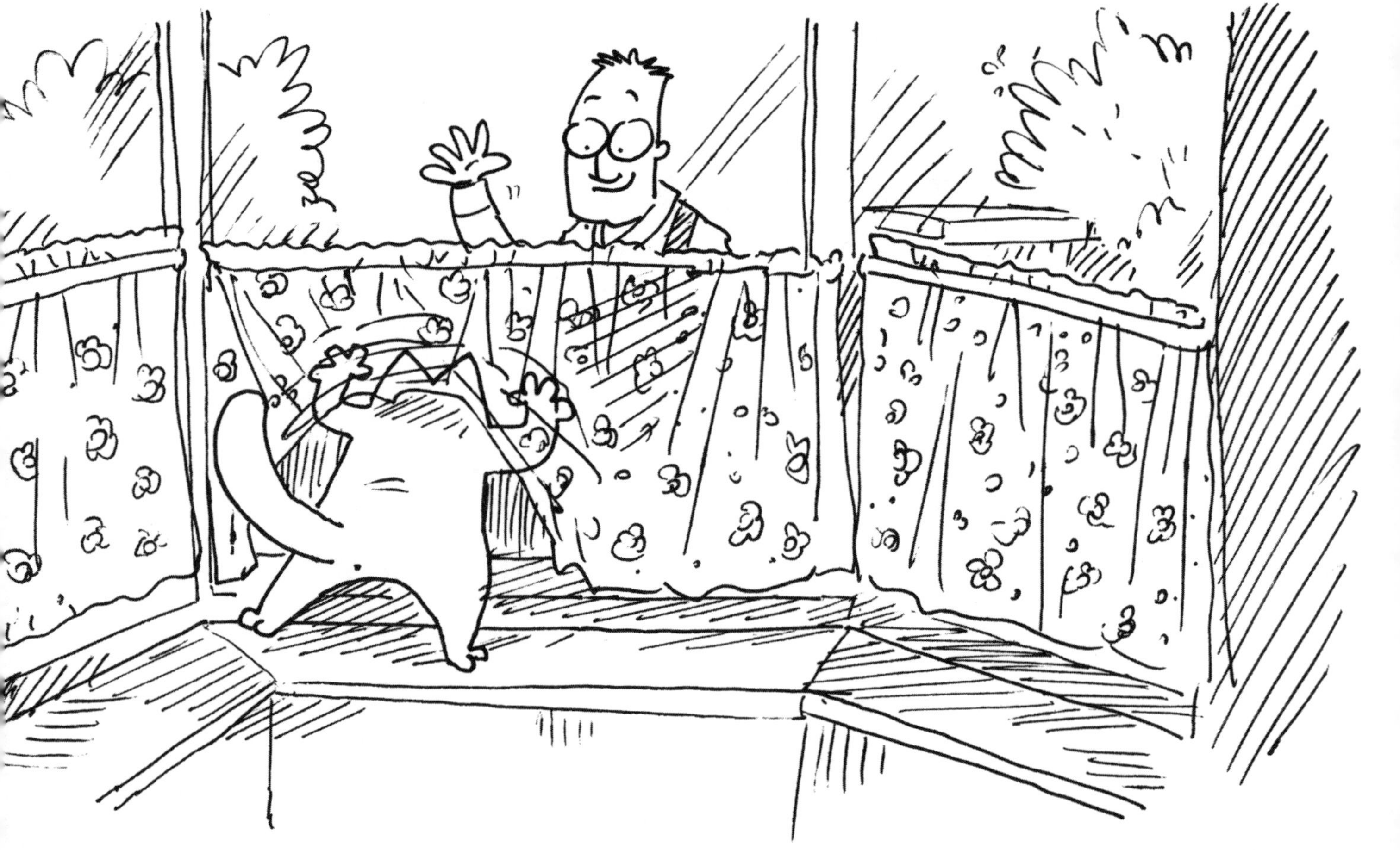

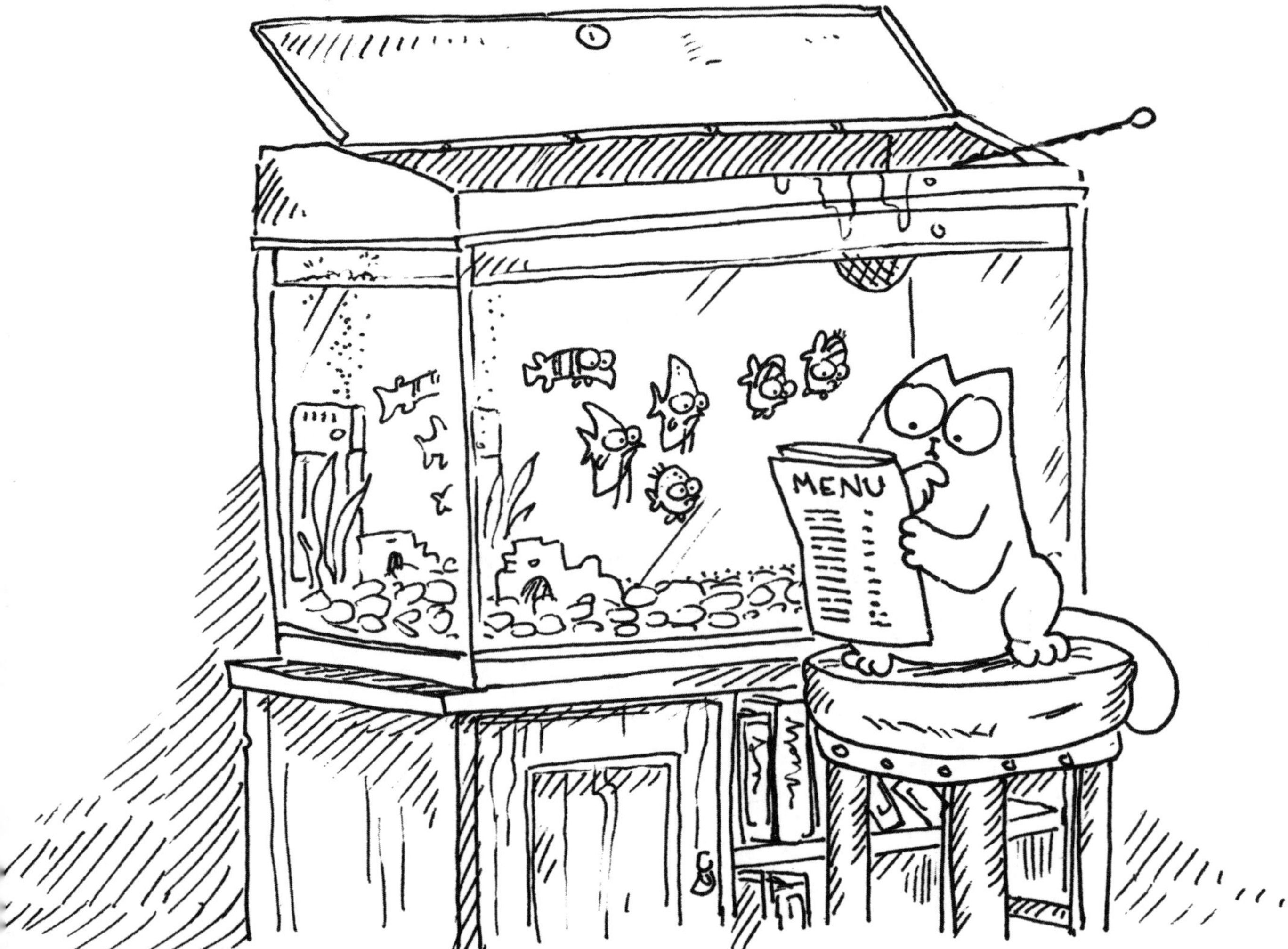
MENU

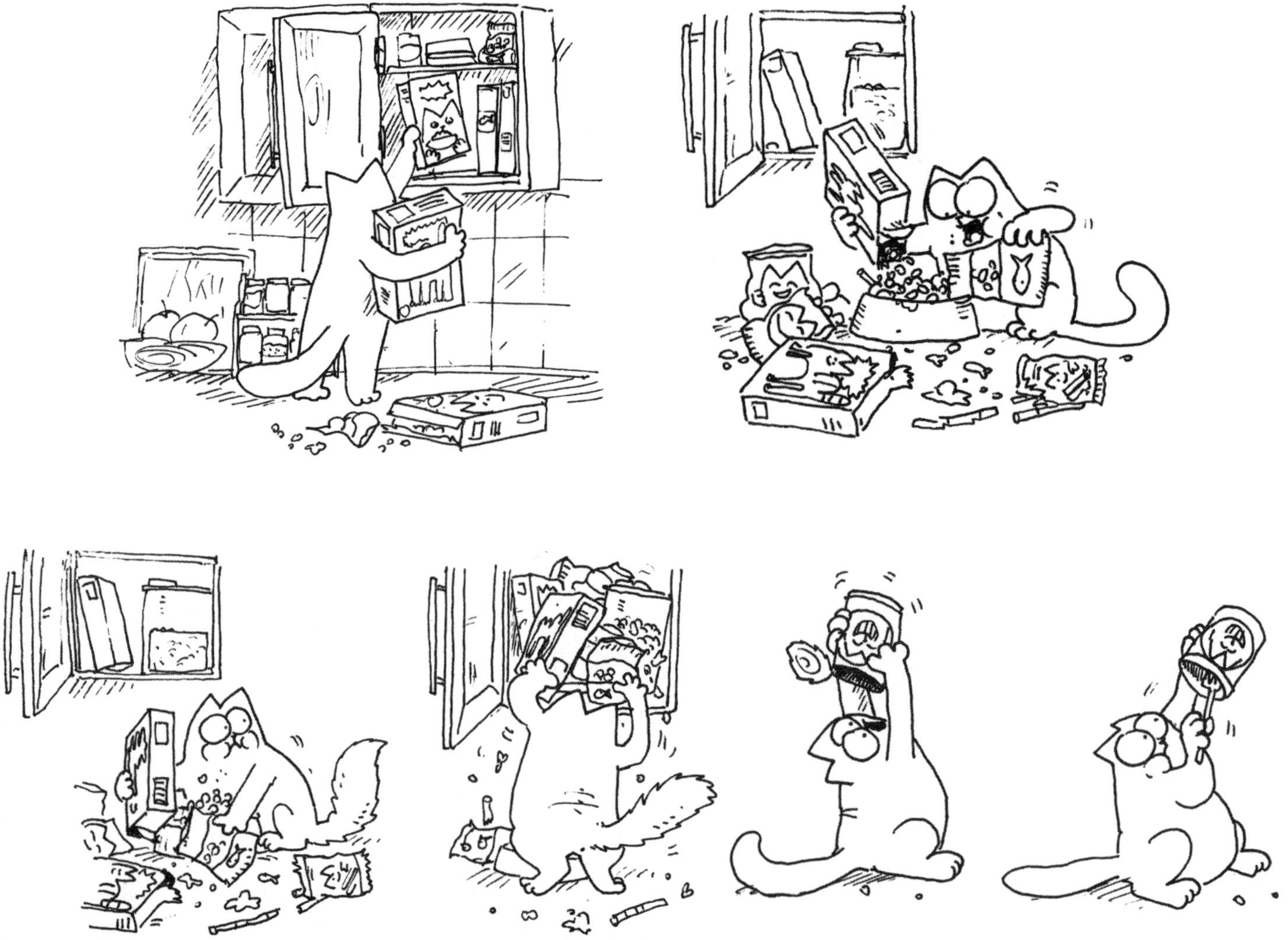

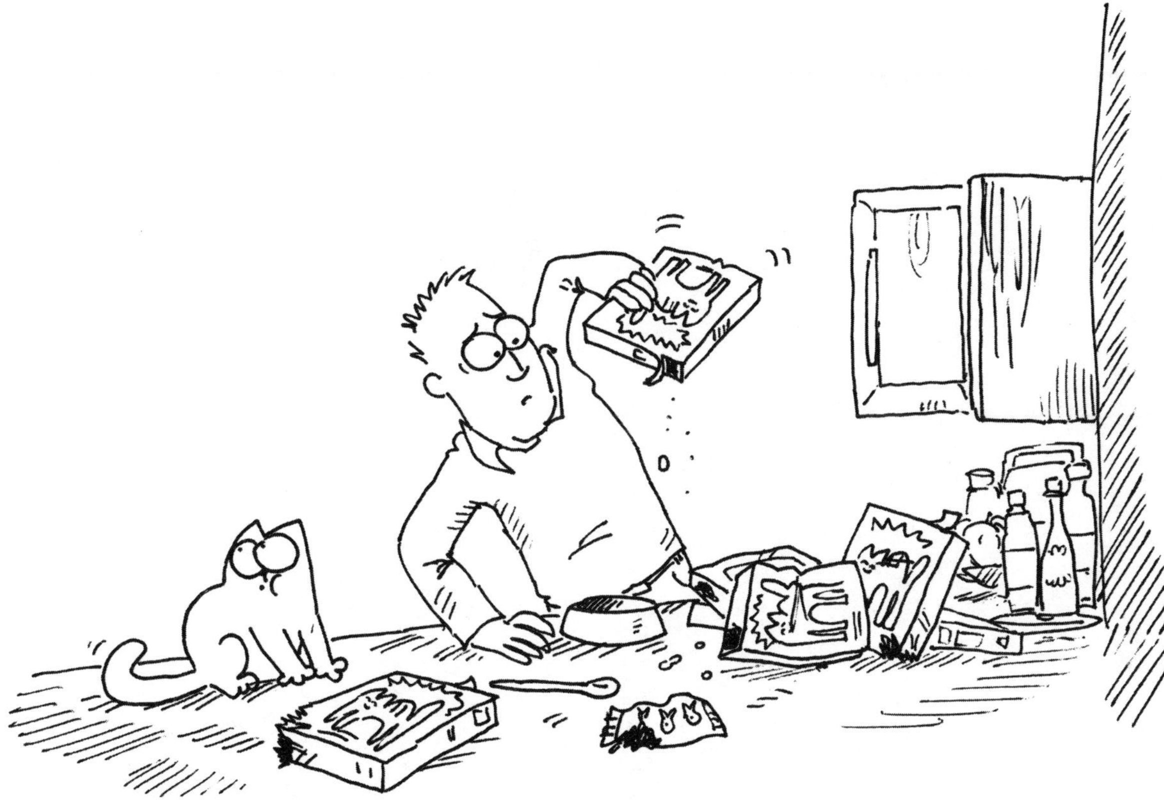

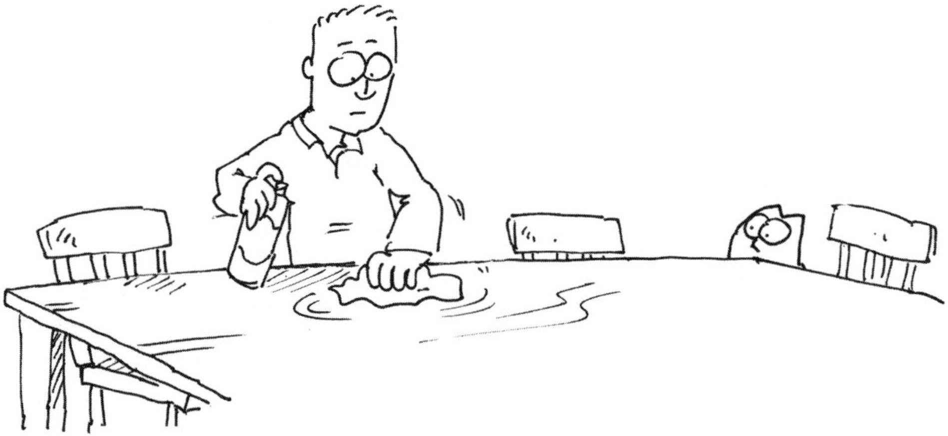

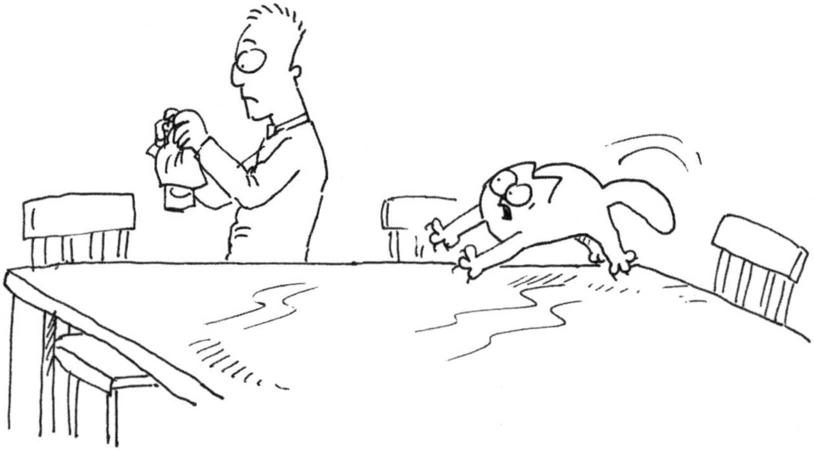

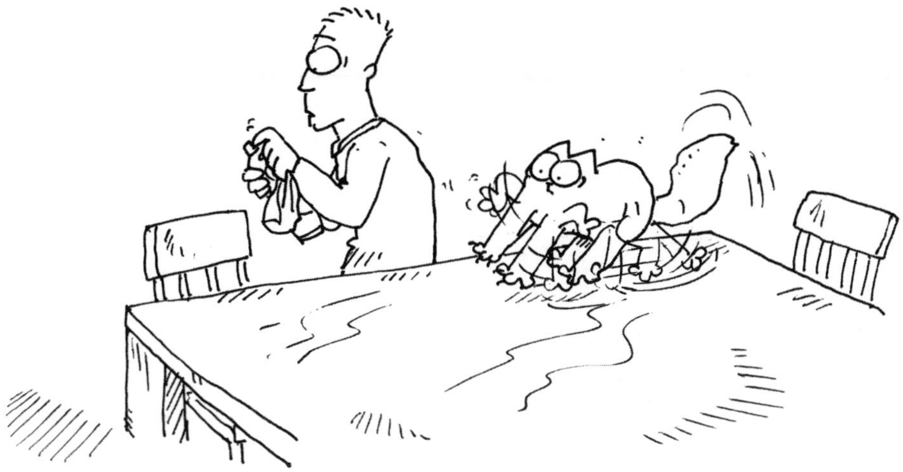

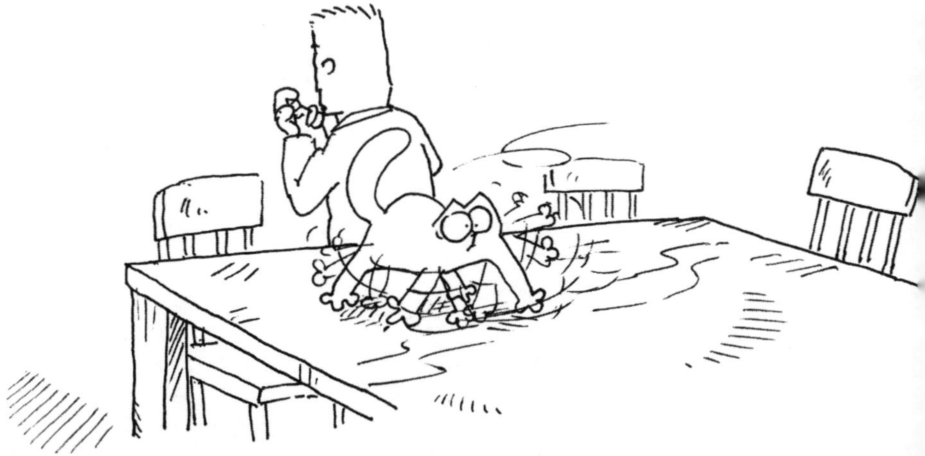

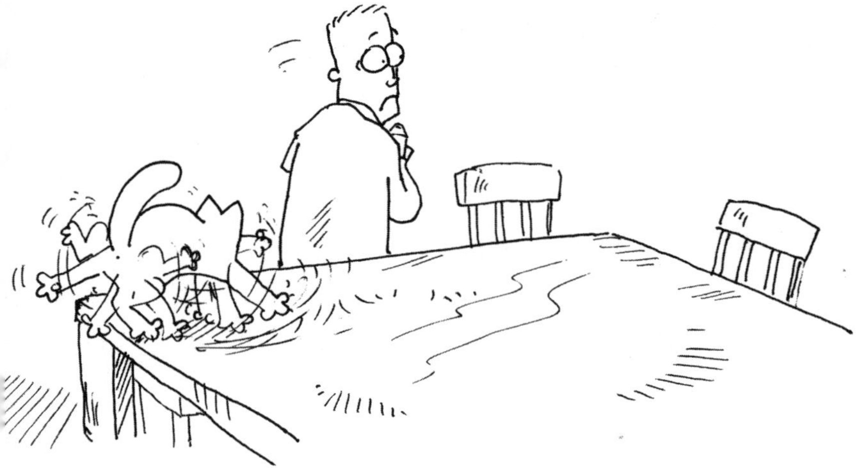

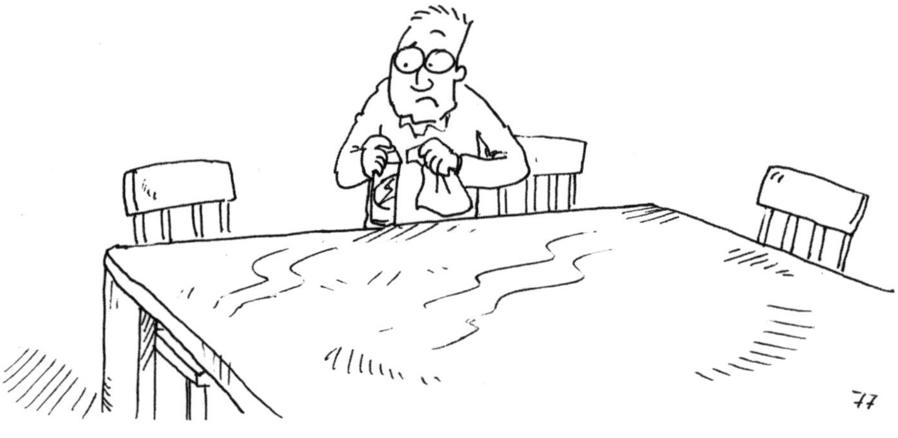

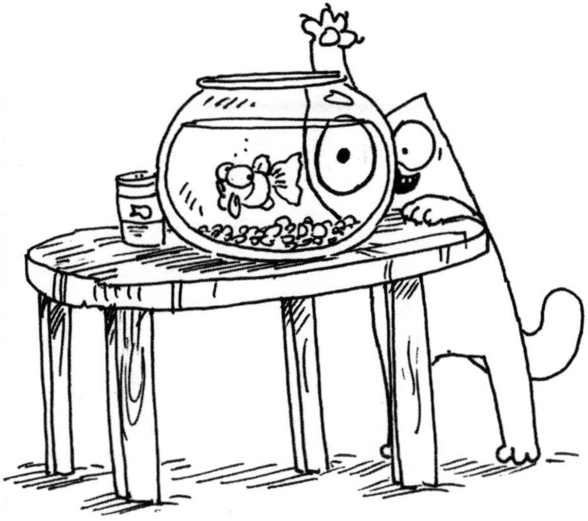

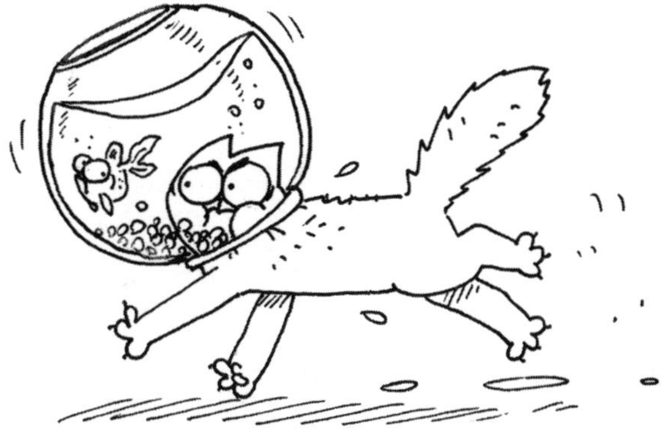

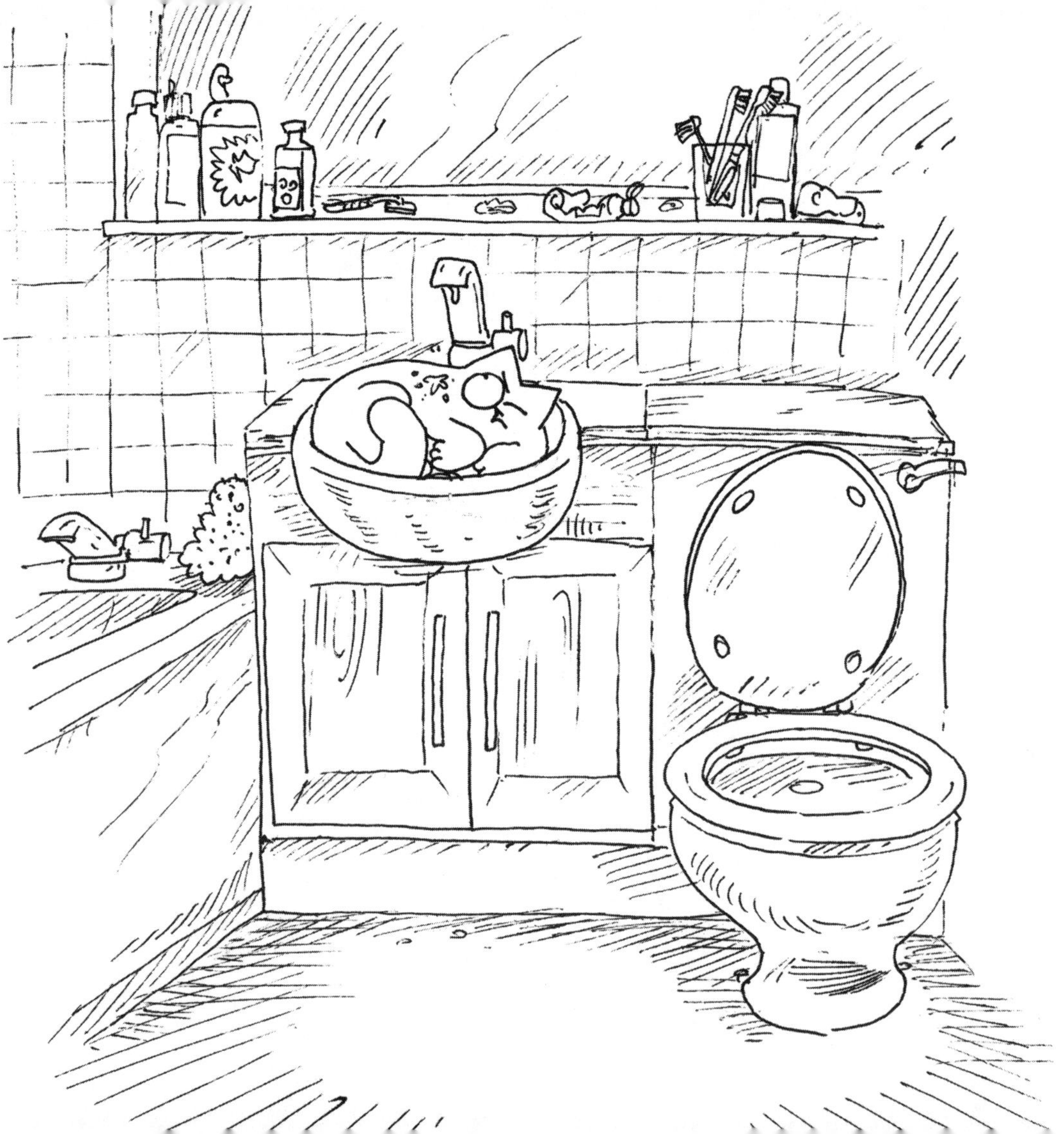

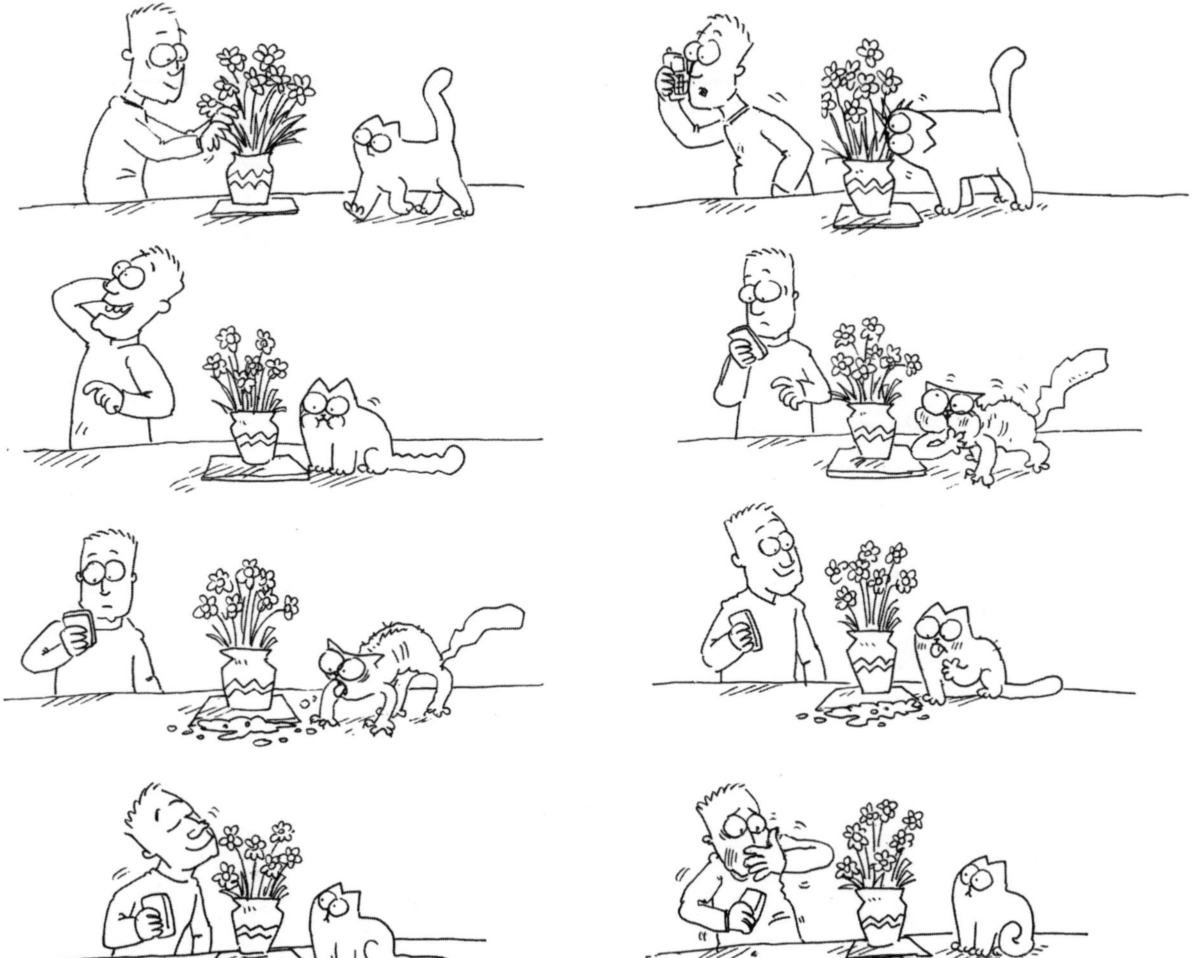

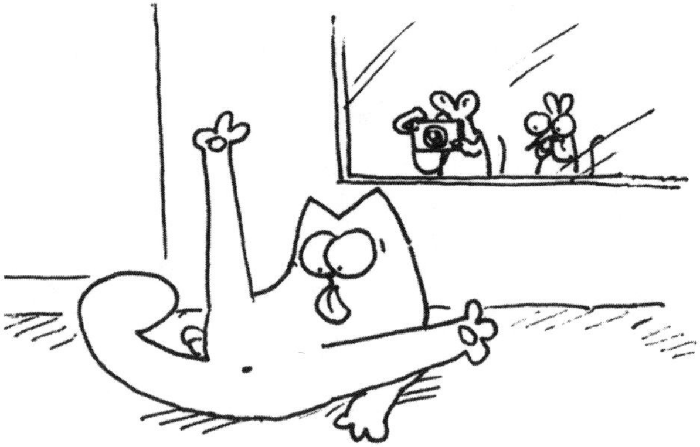

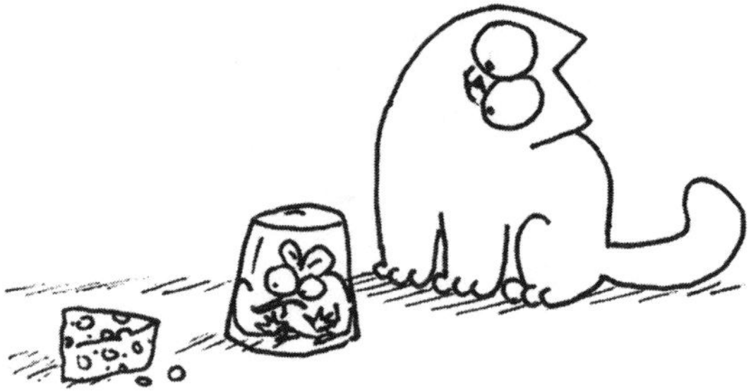

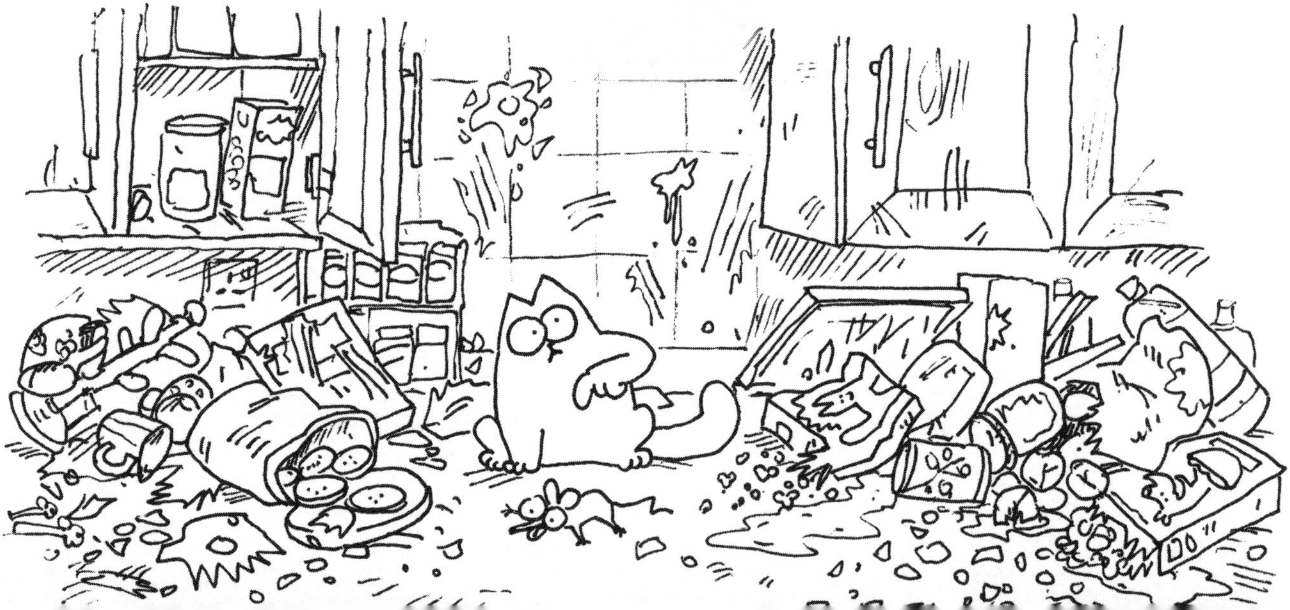

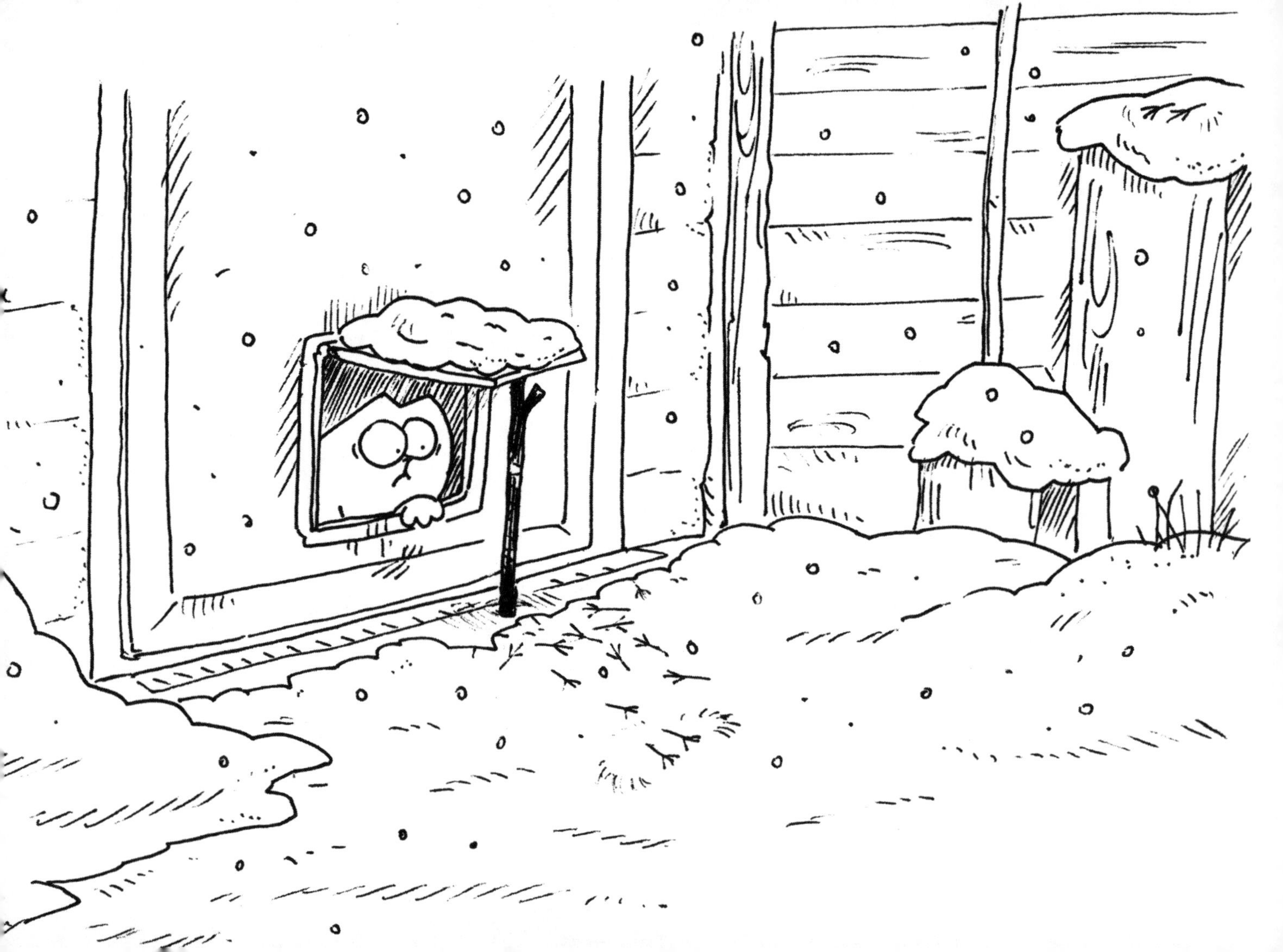

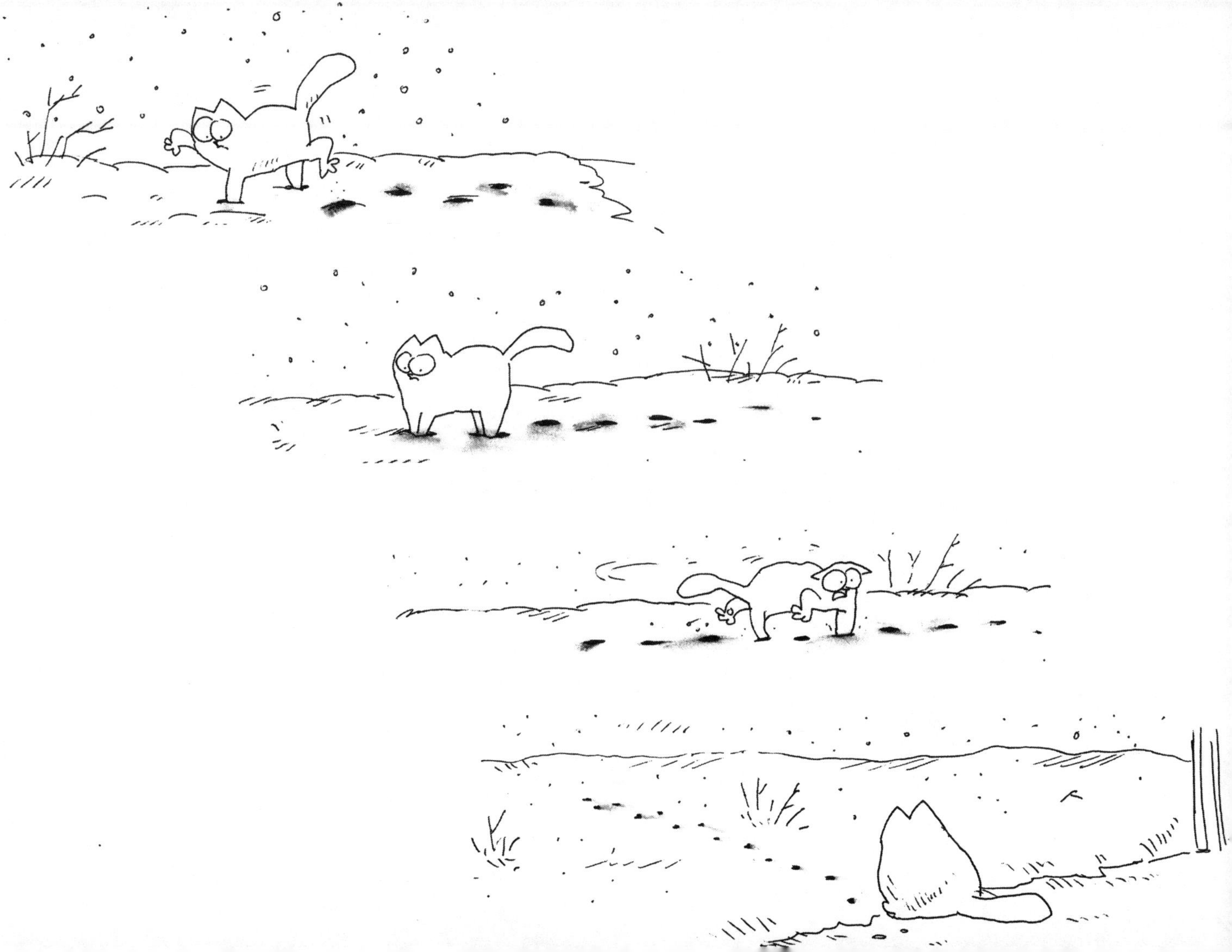

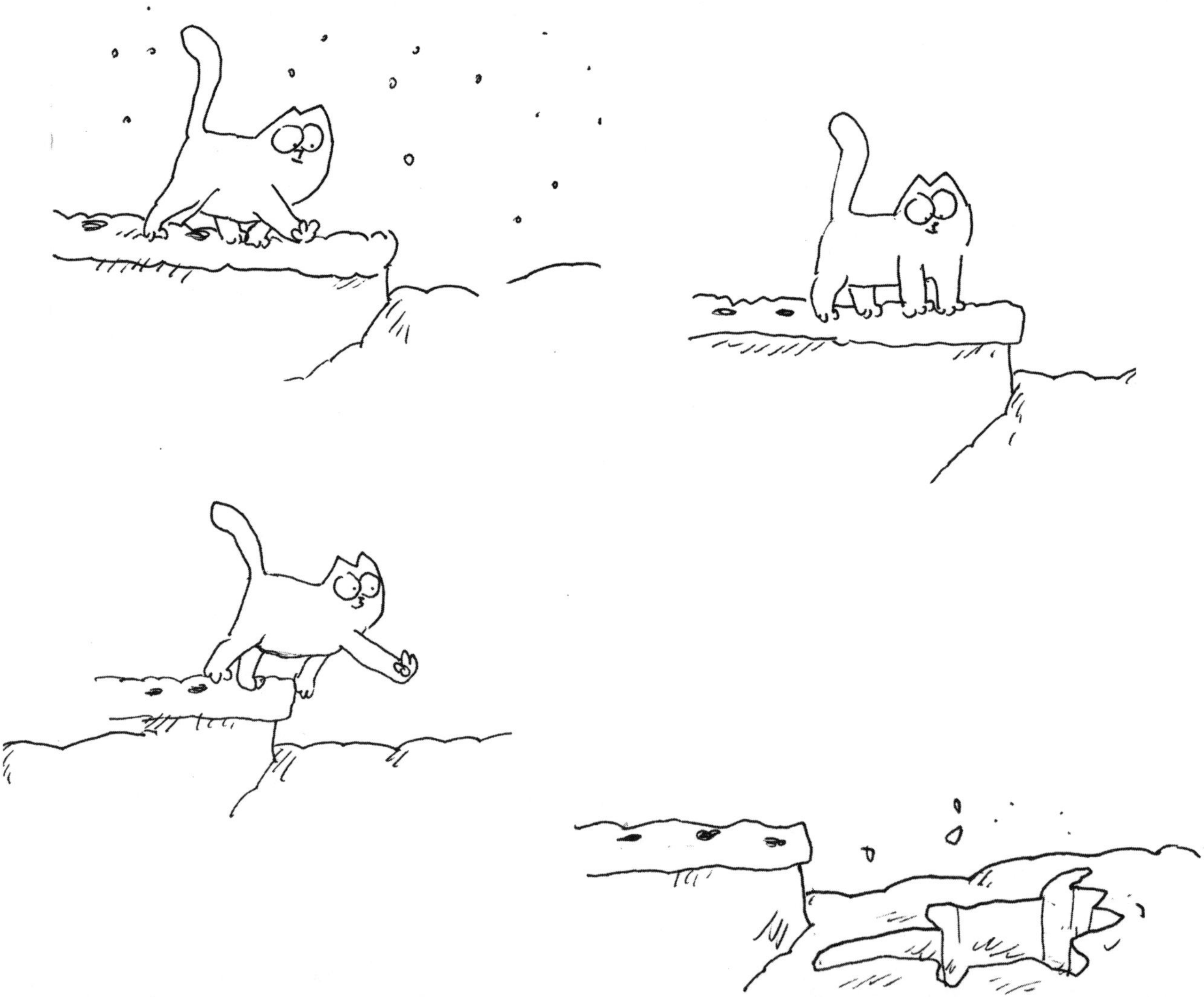

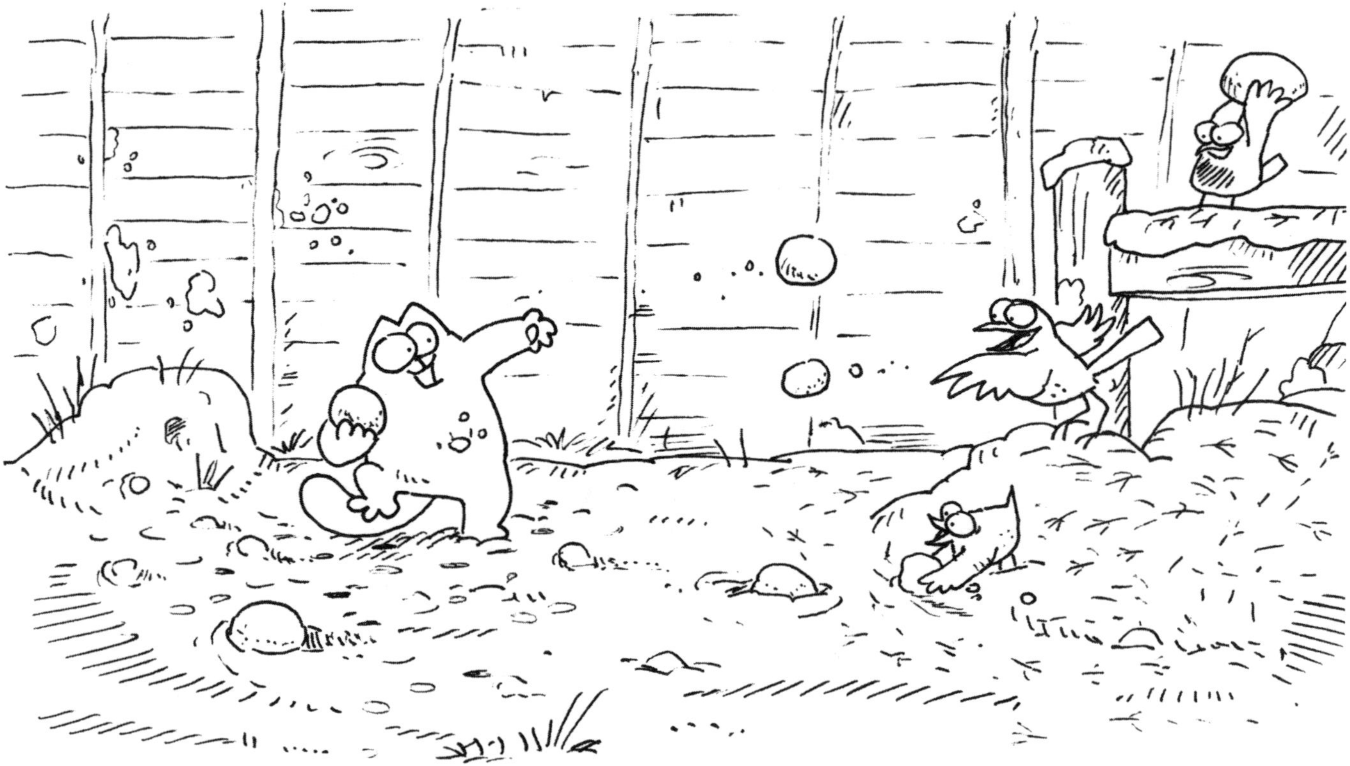

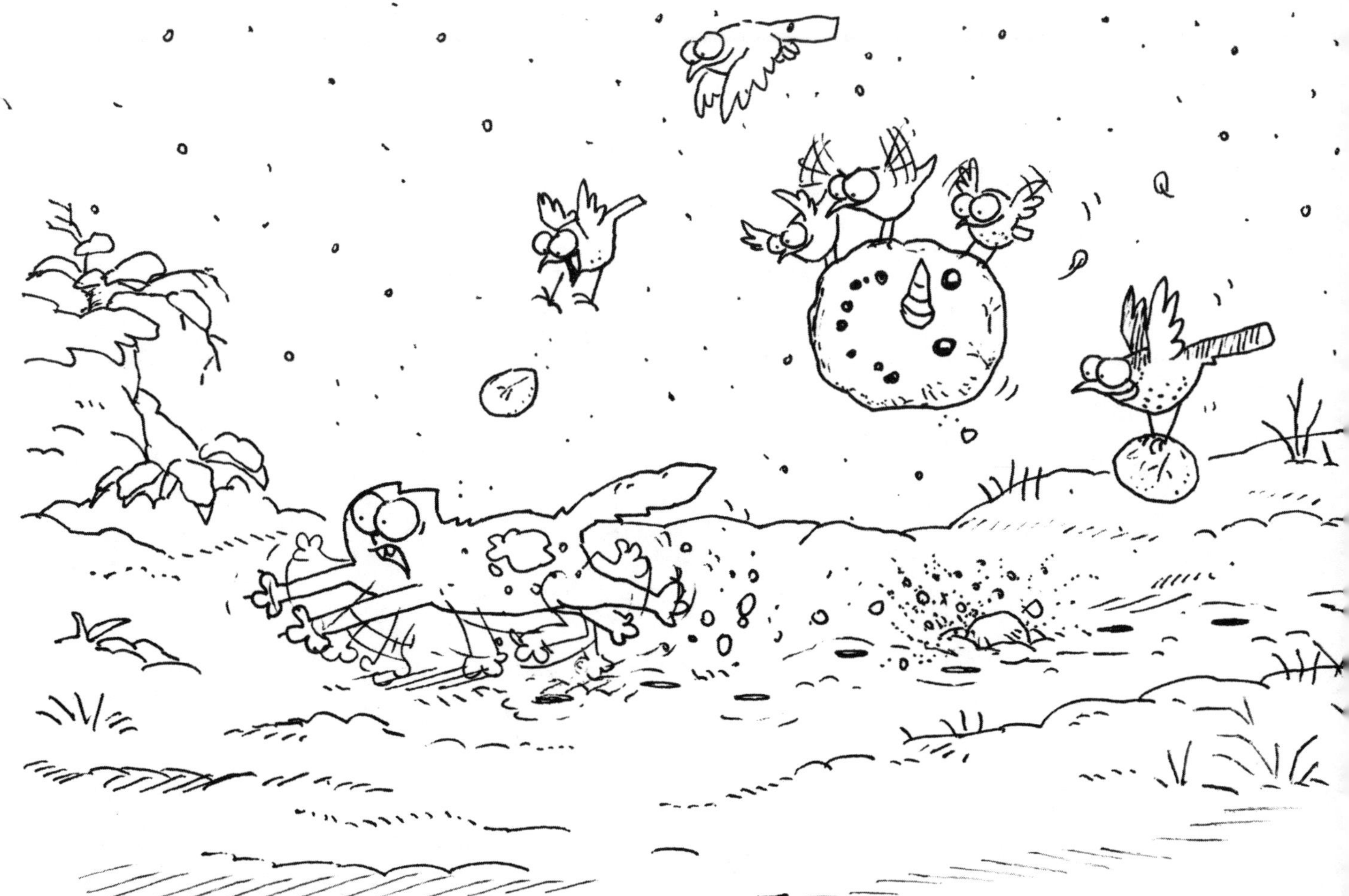

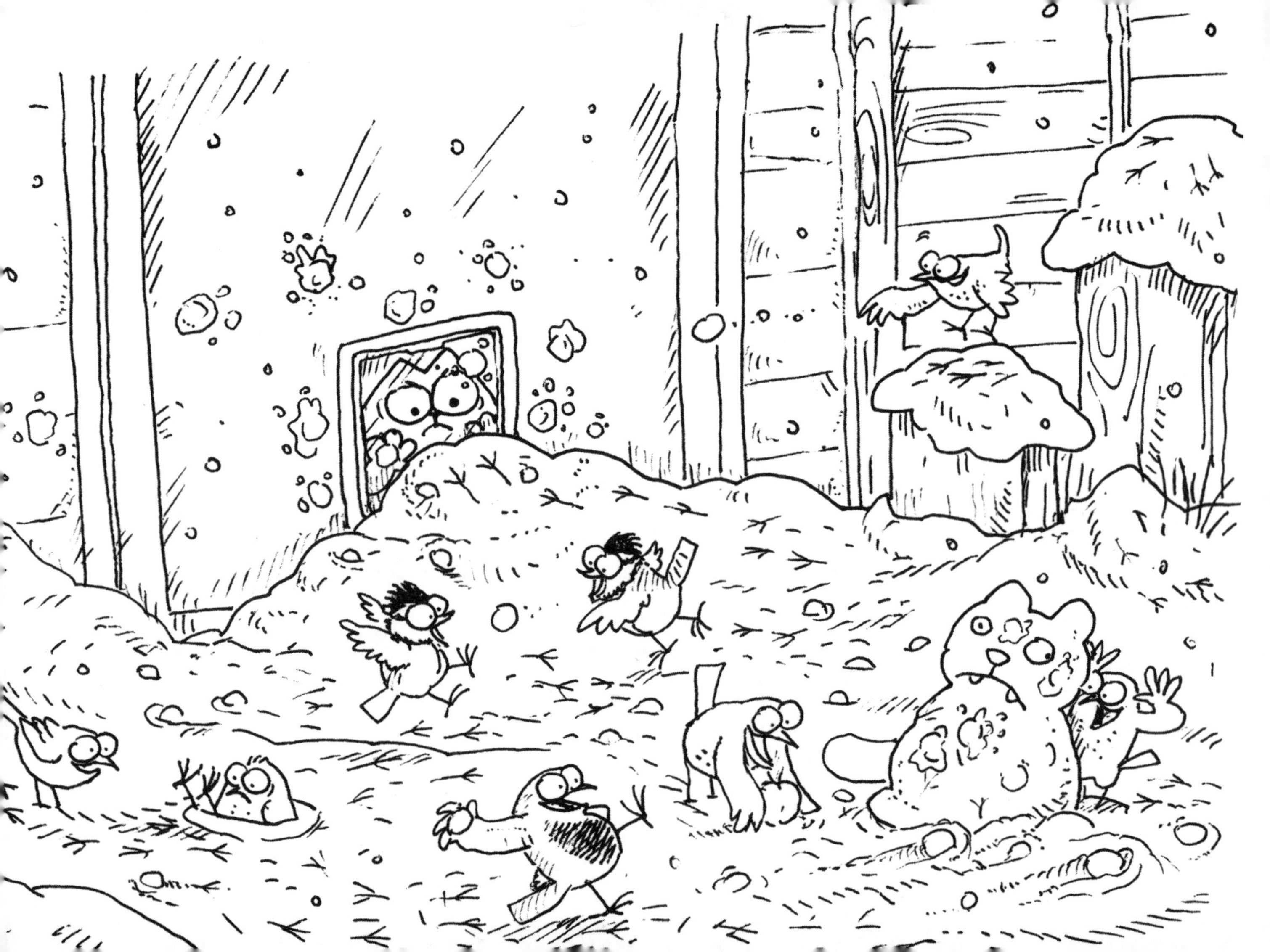

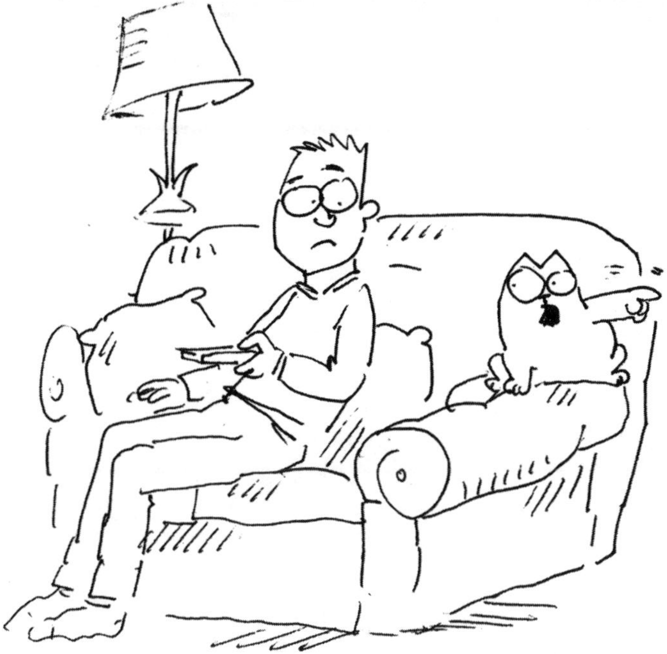

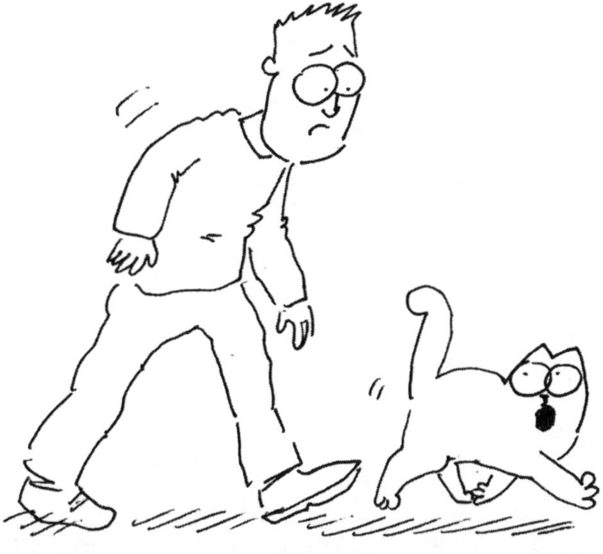

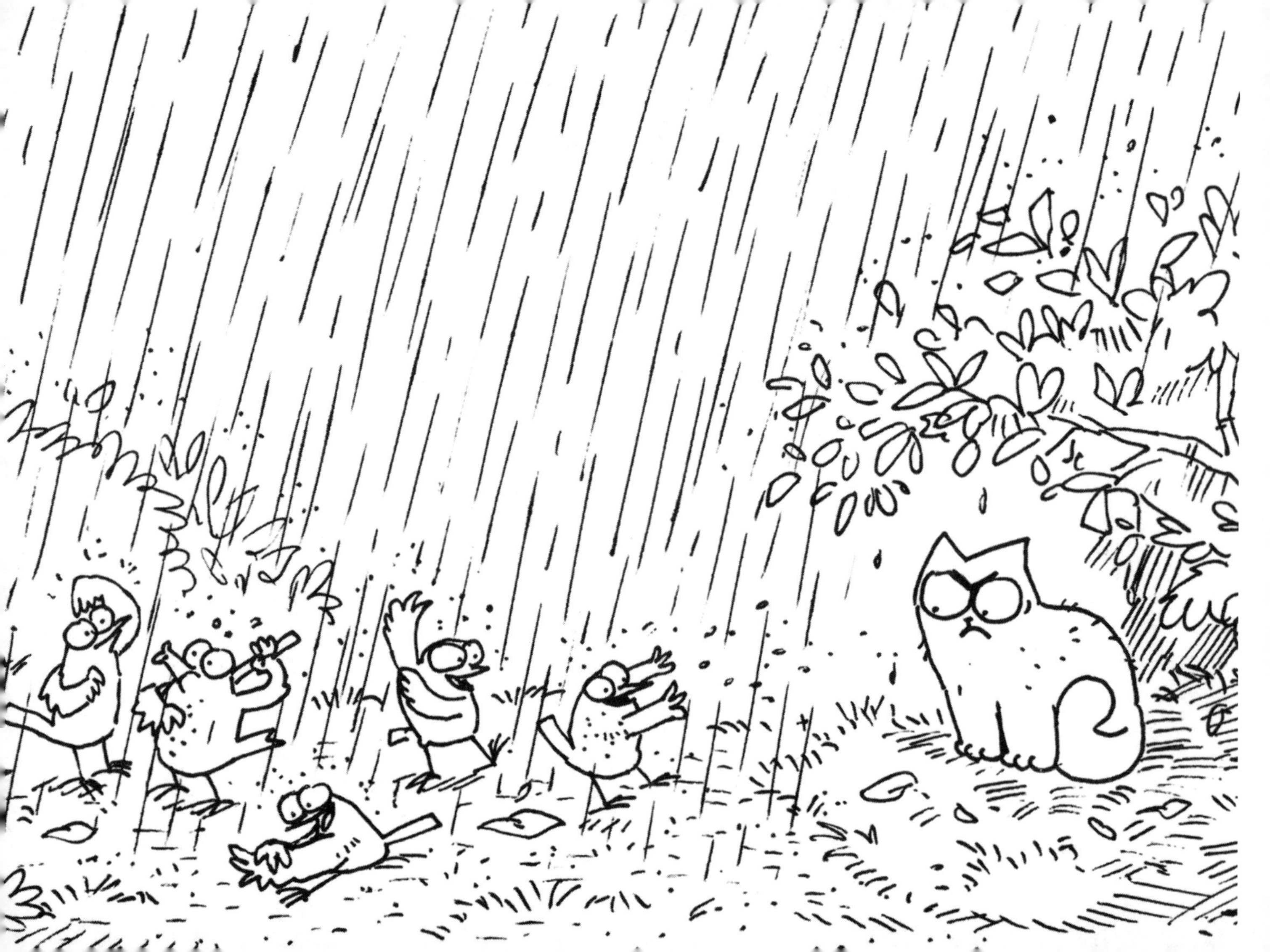

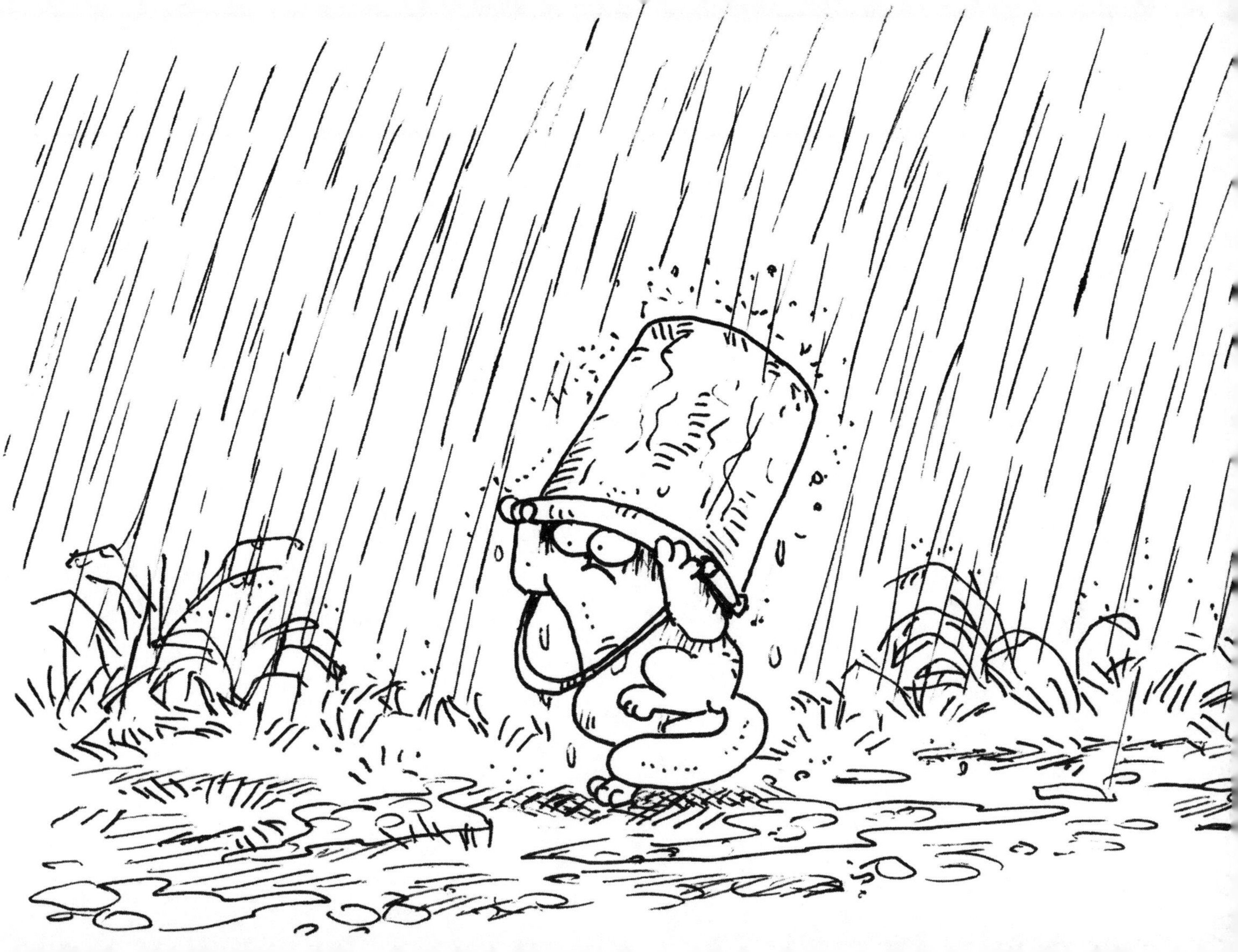

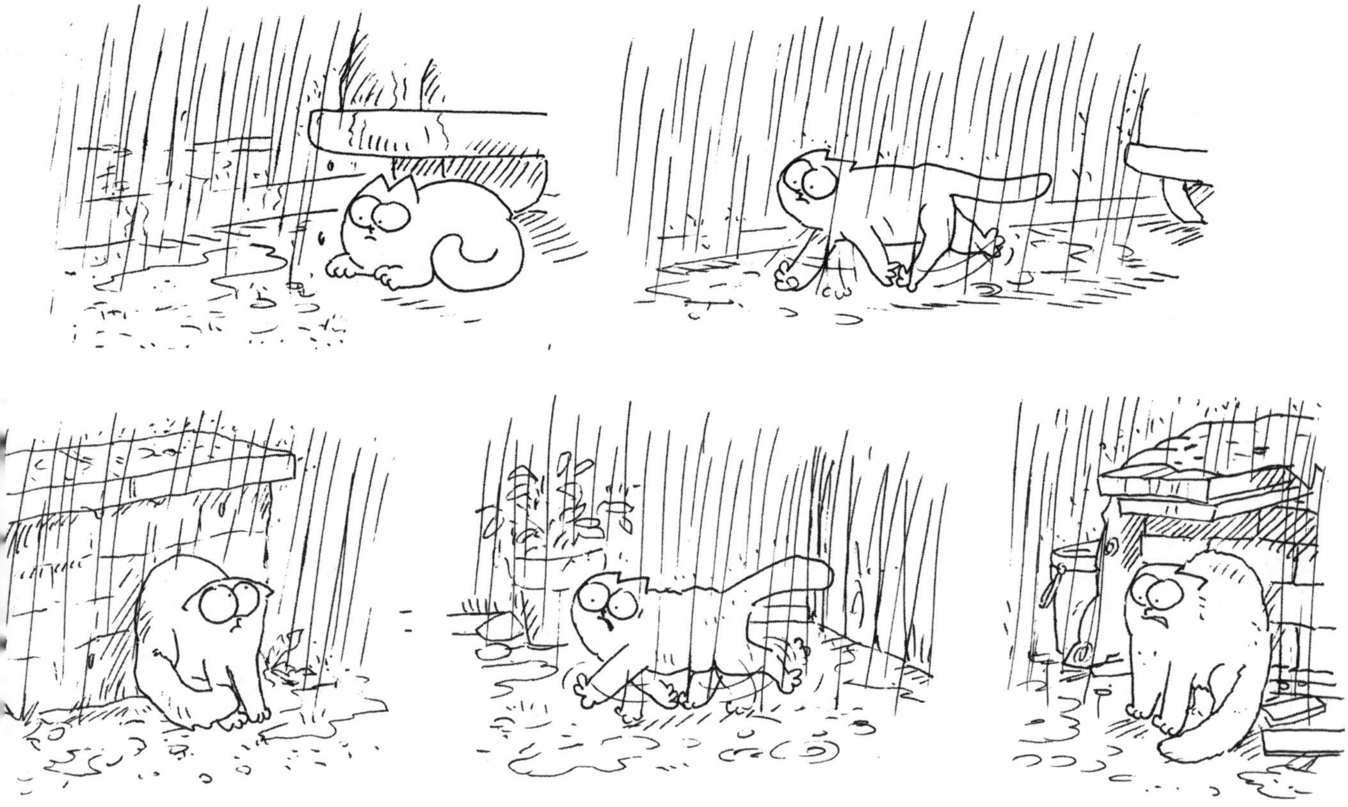

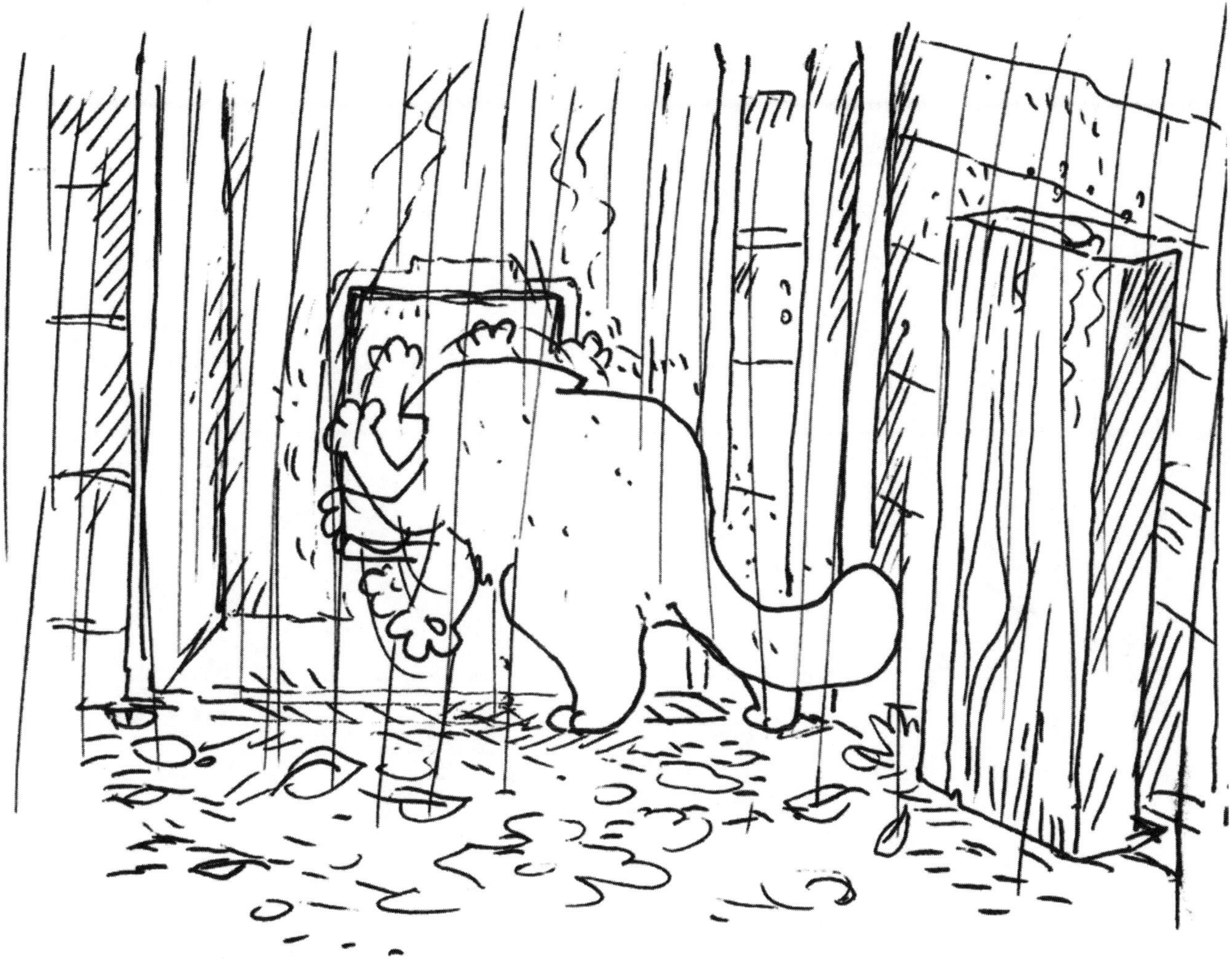

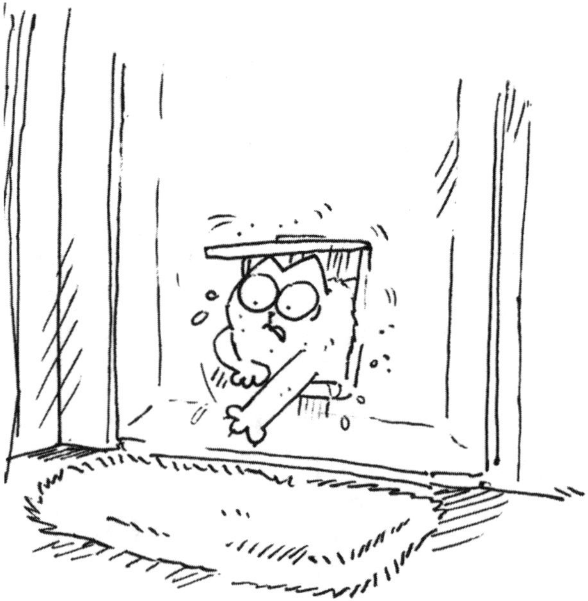

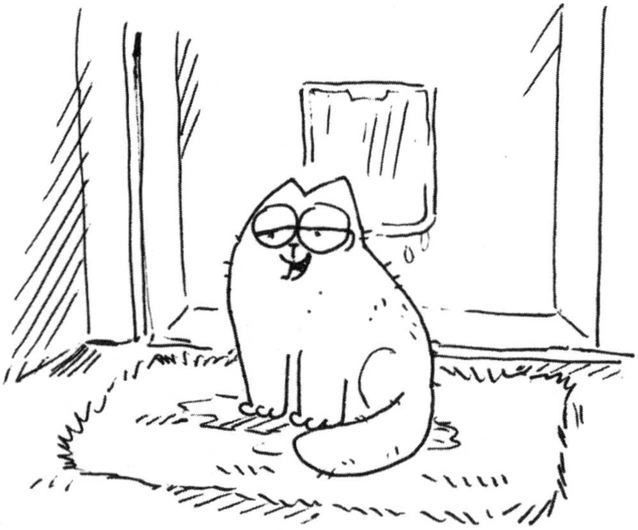

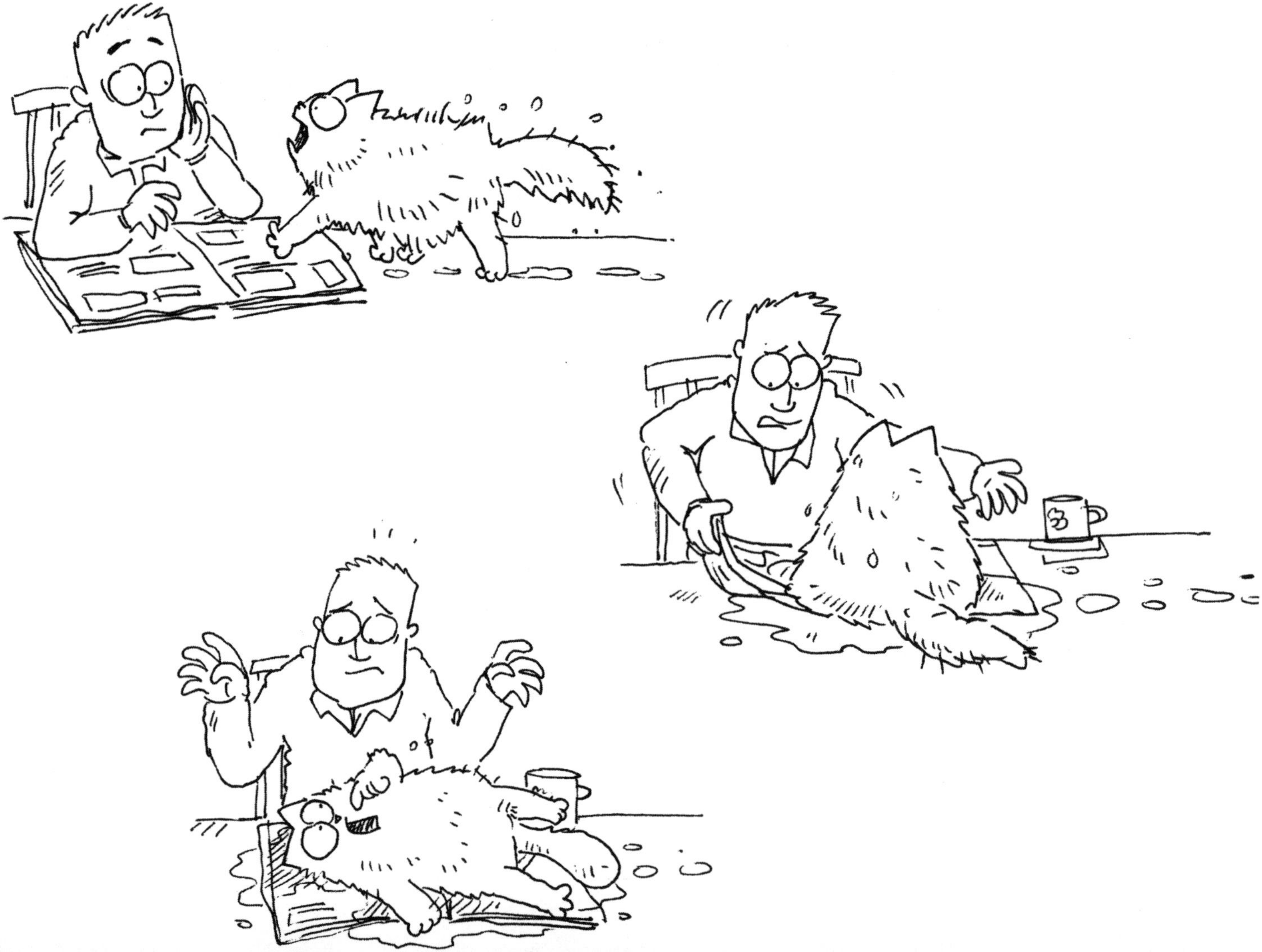

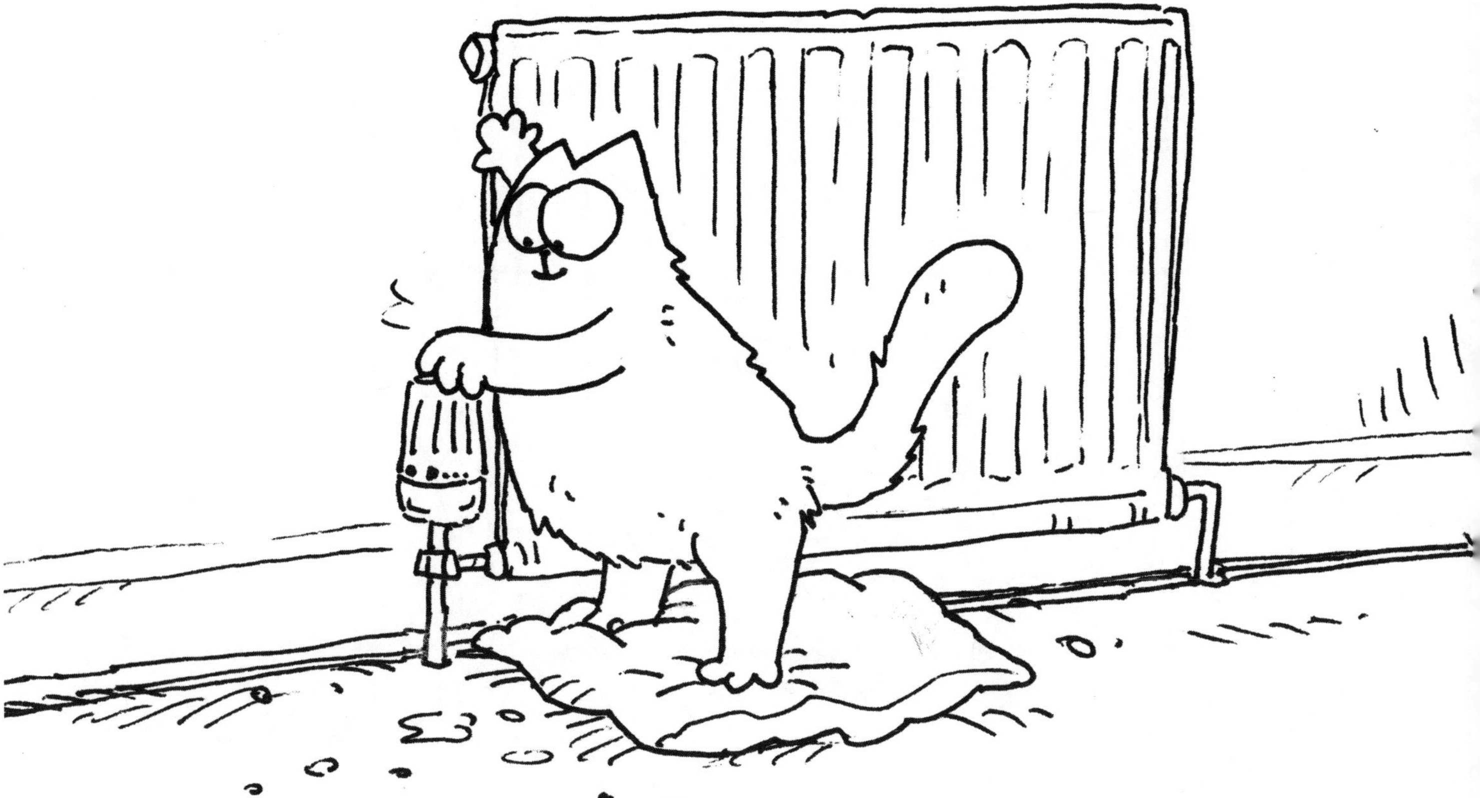

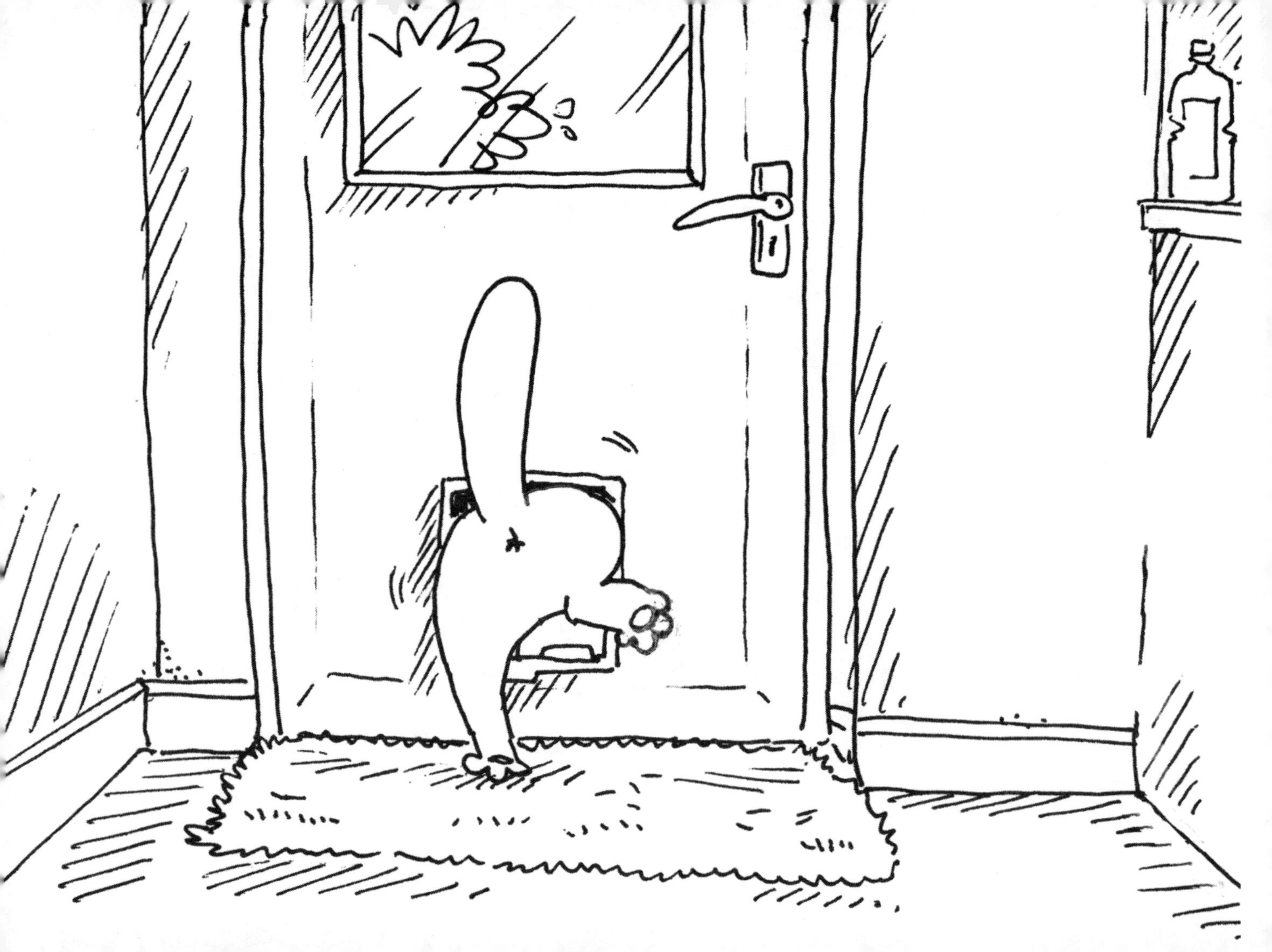

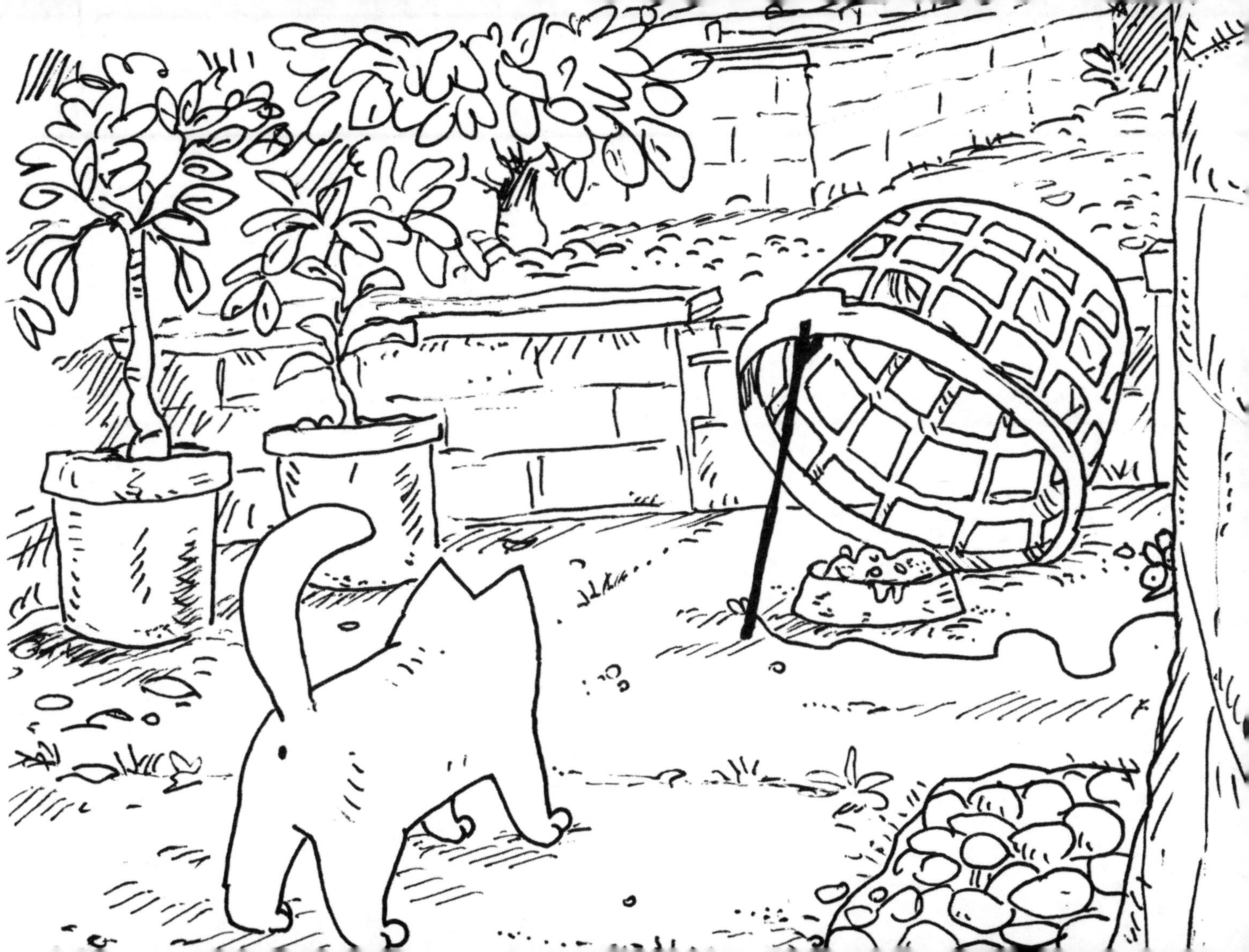

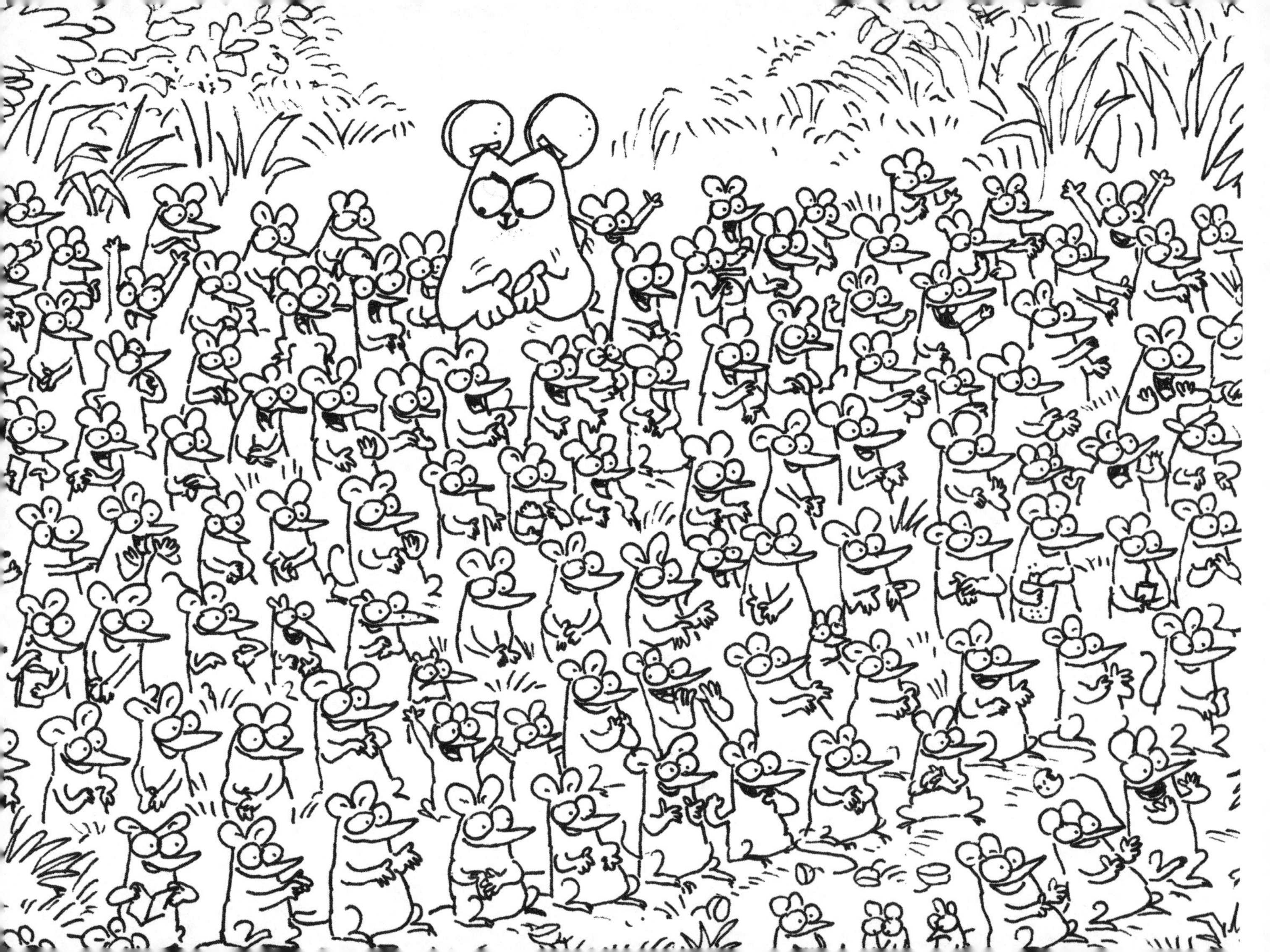

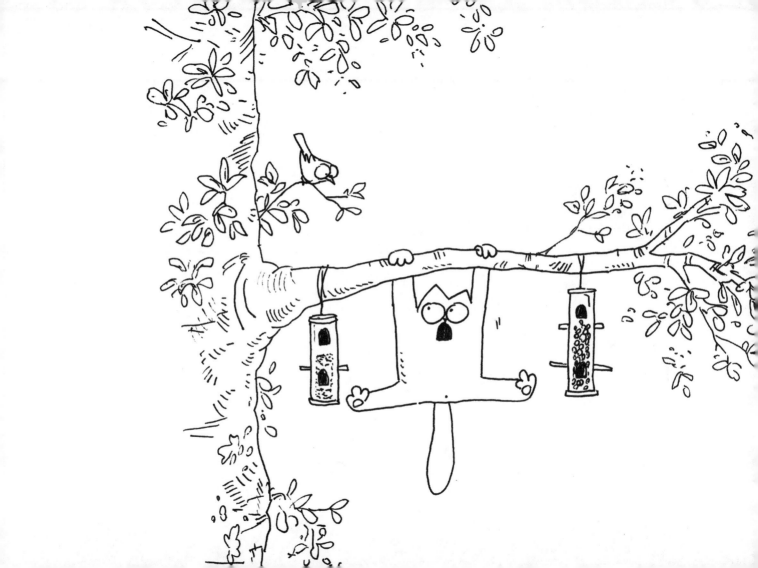

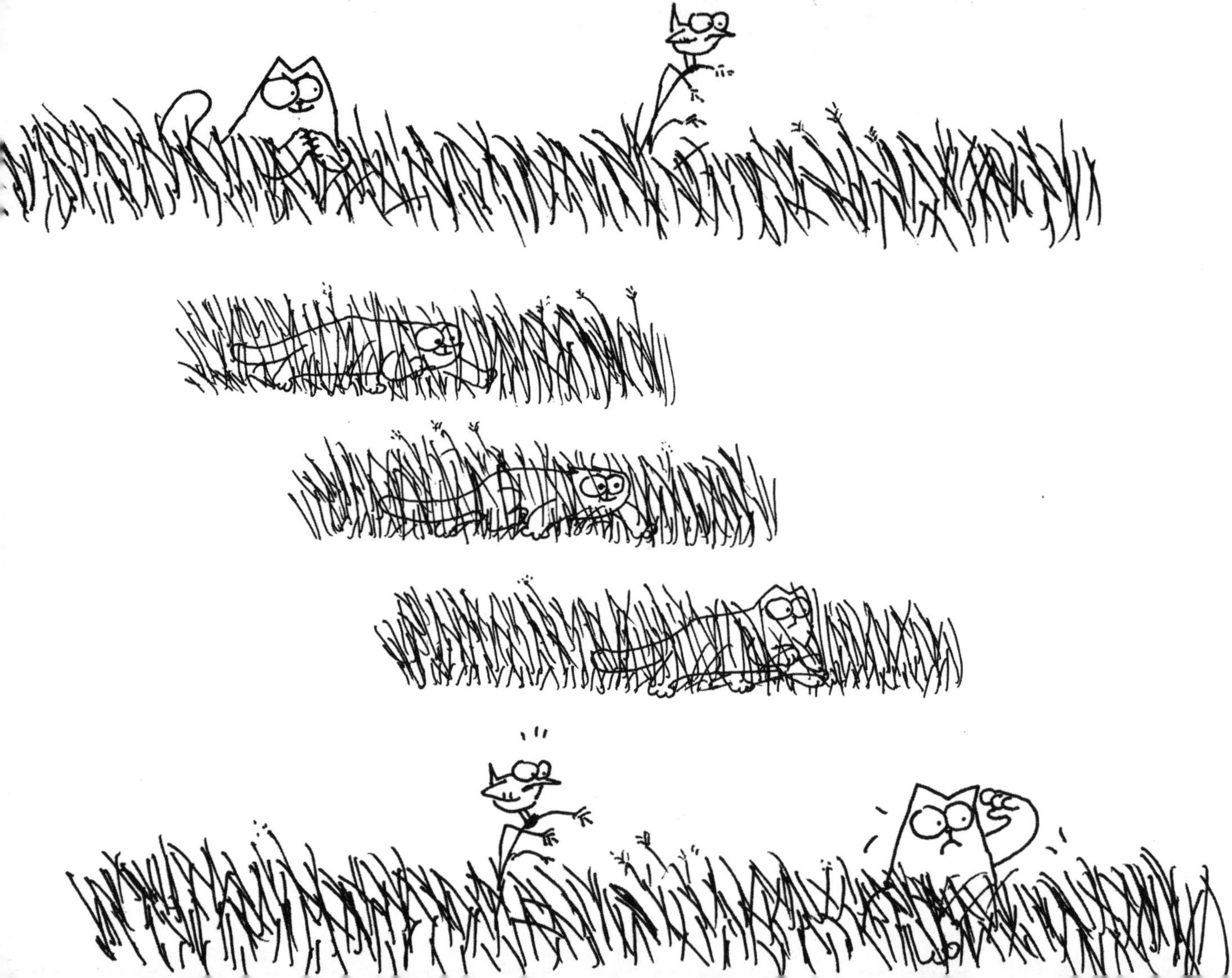

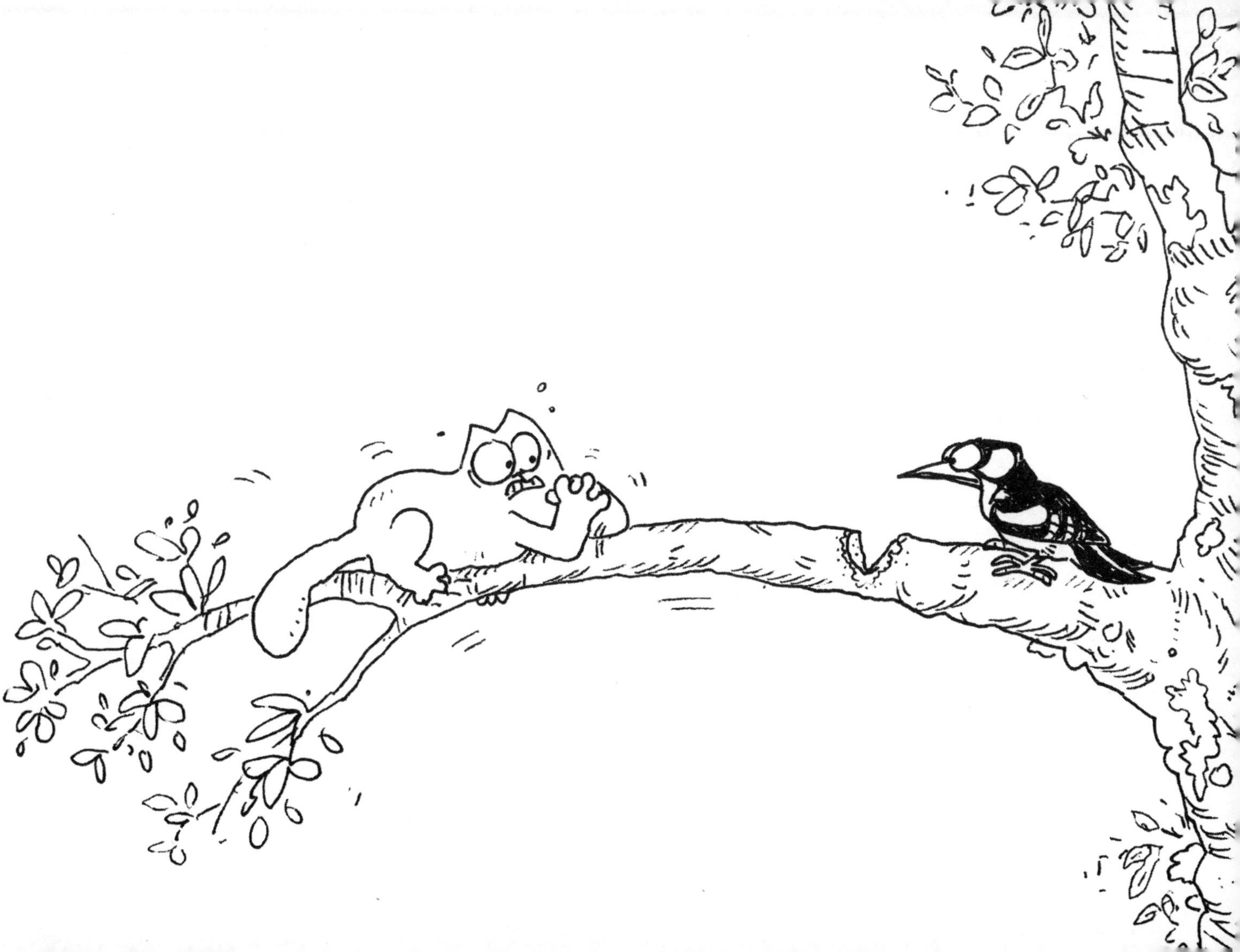

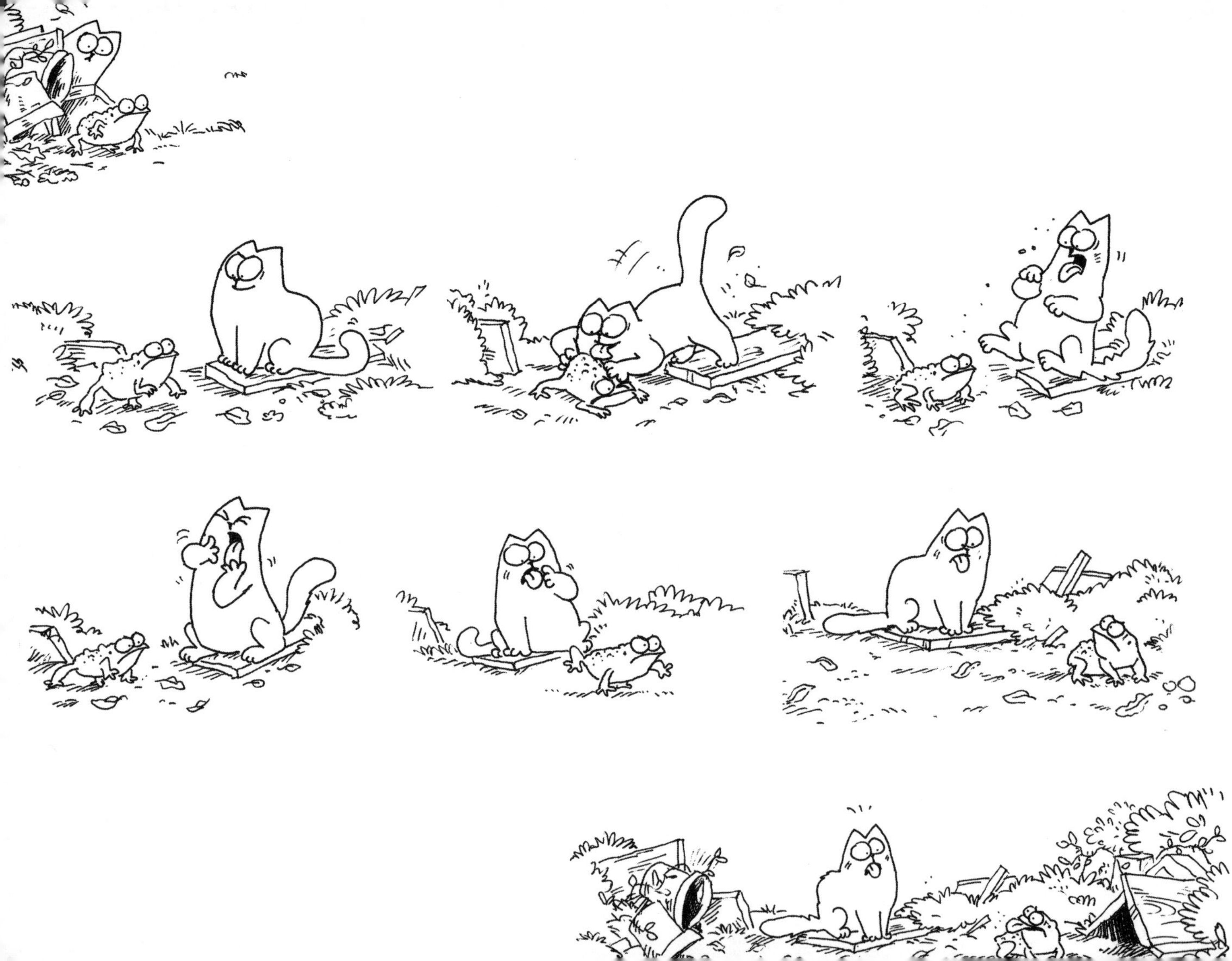

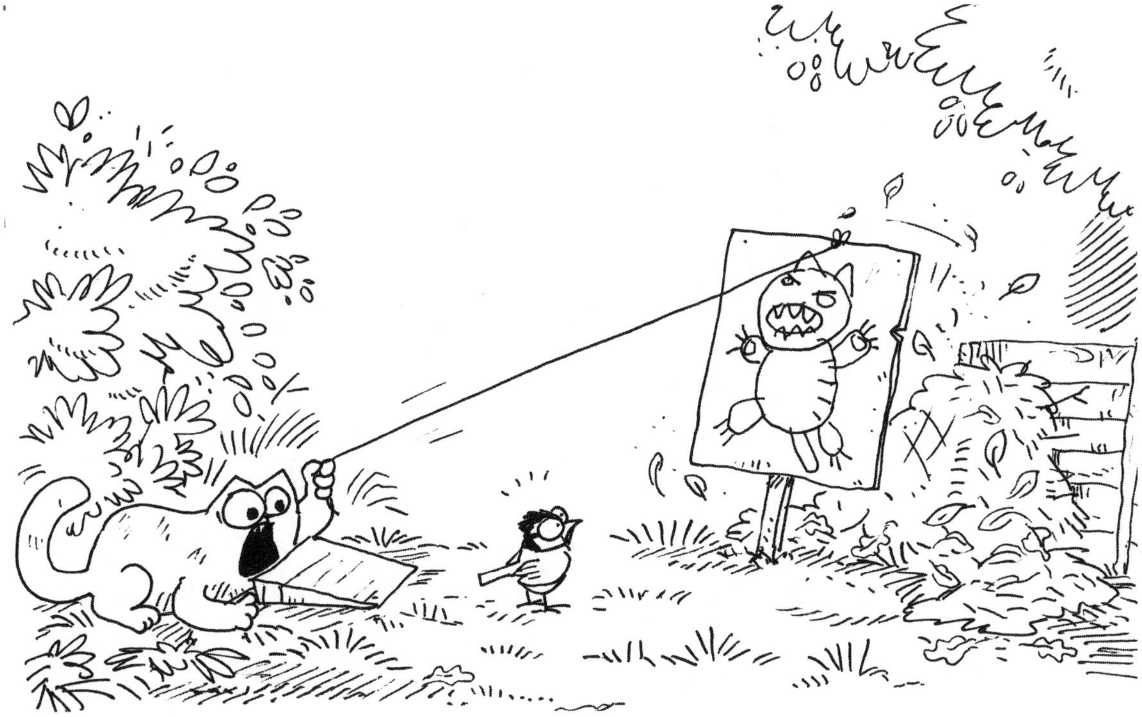

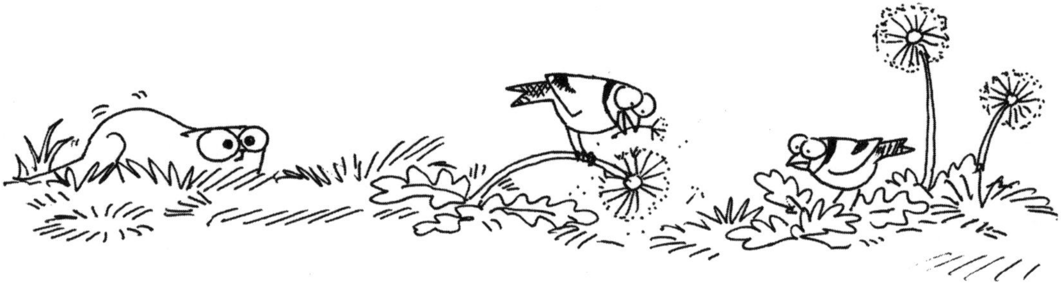

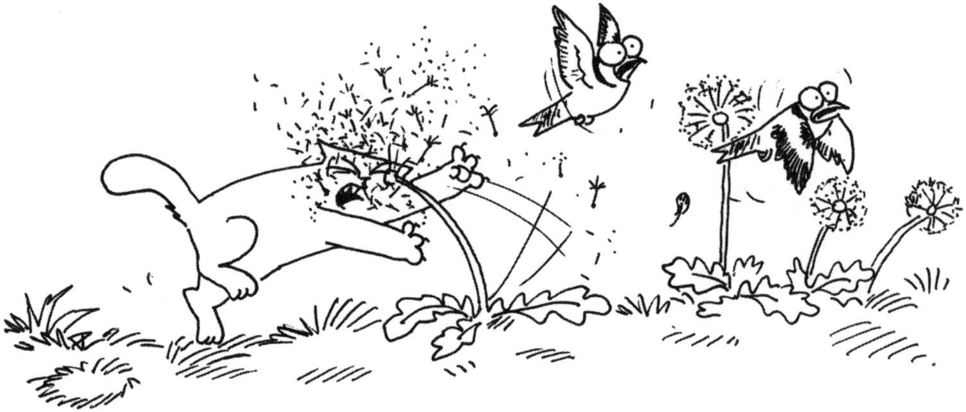

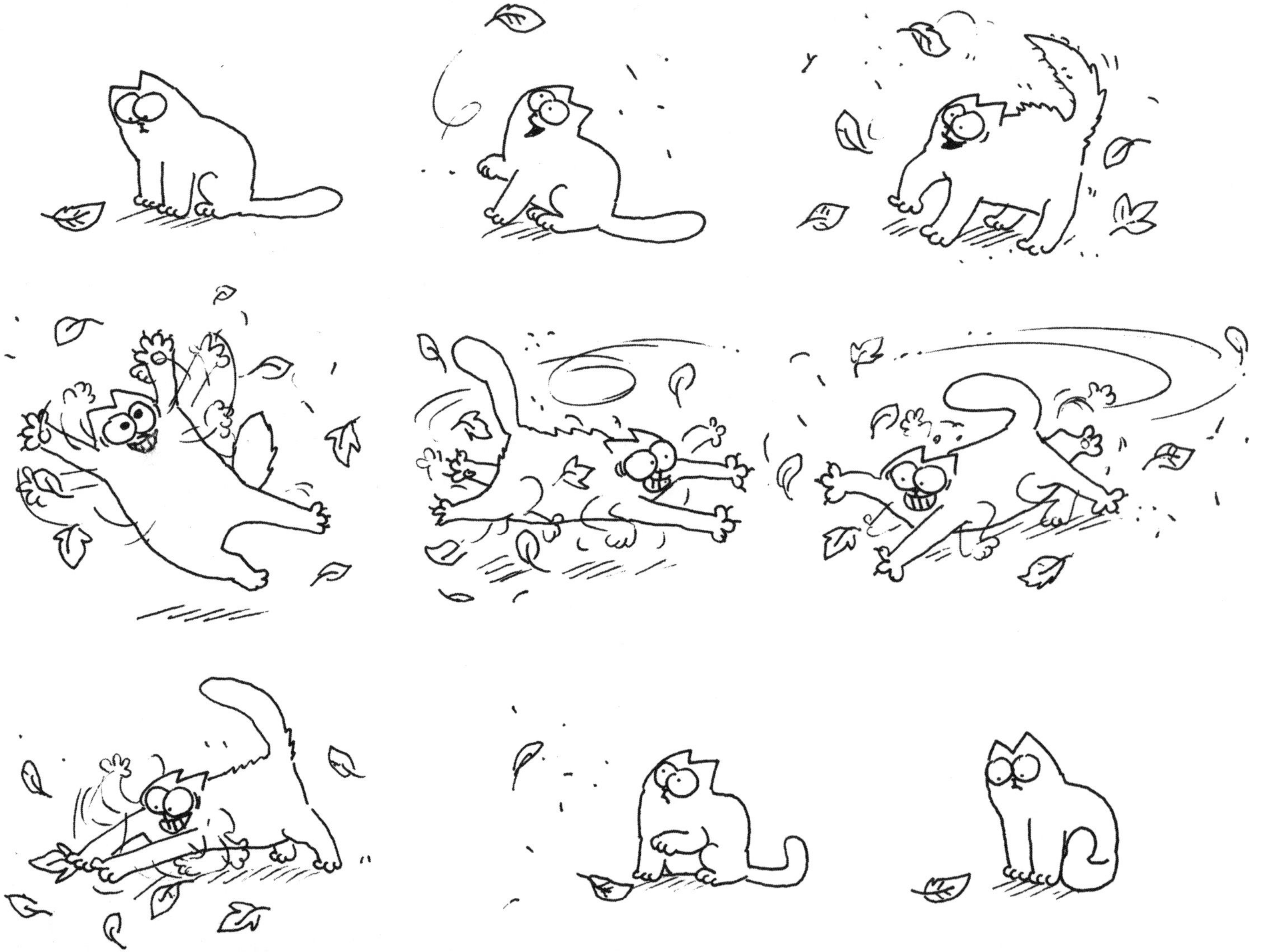

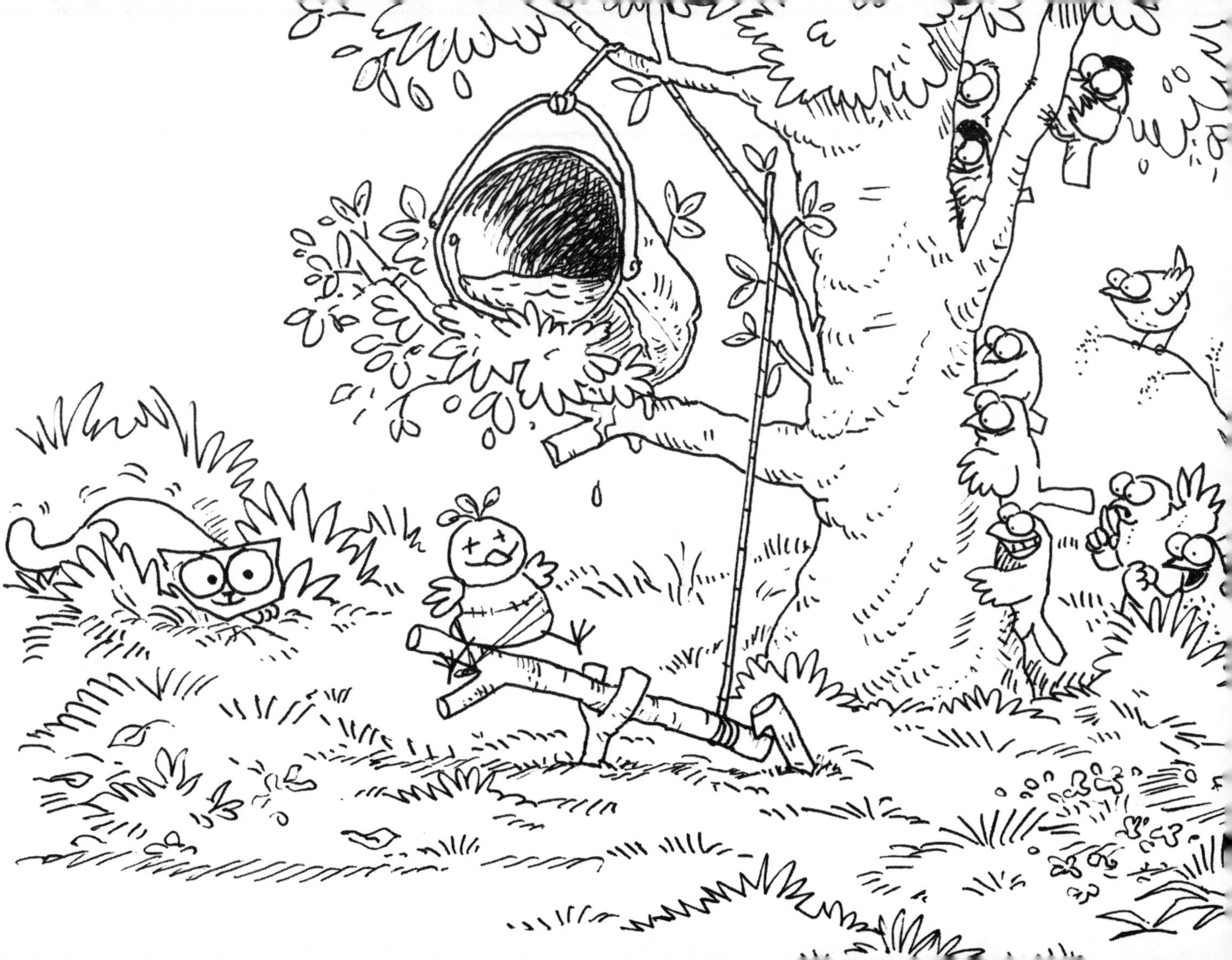

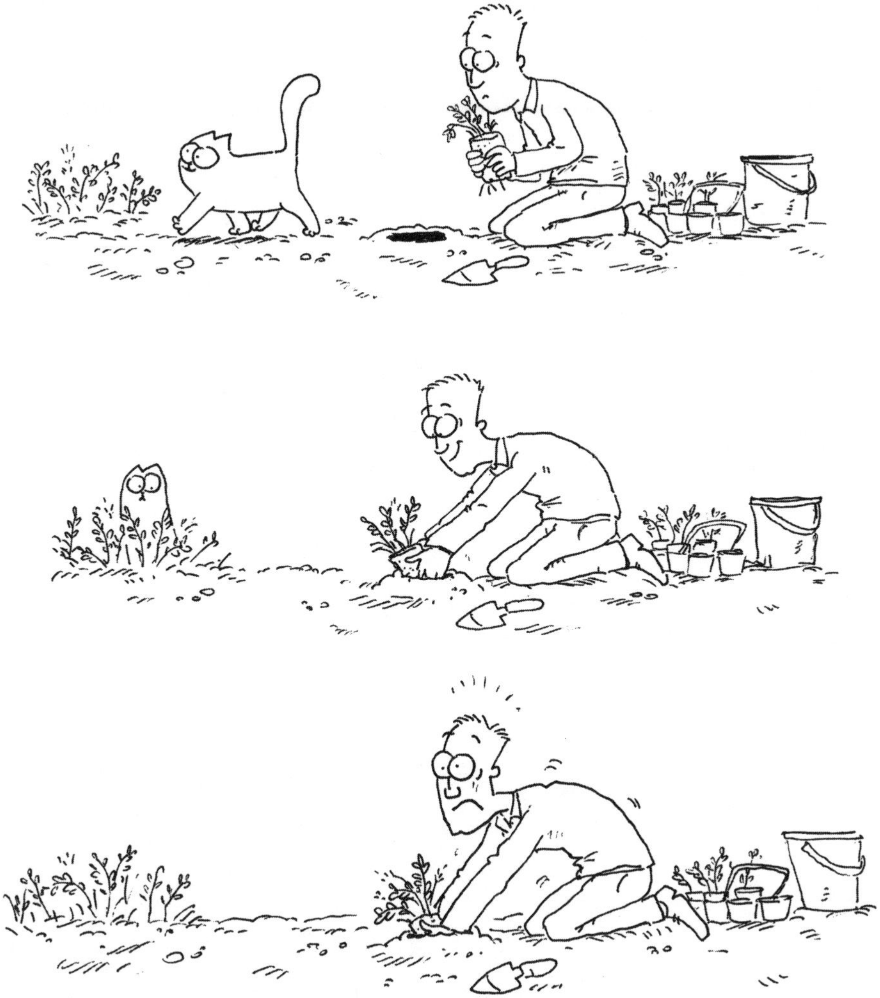

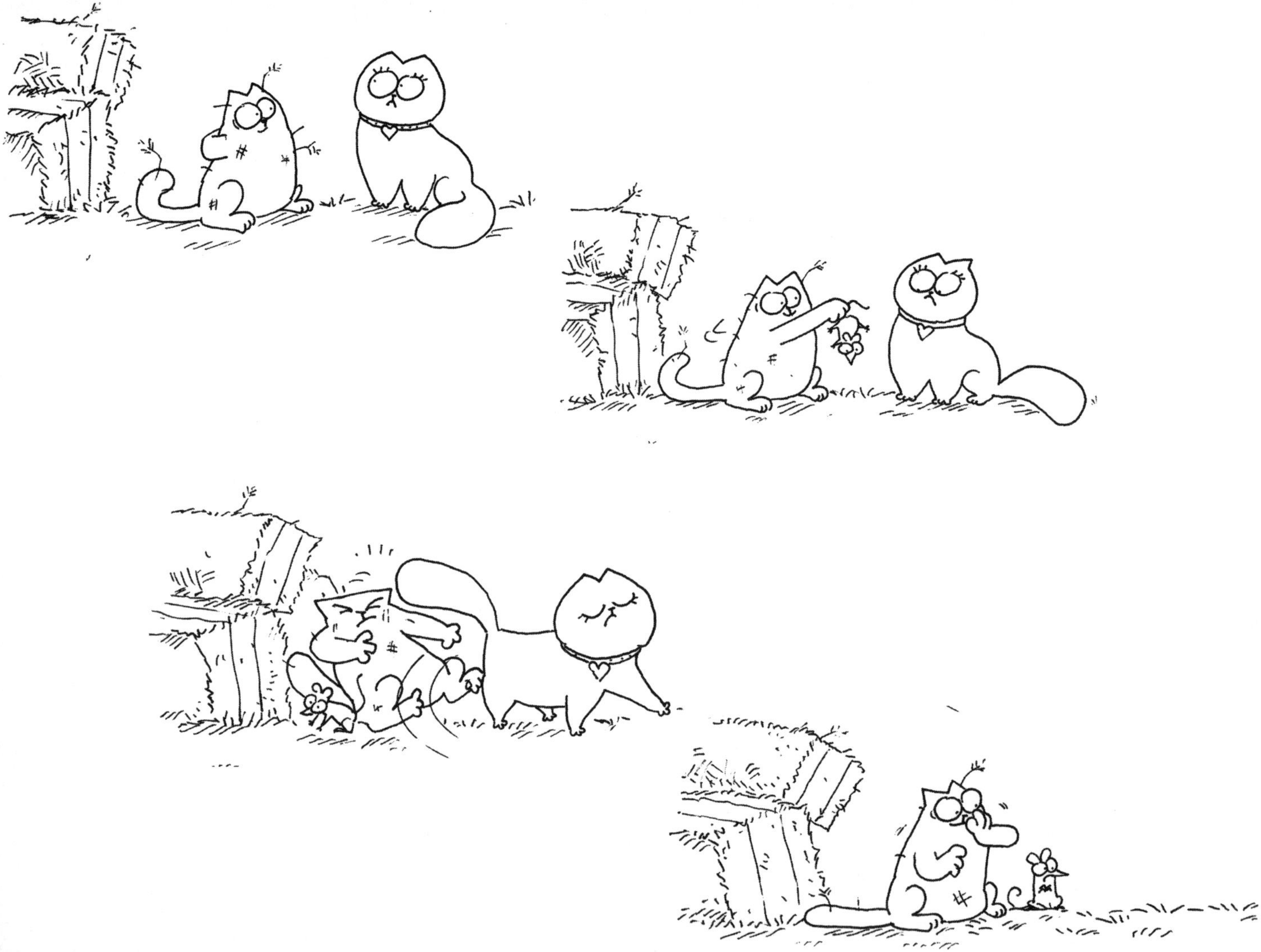

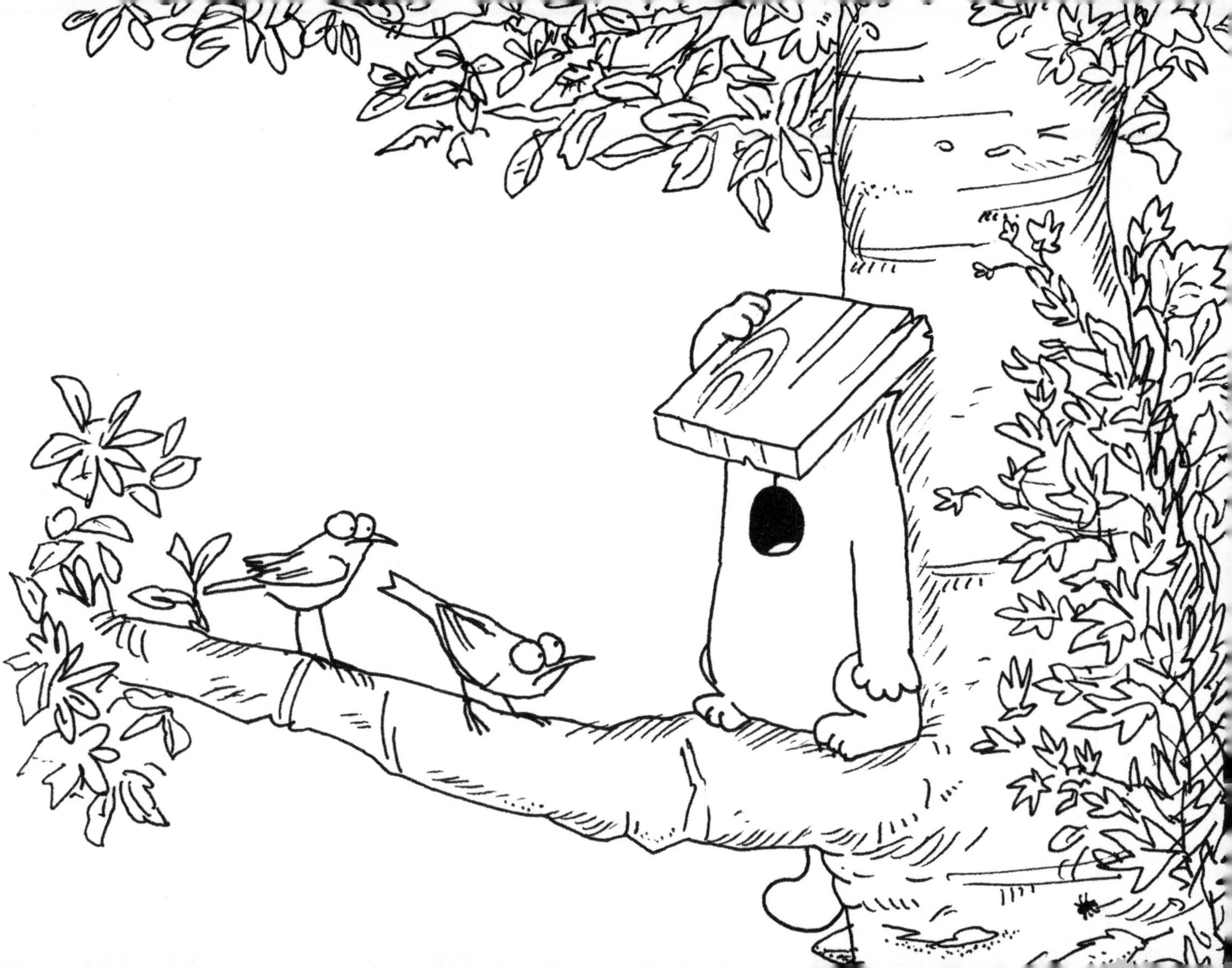

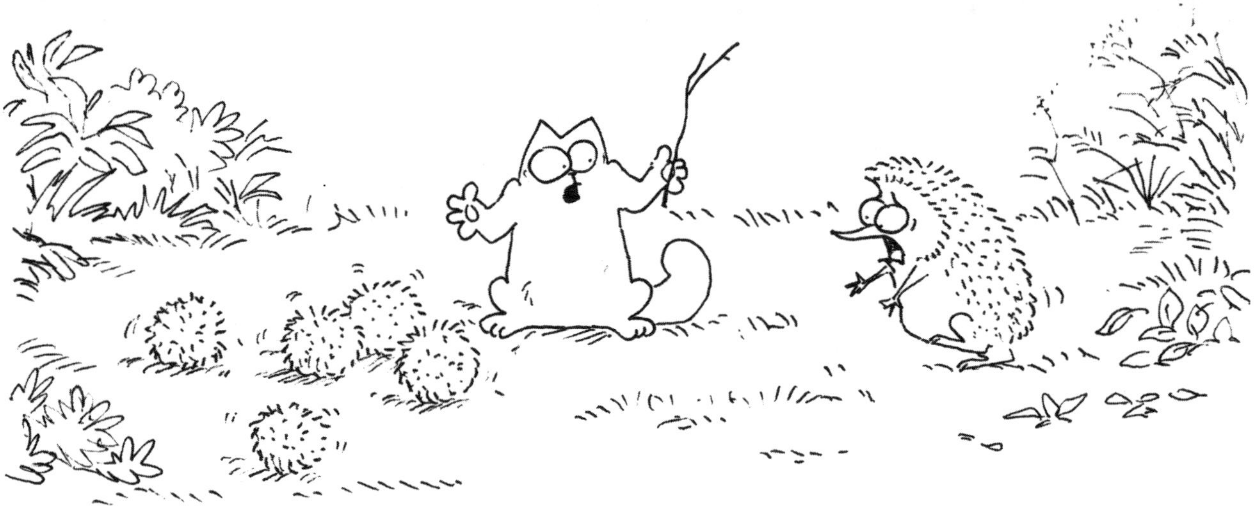

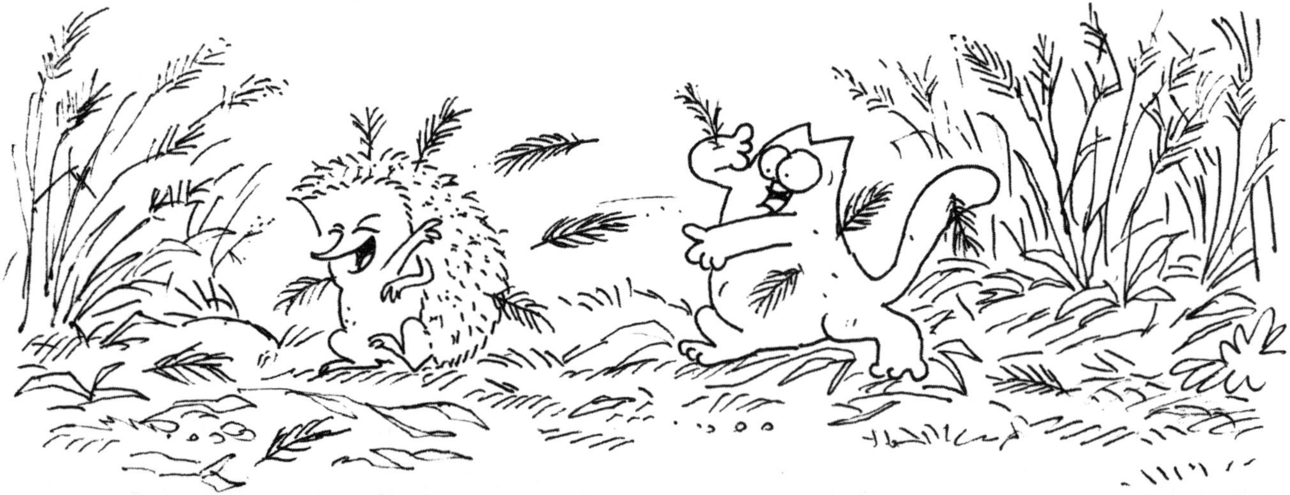

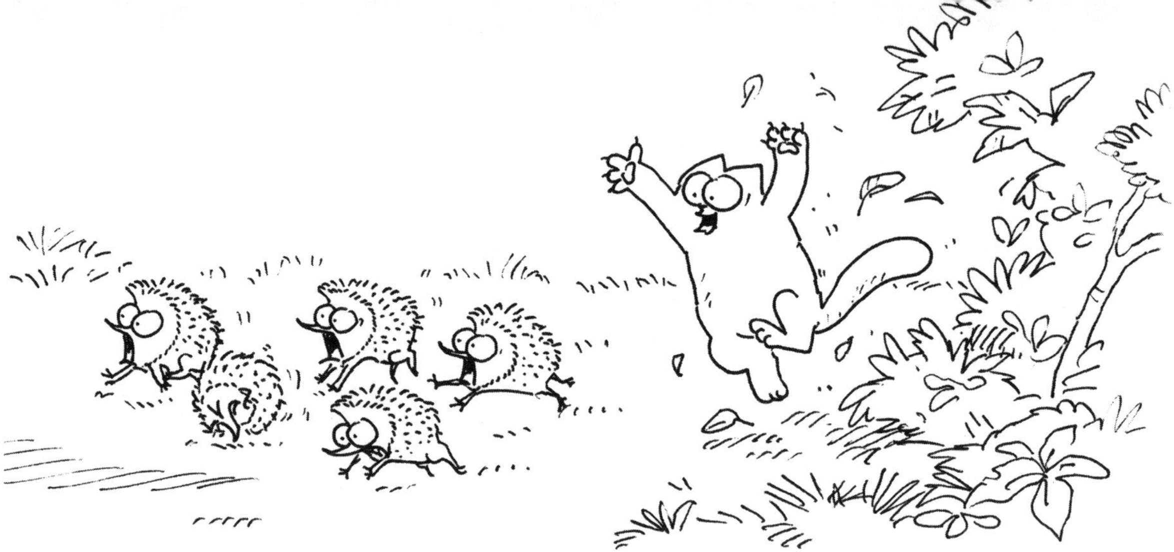

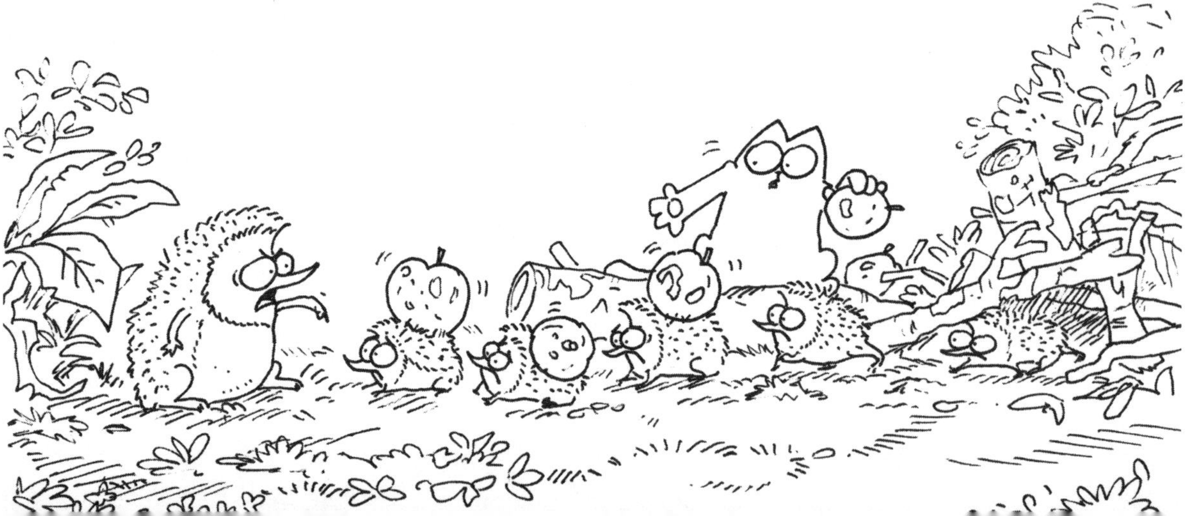

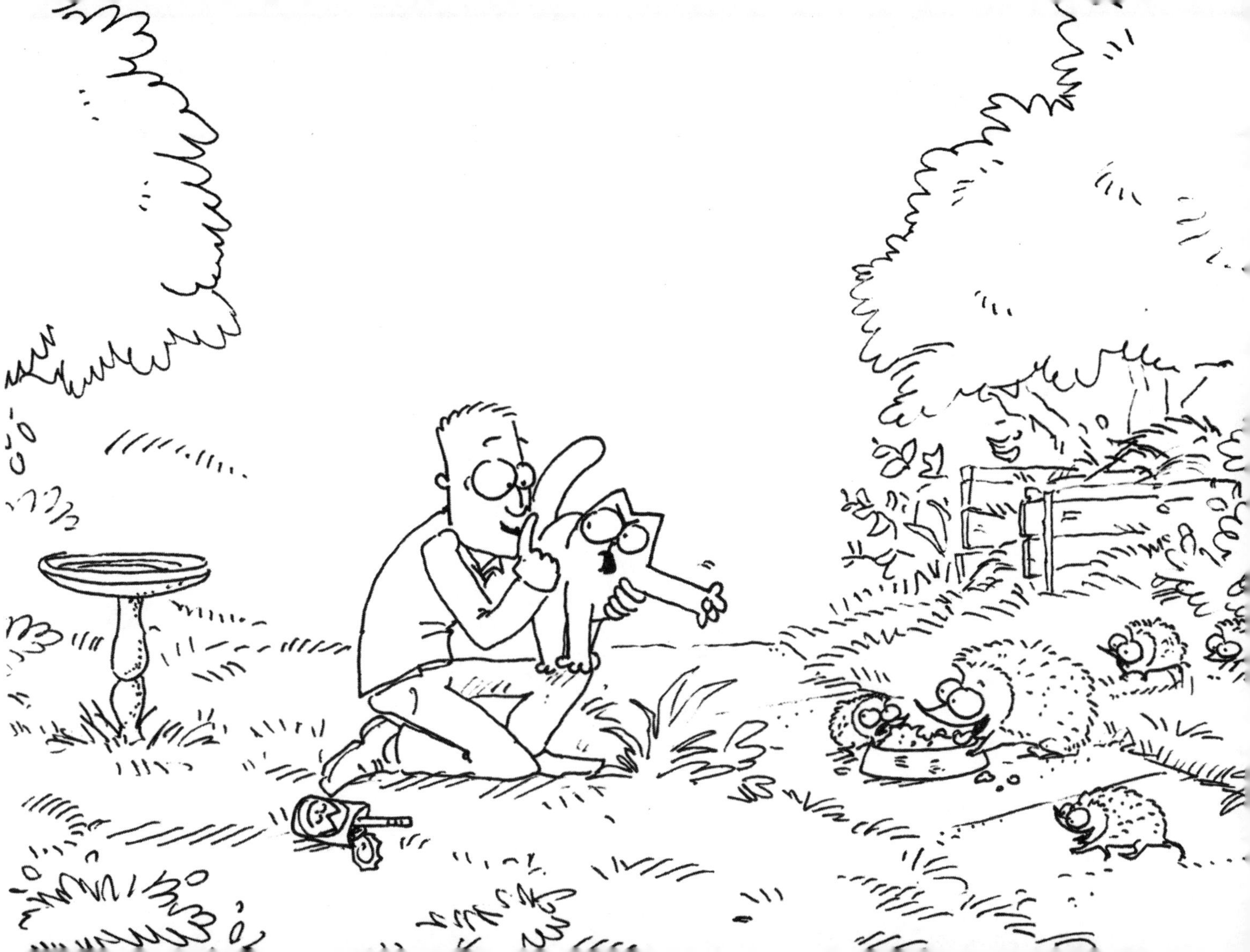

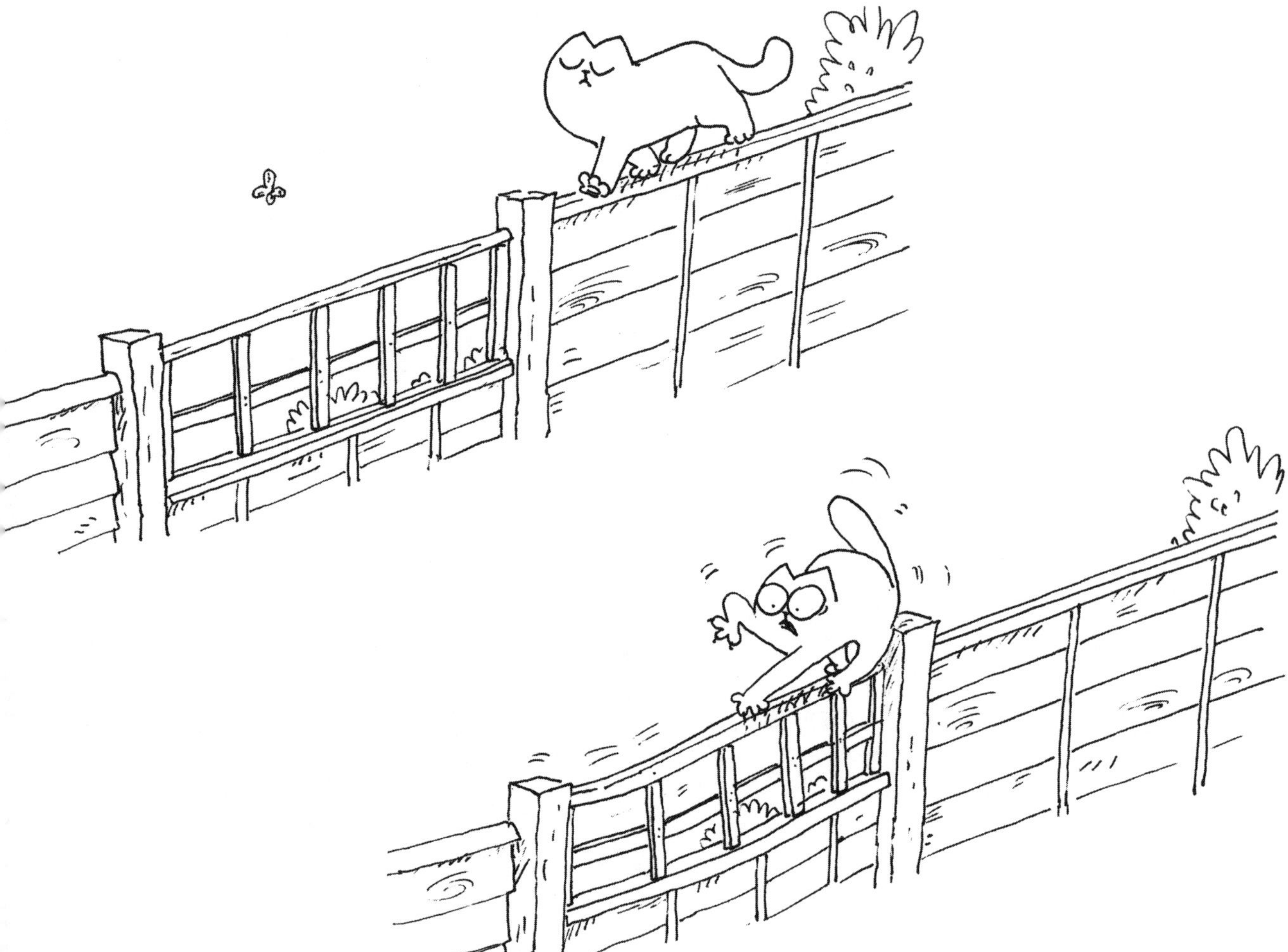

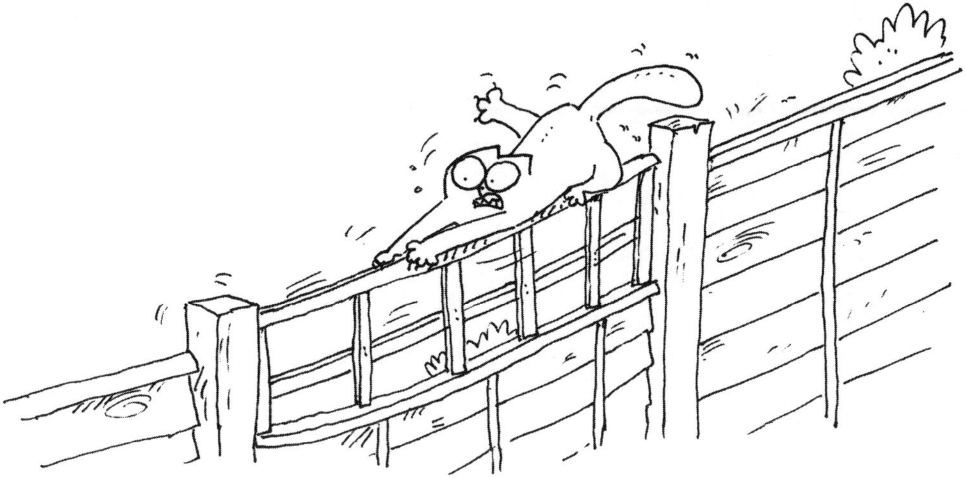
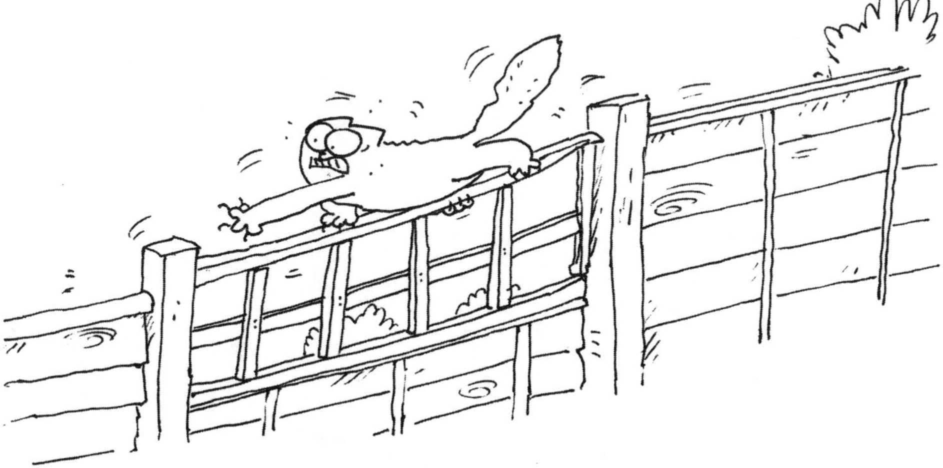

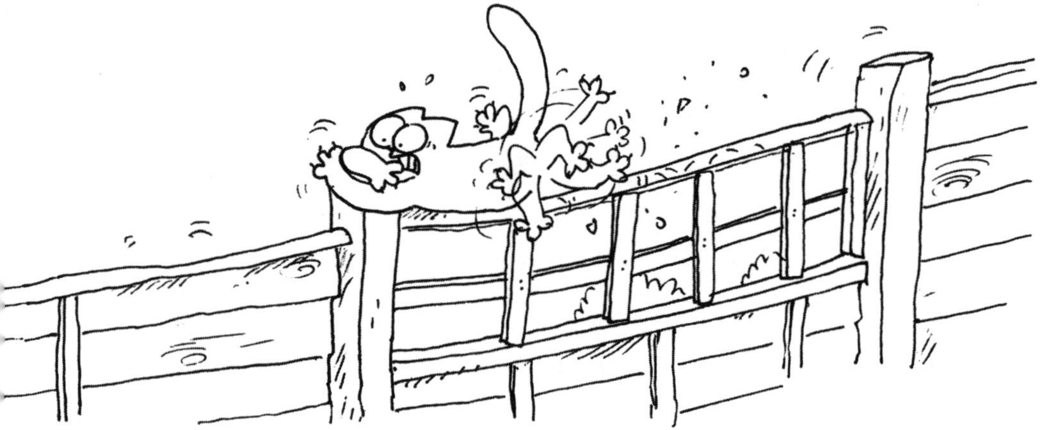

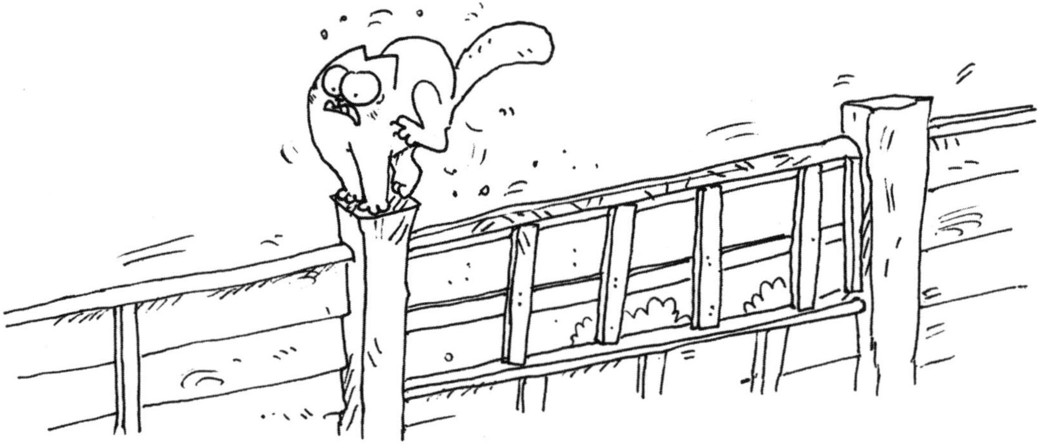

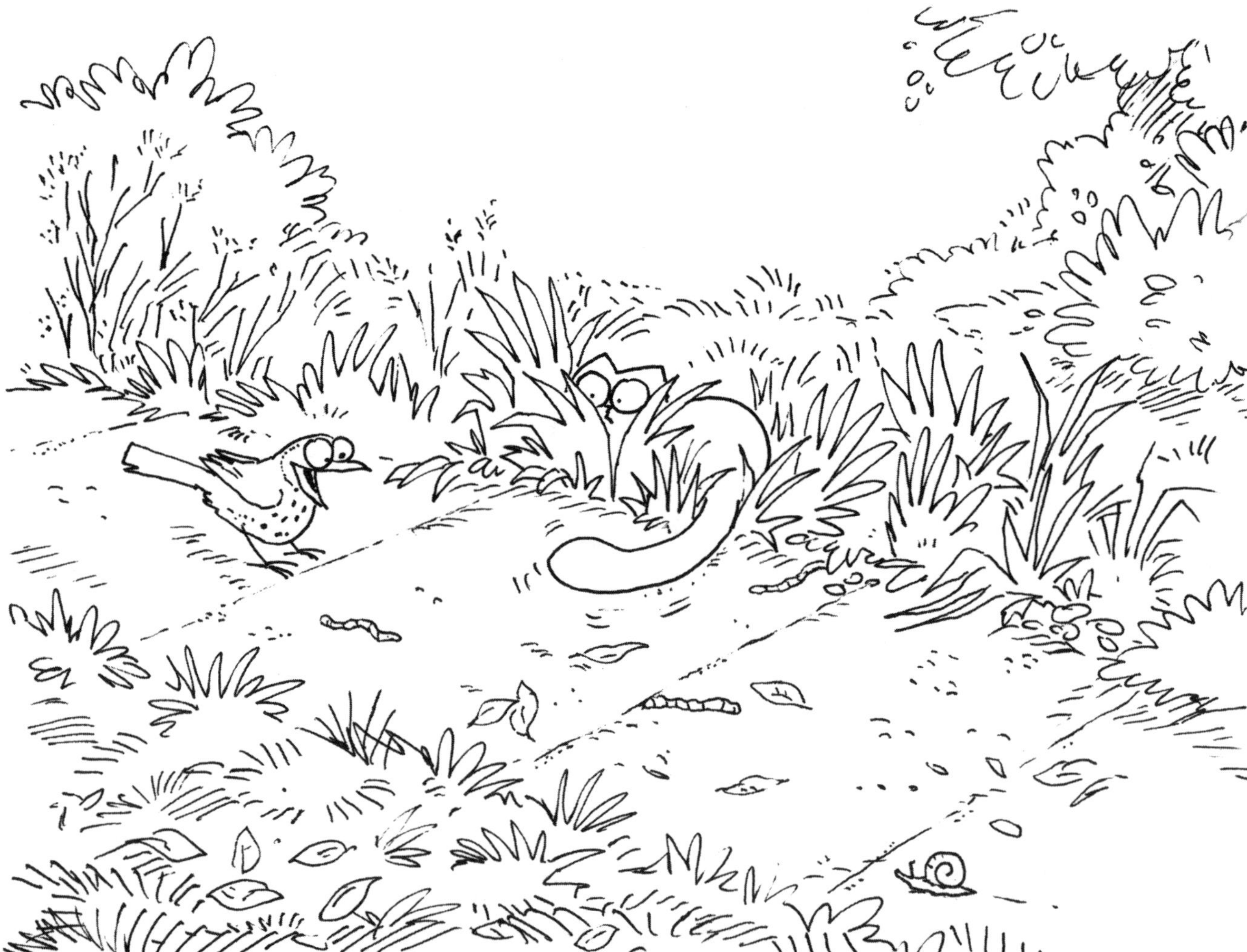

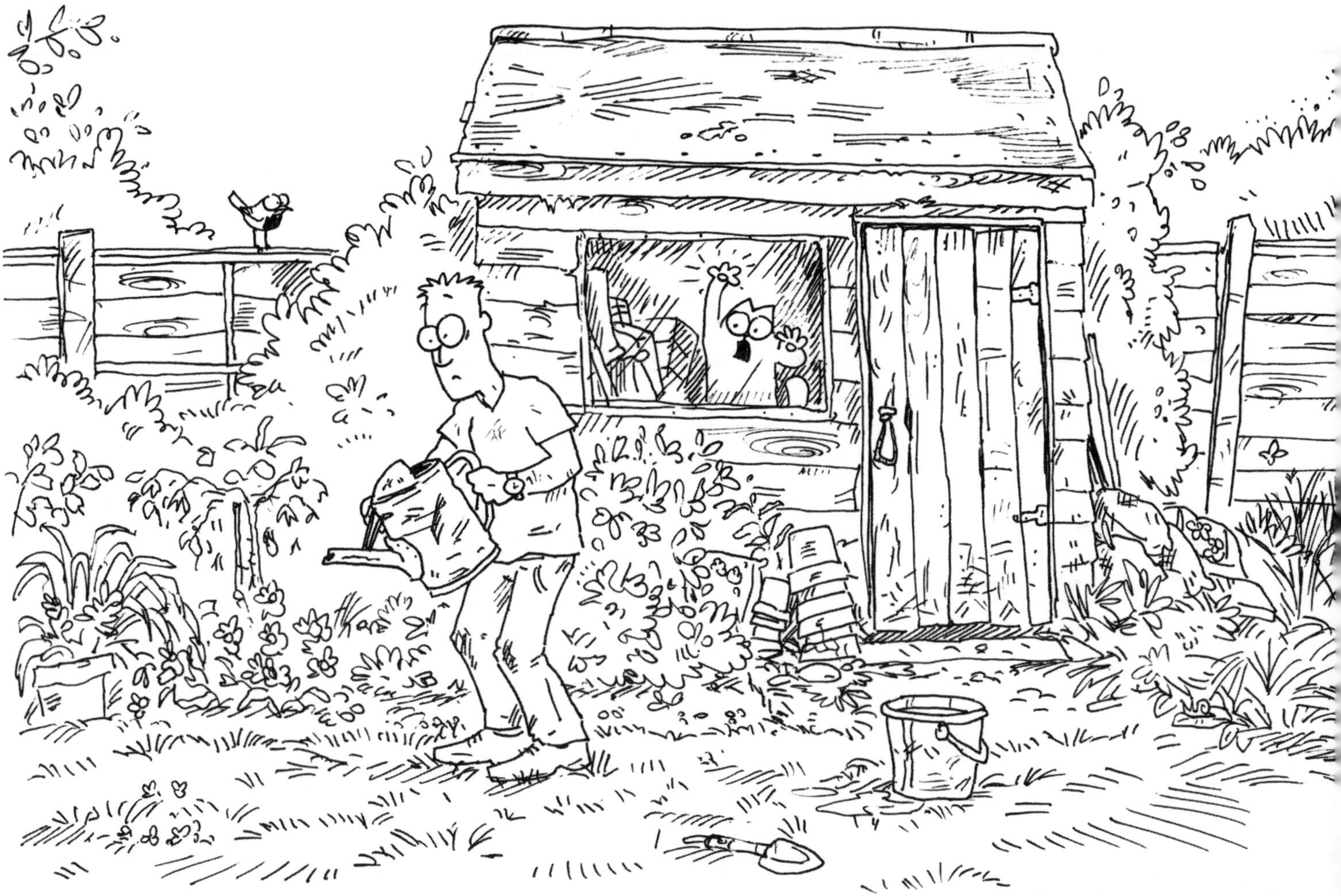

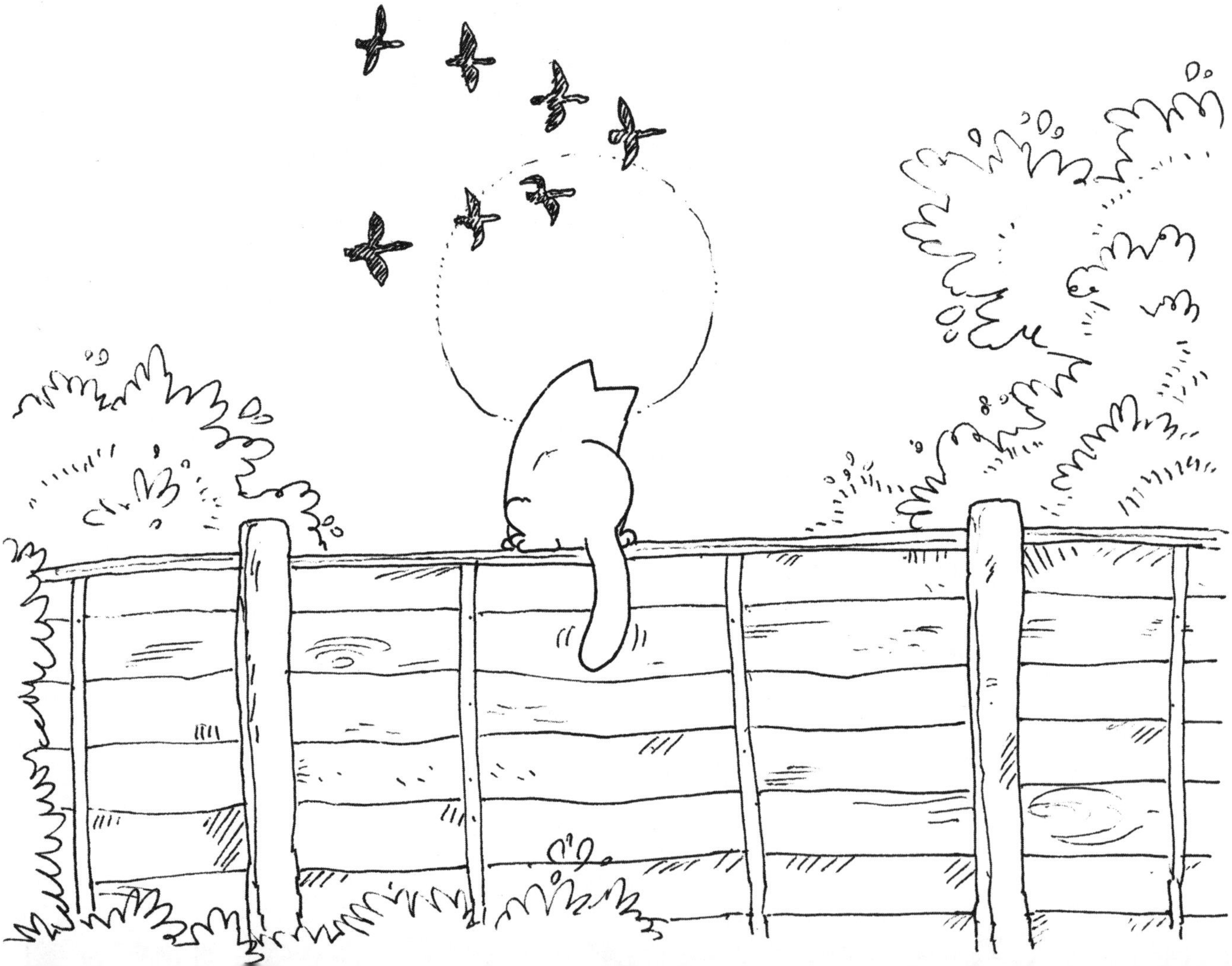

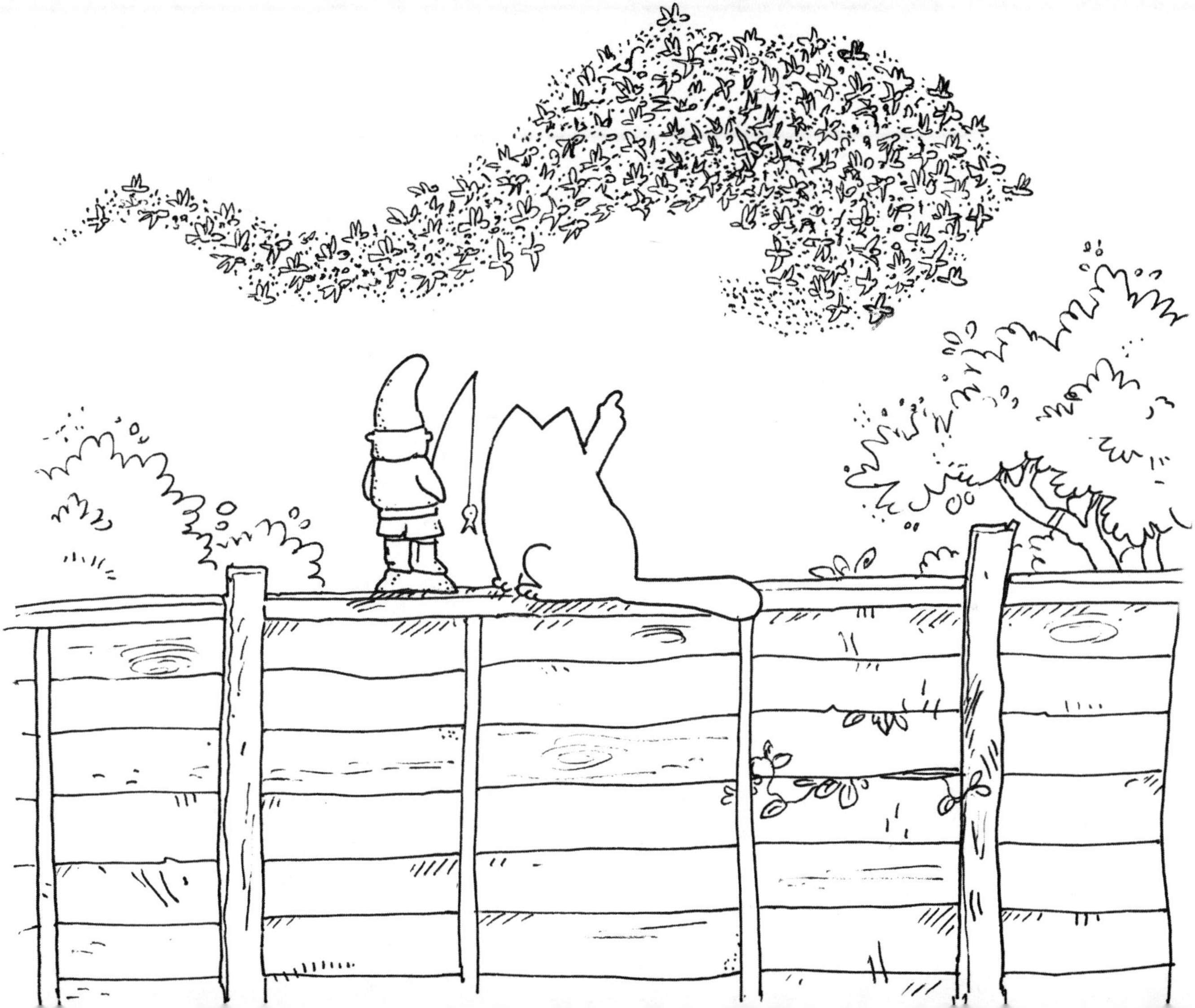

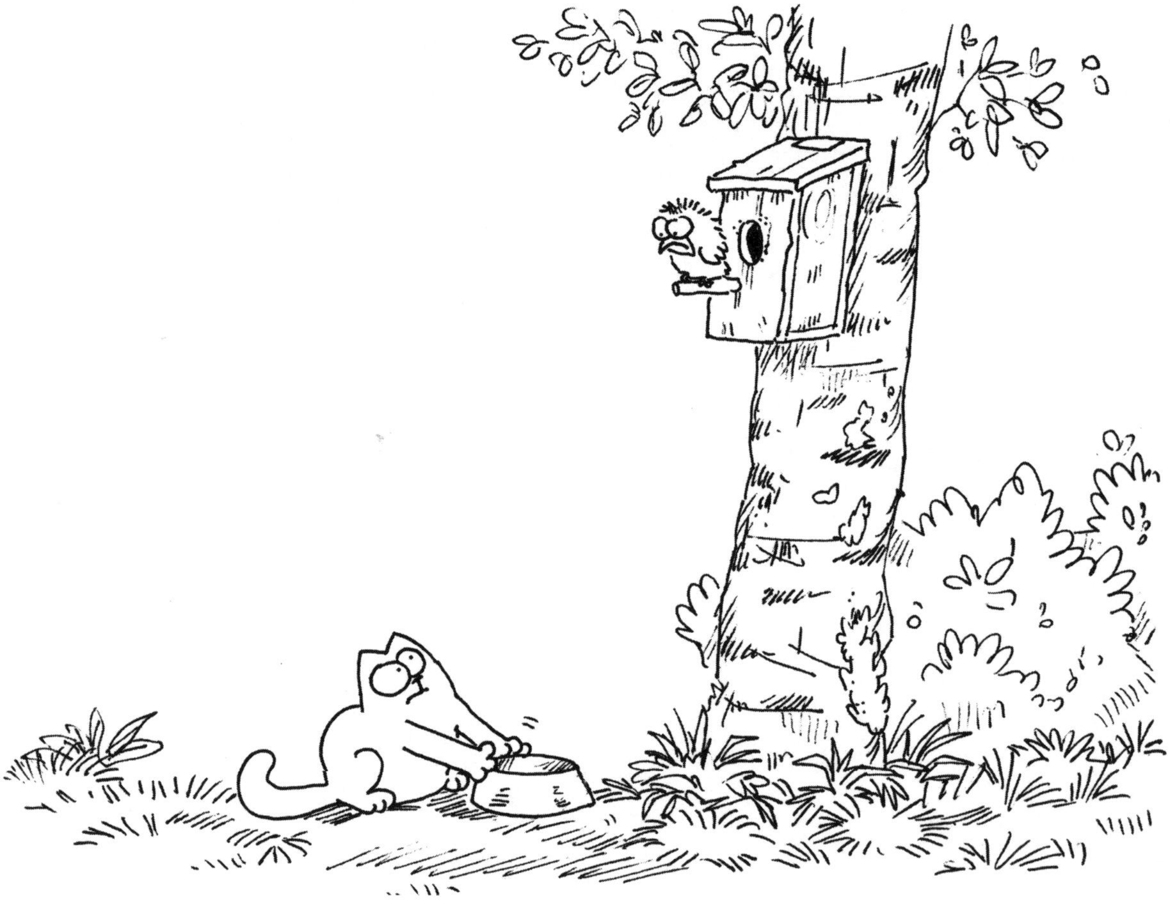

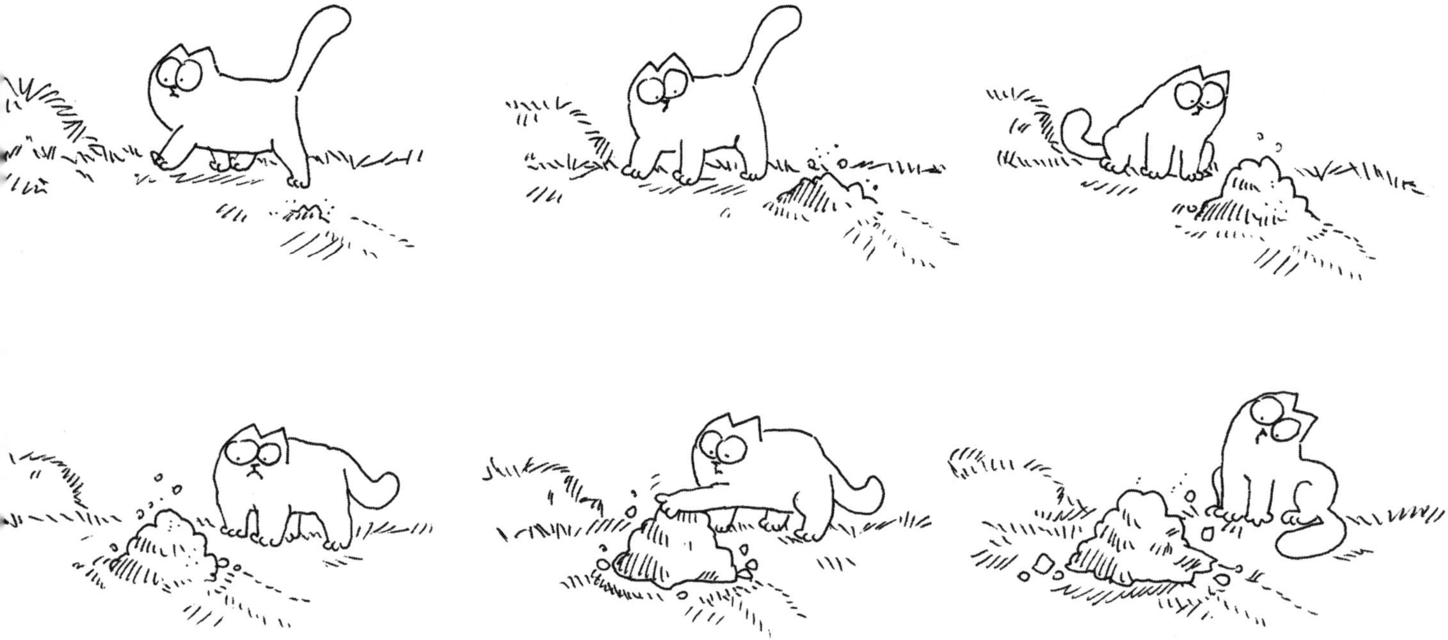

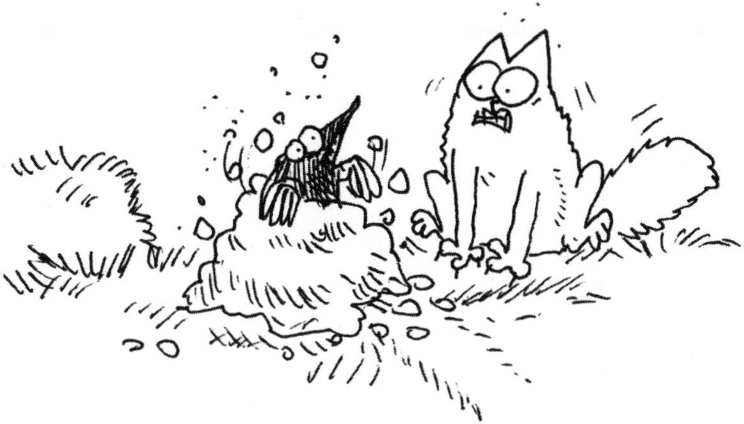

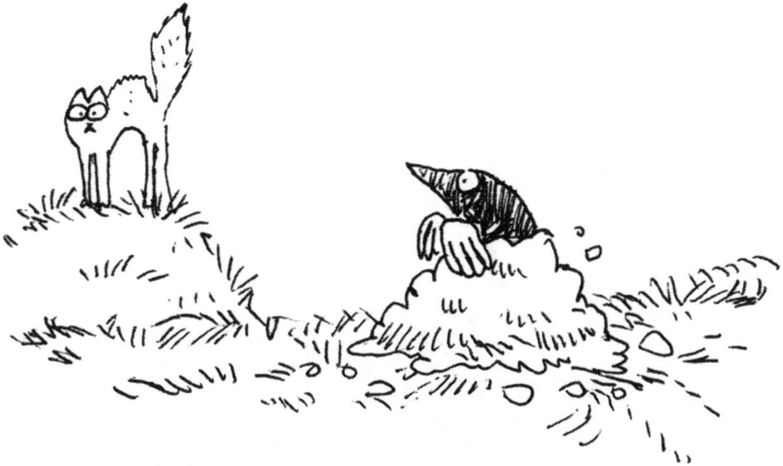

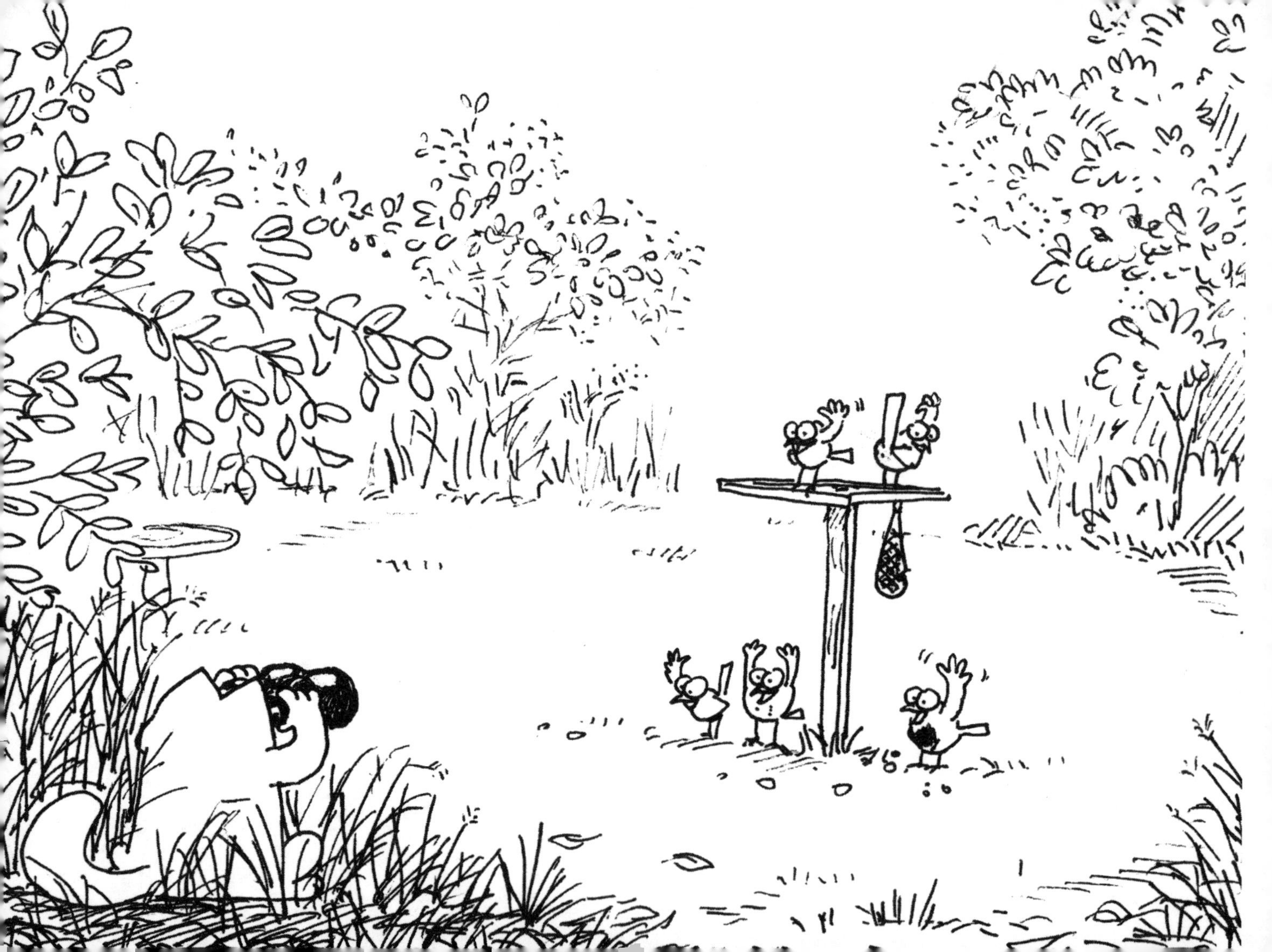

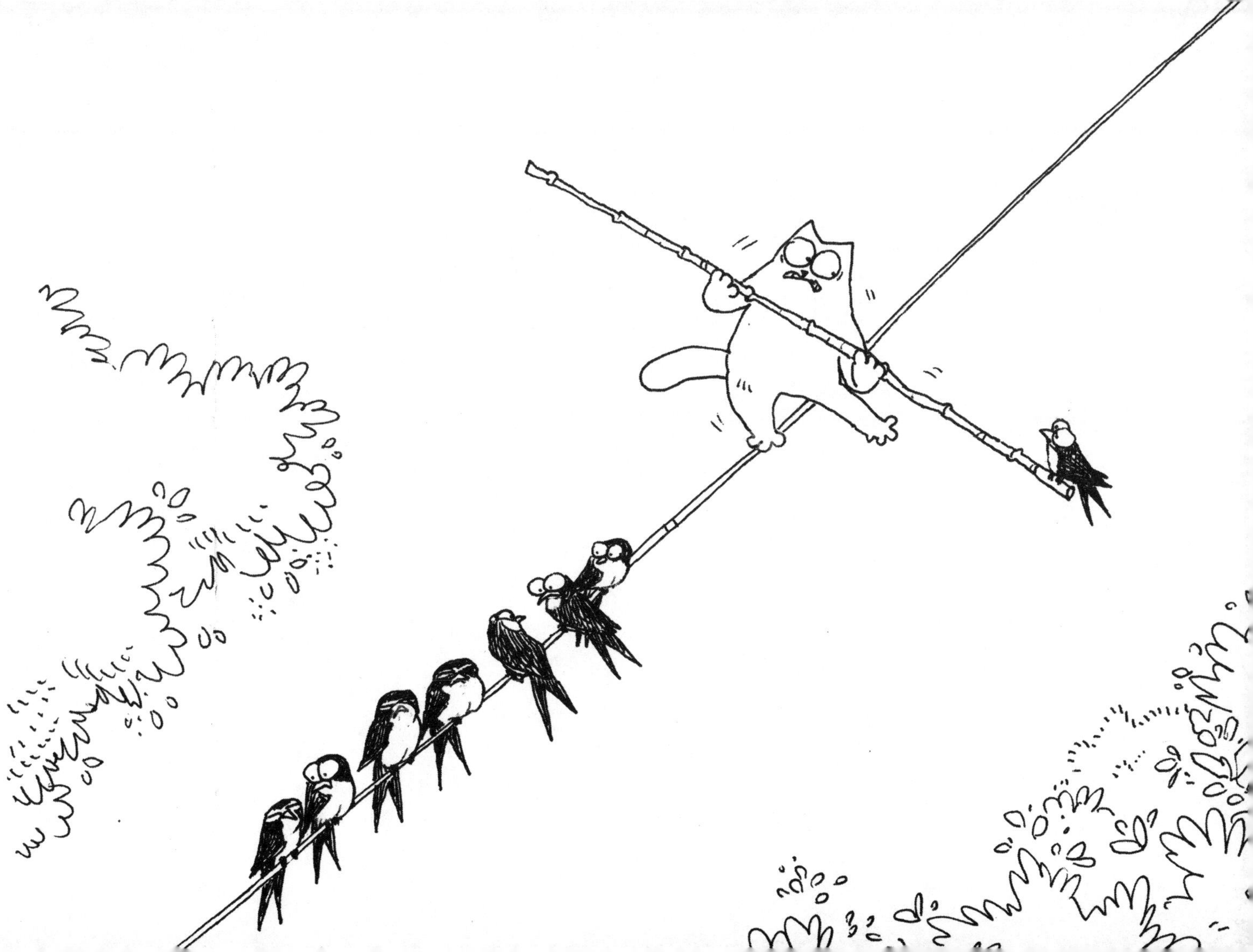

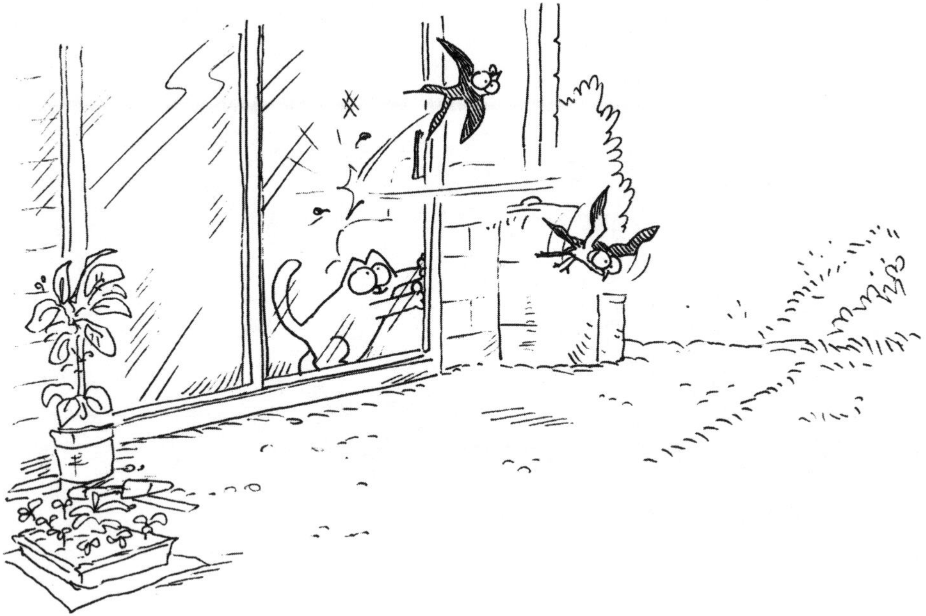

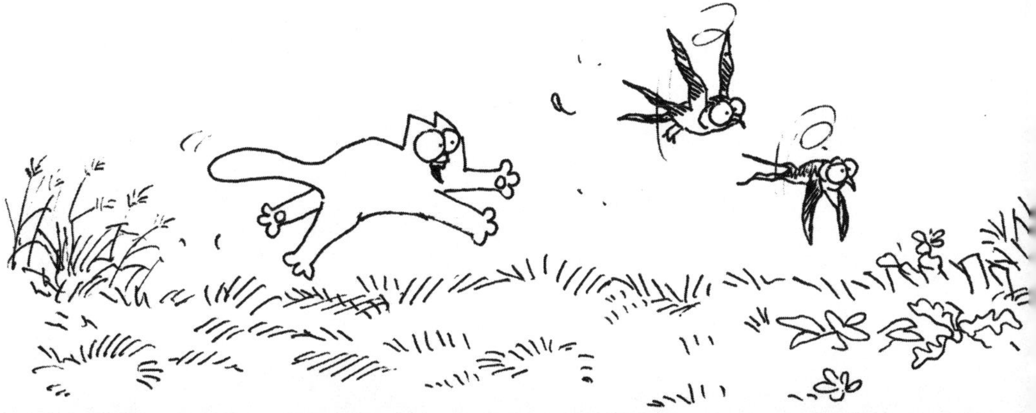

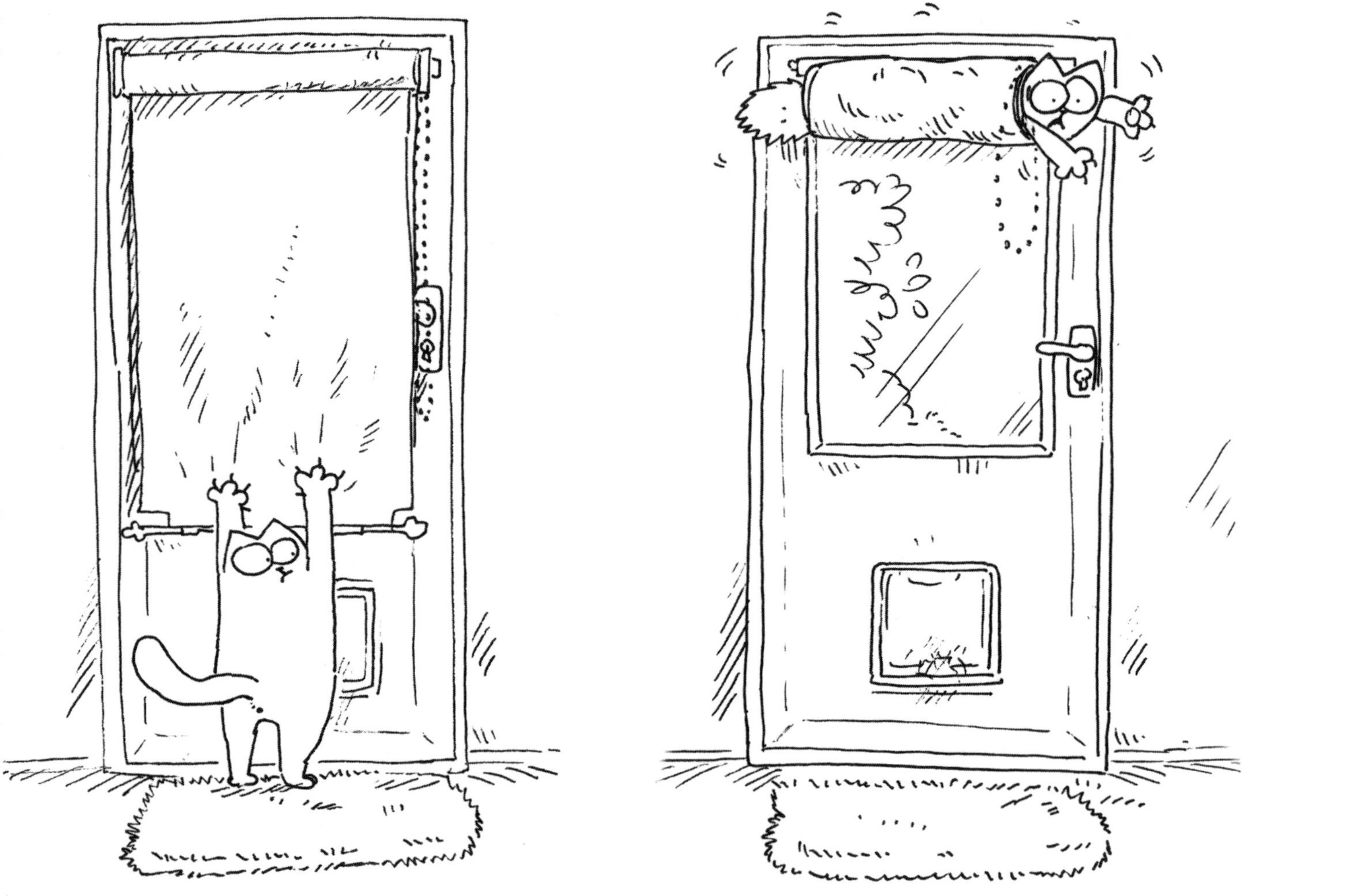

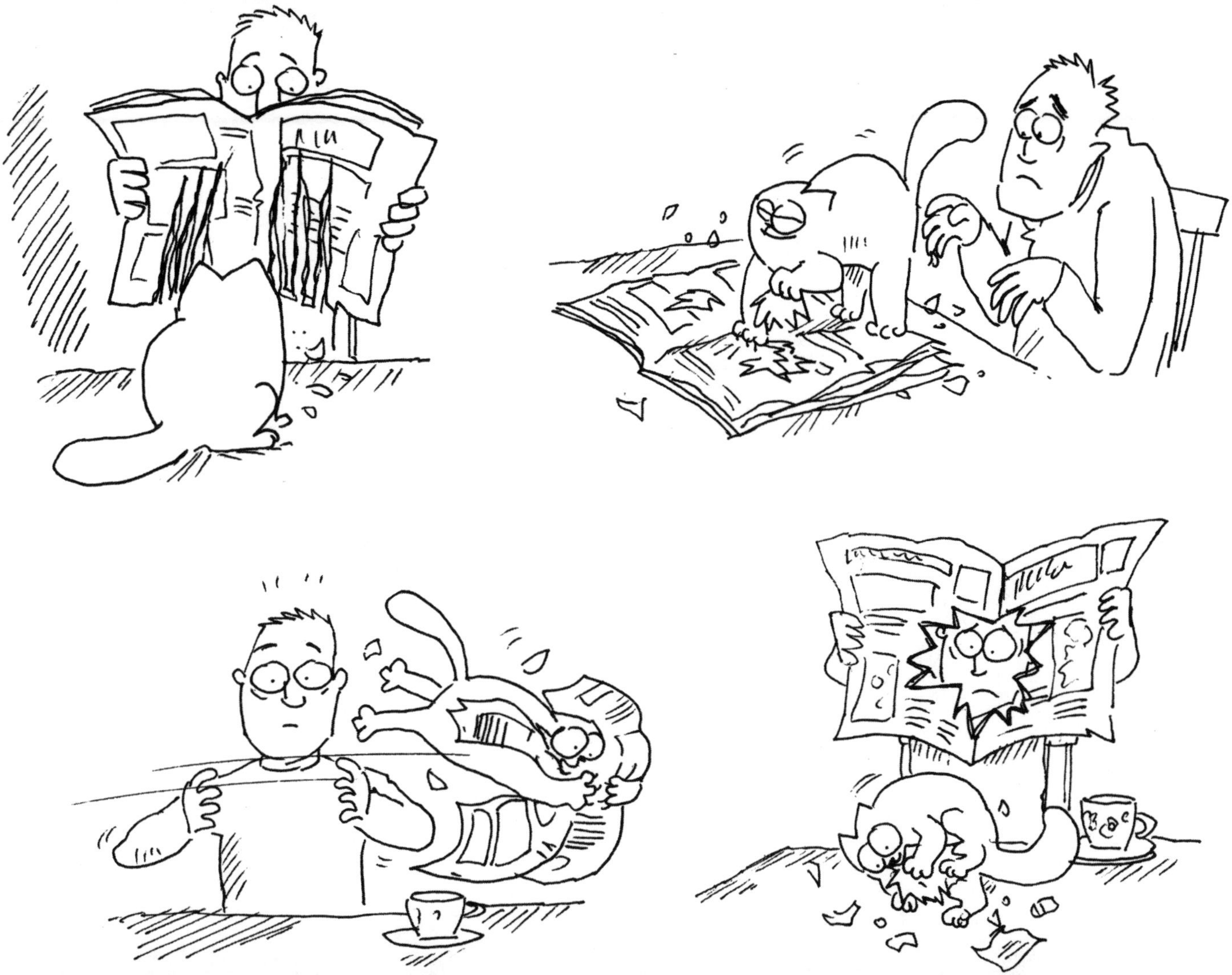

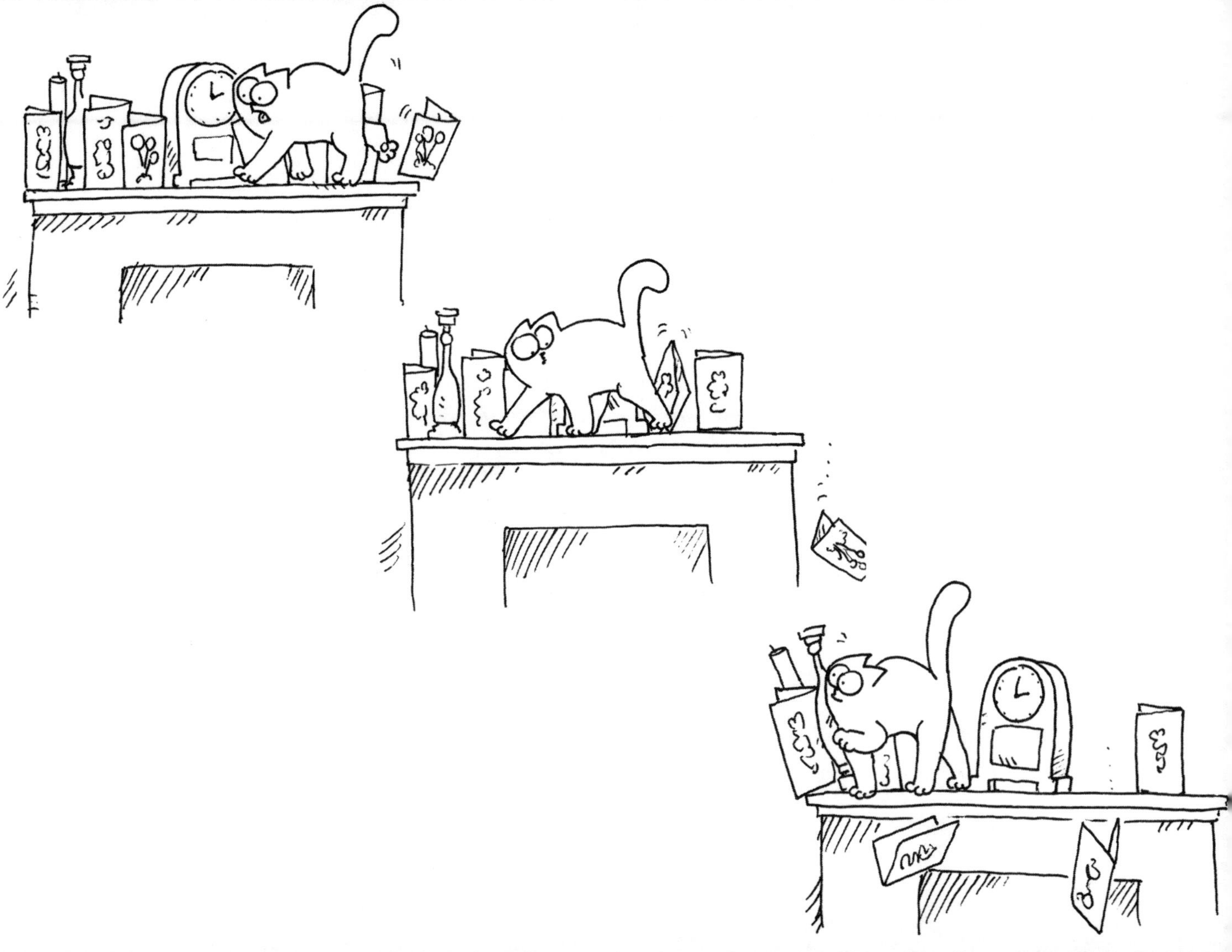

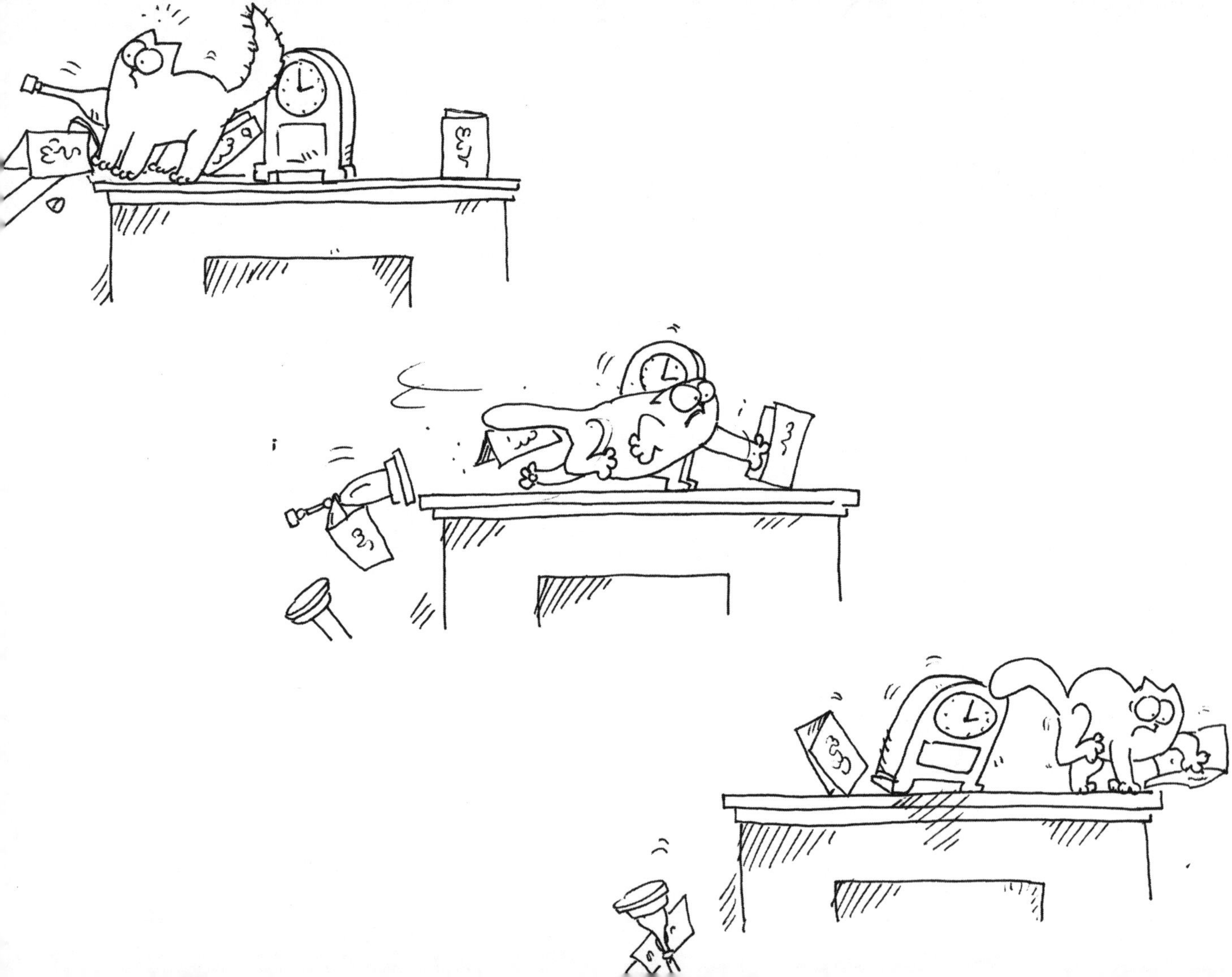

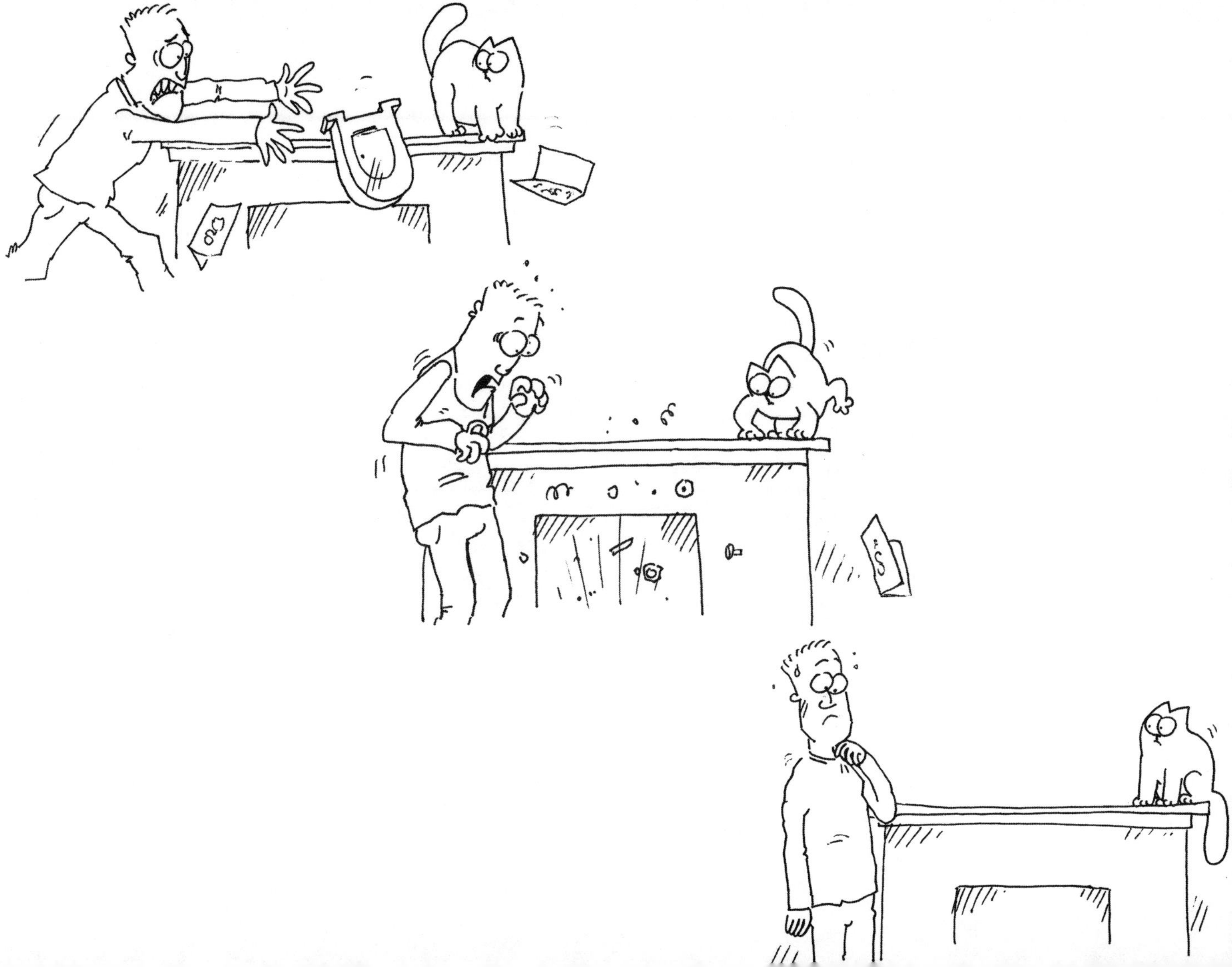

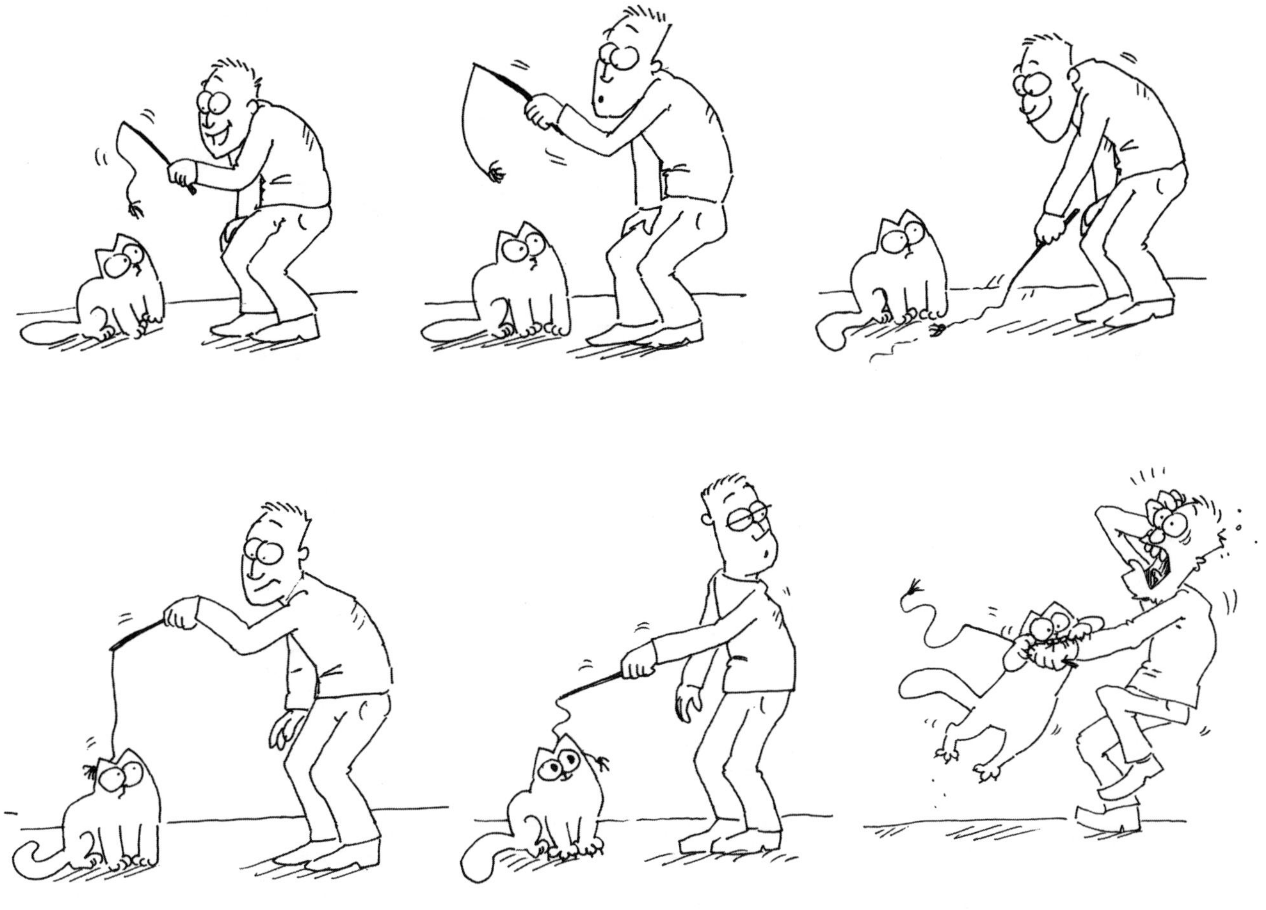

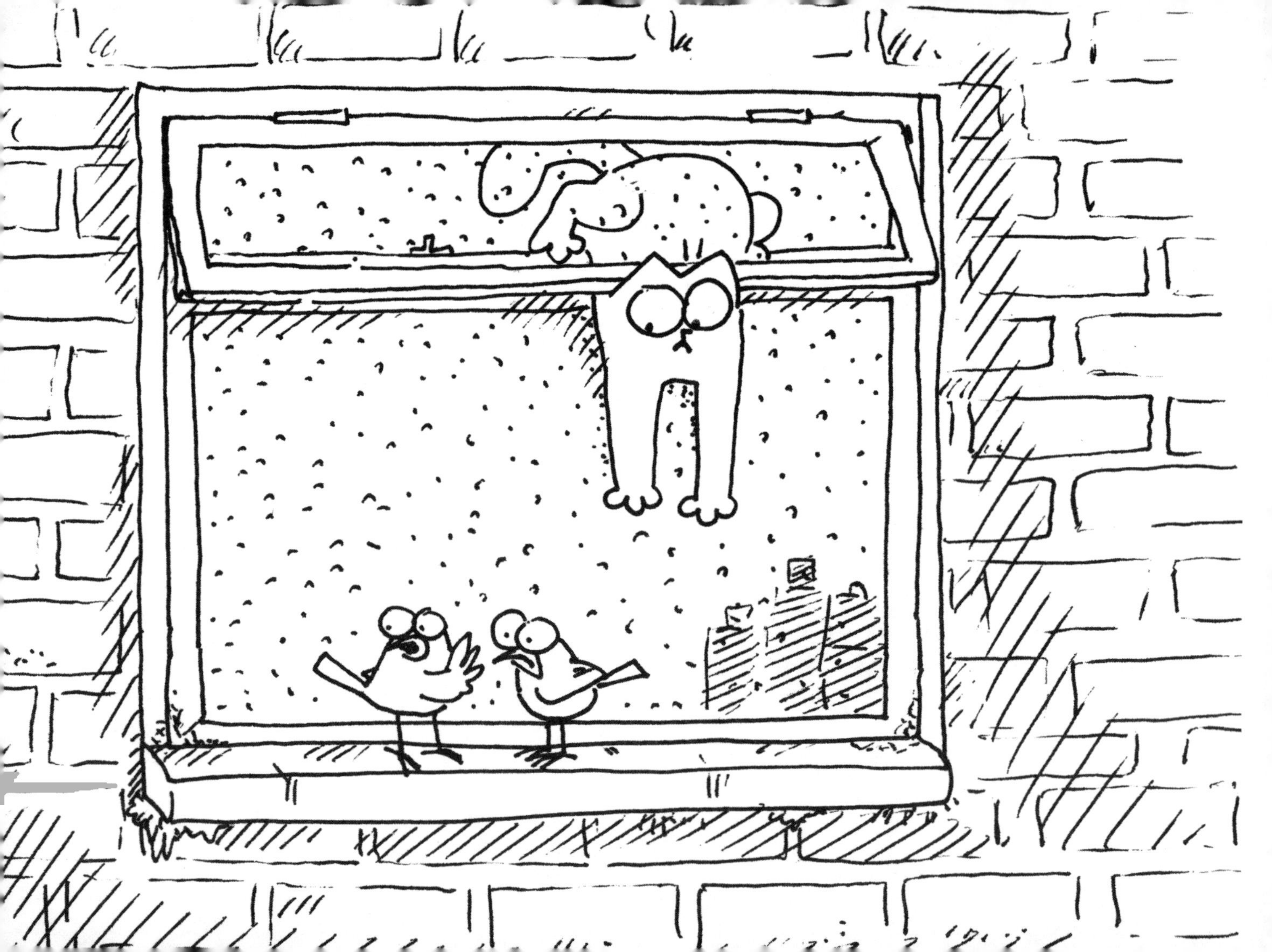

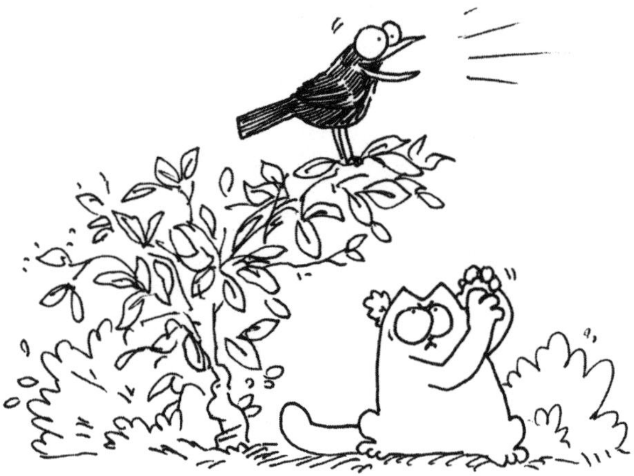

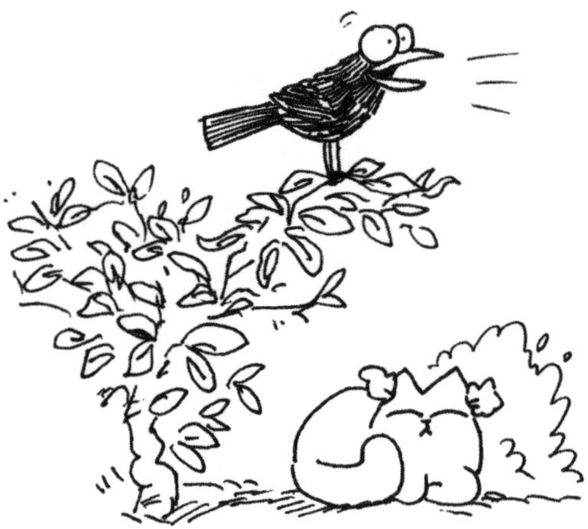

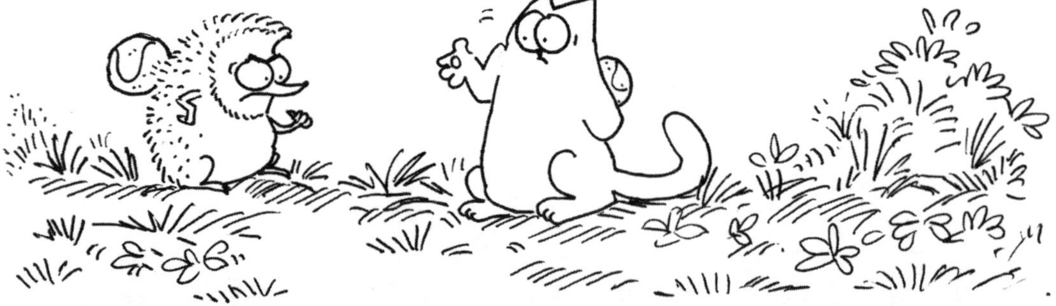

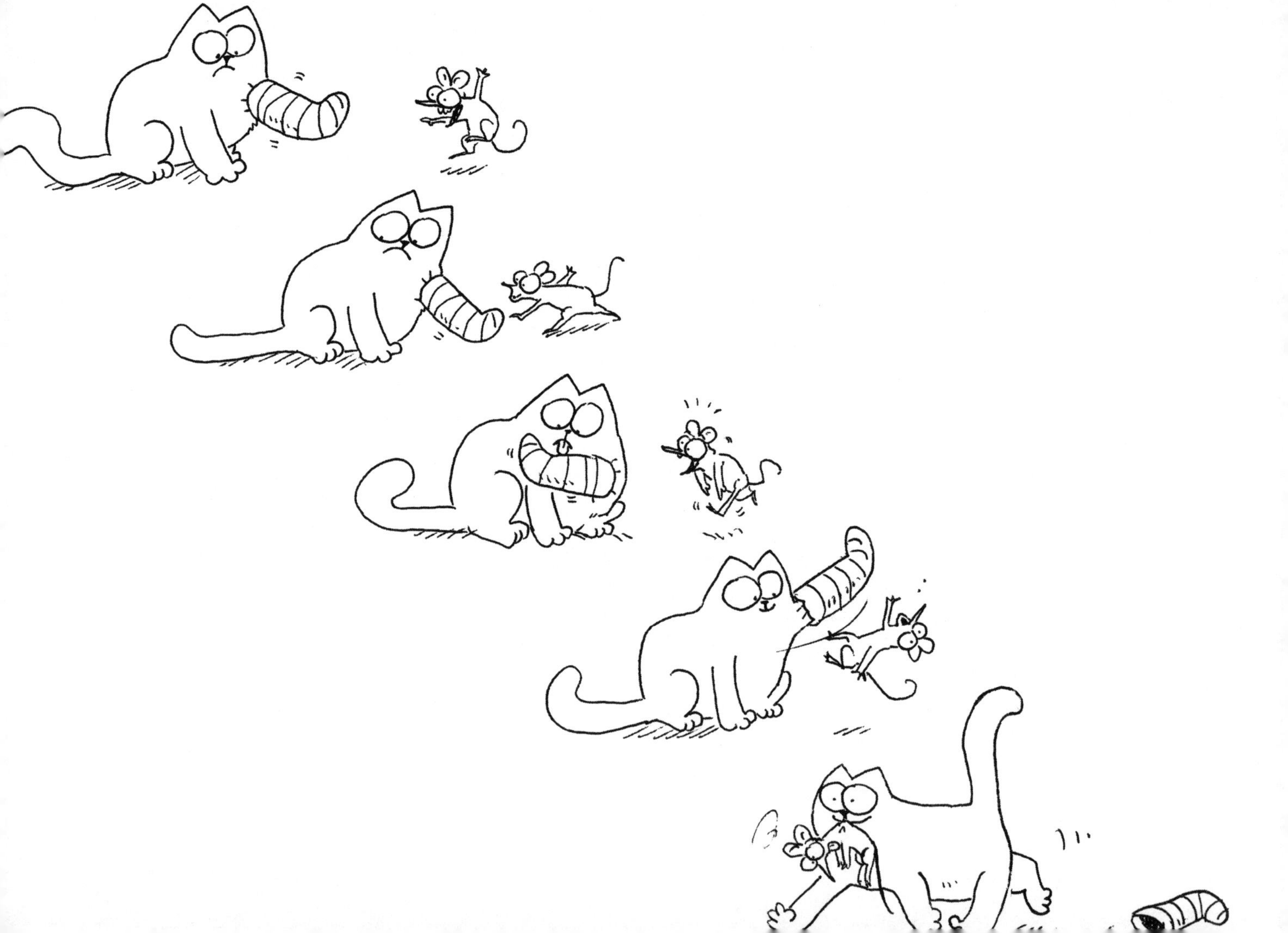

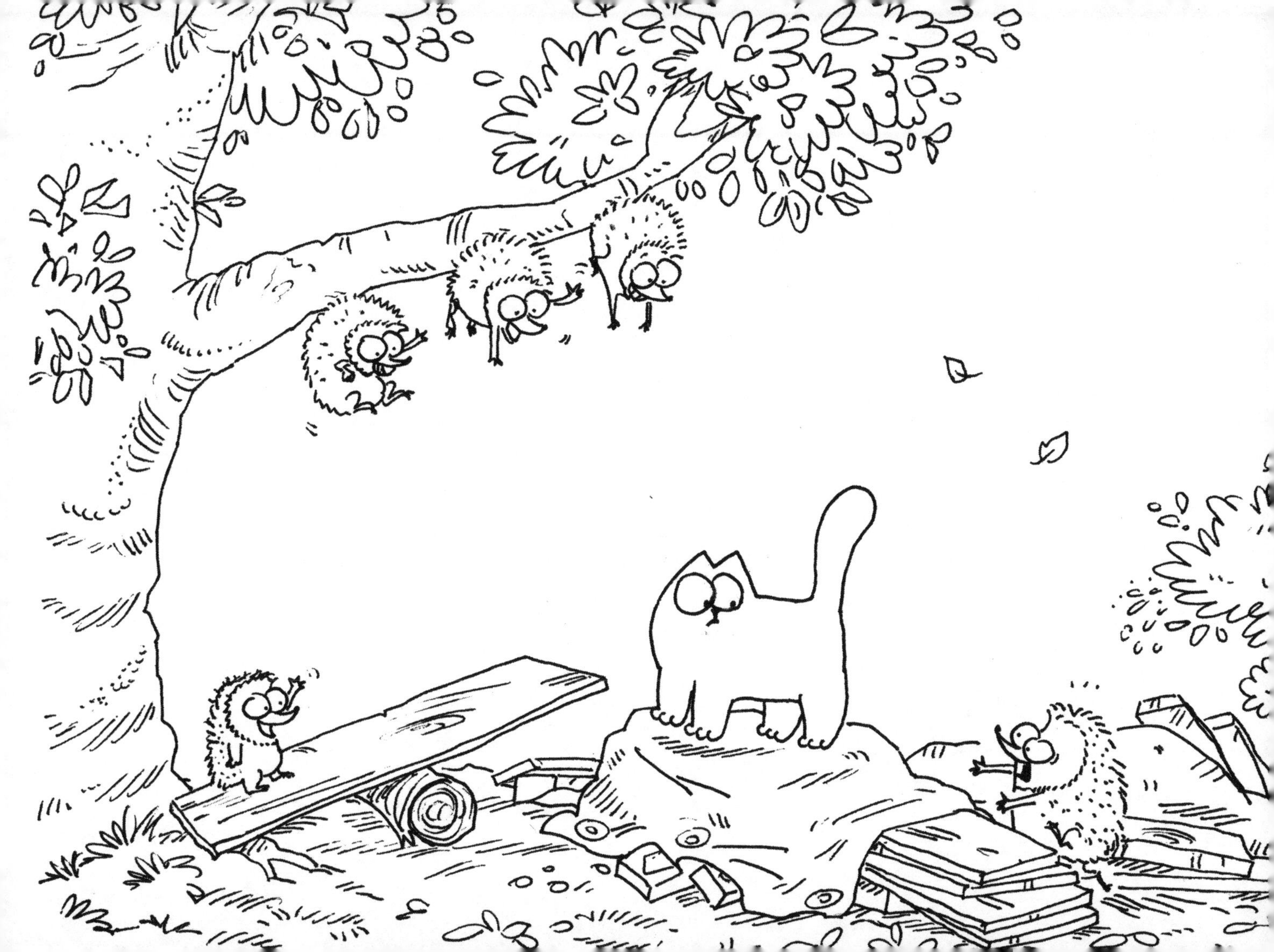

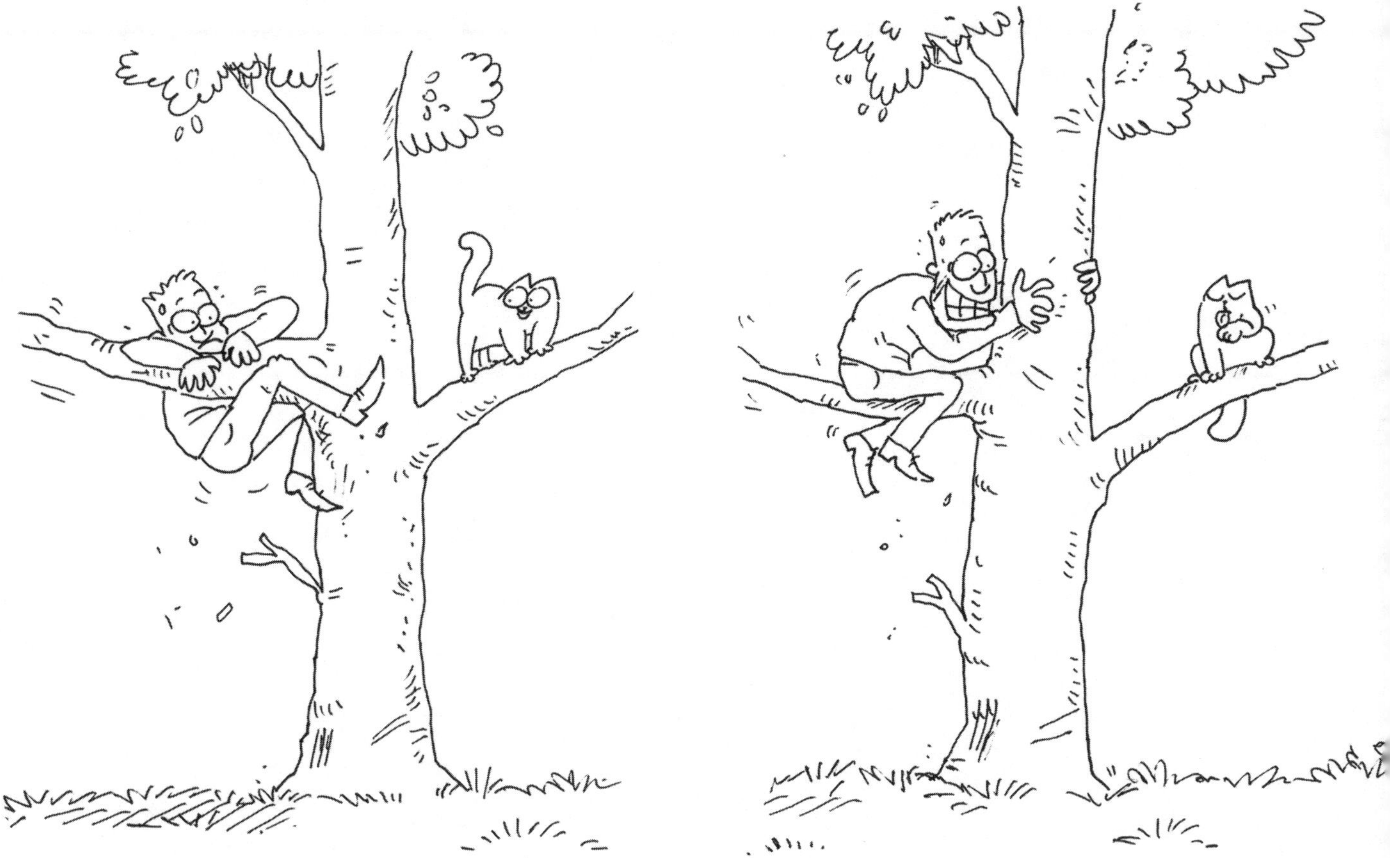

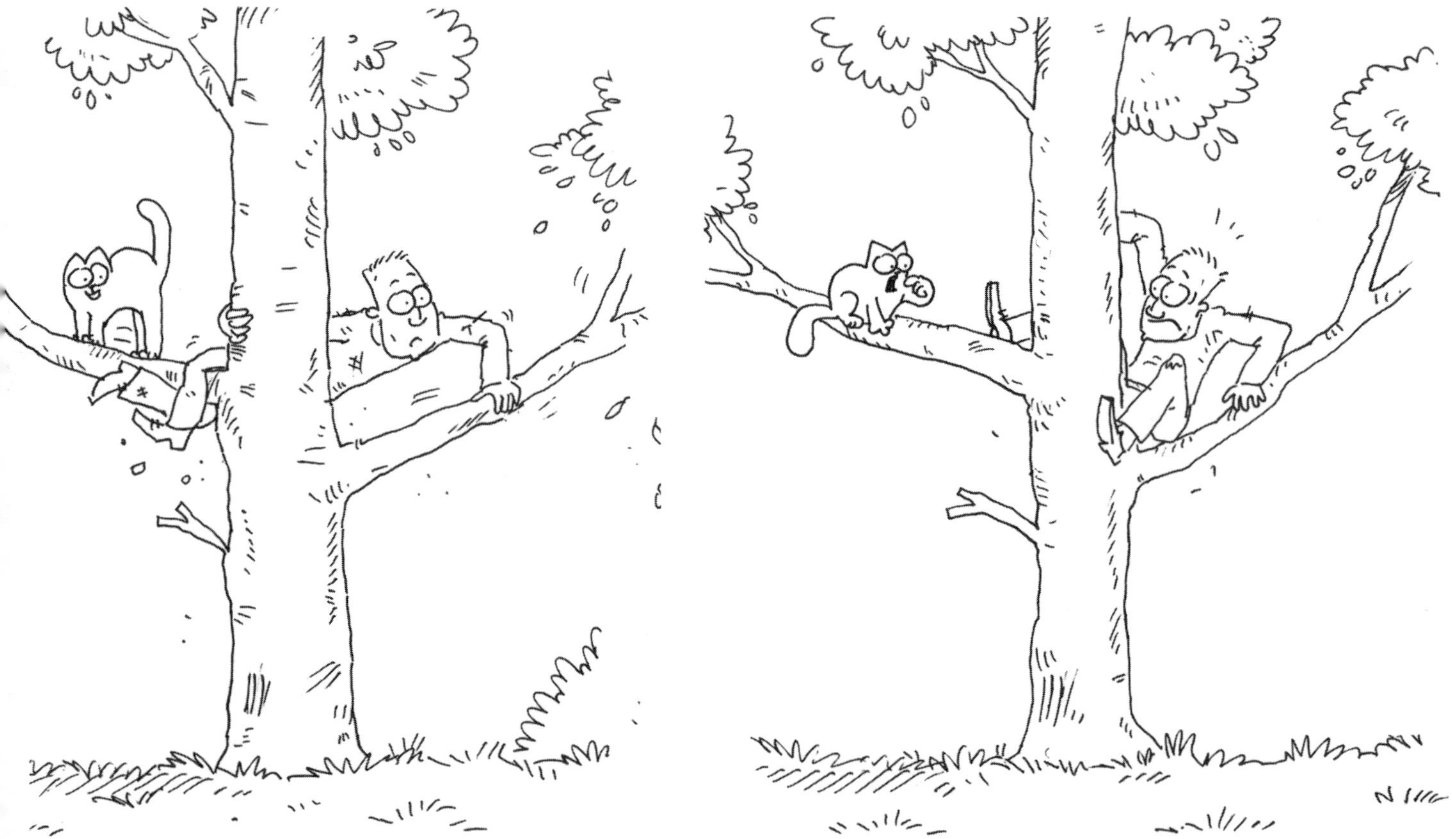

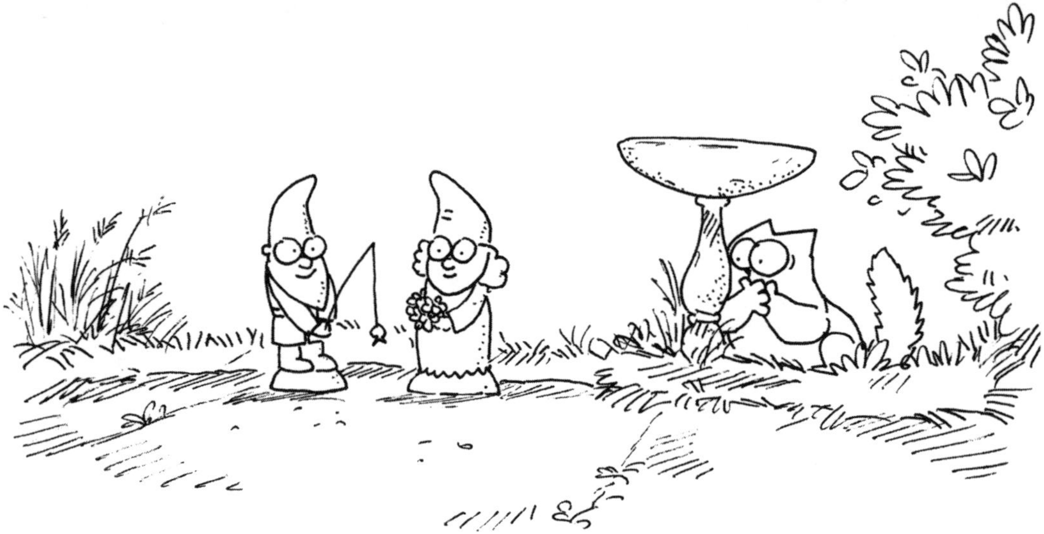

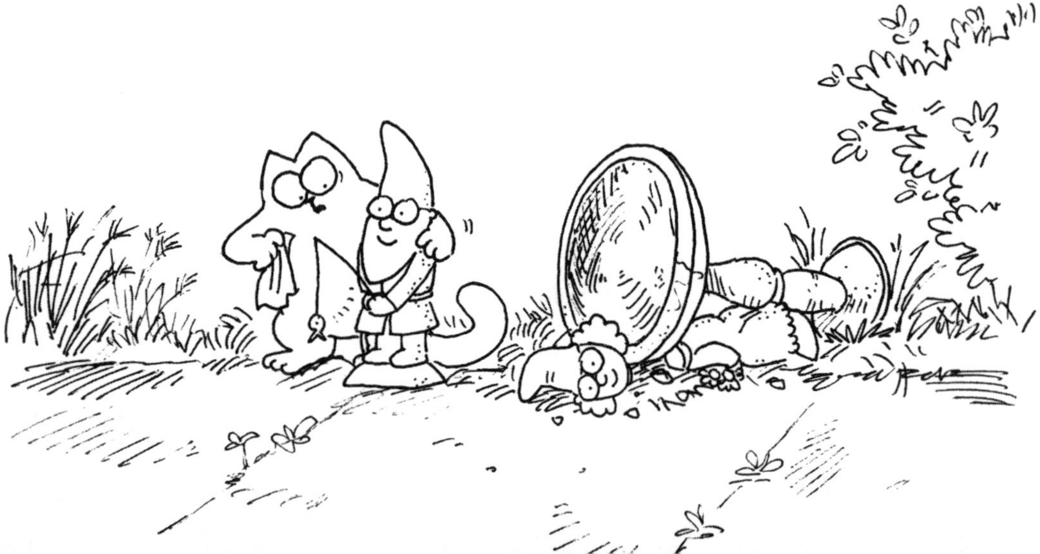

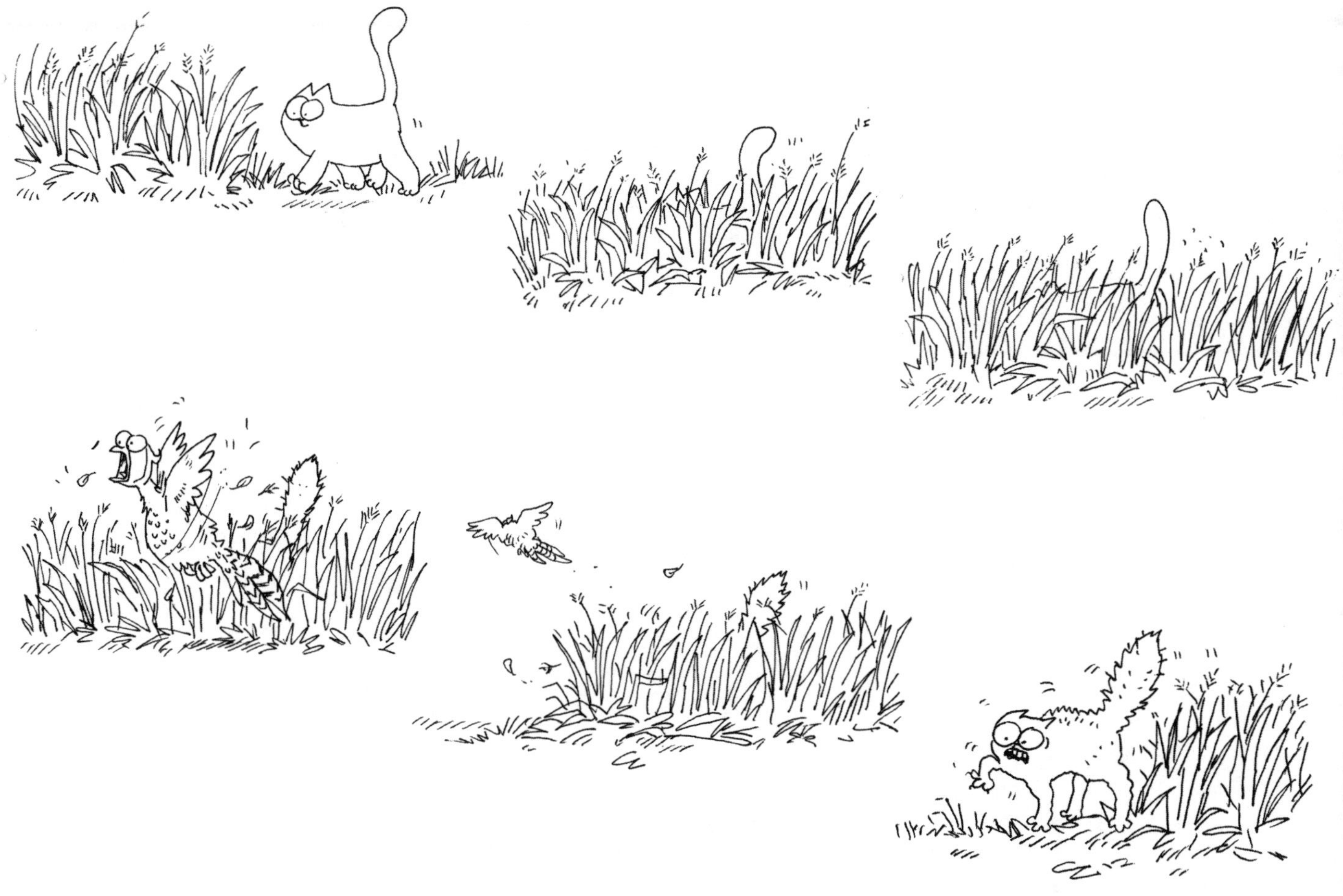

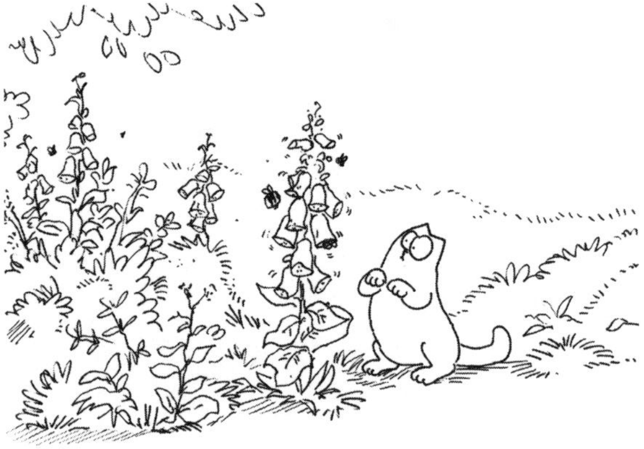

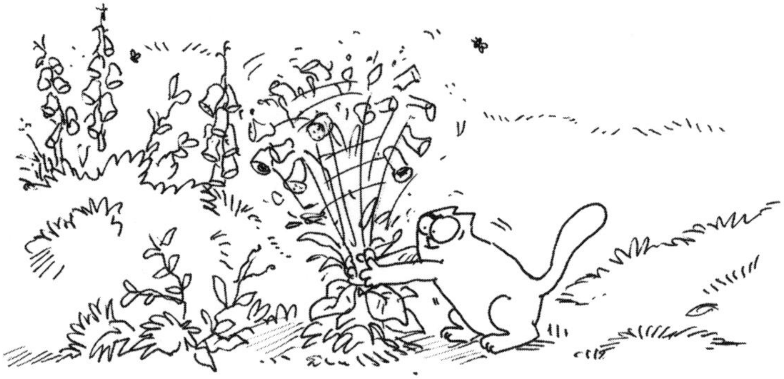

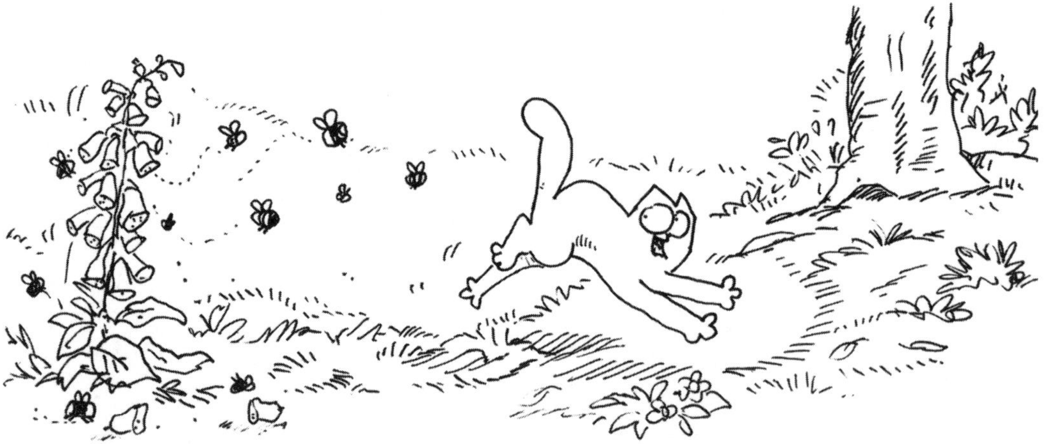

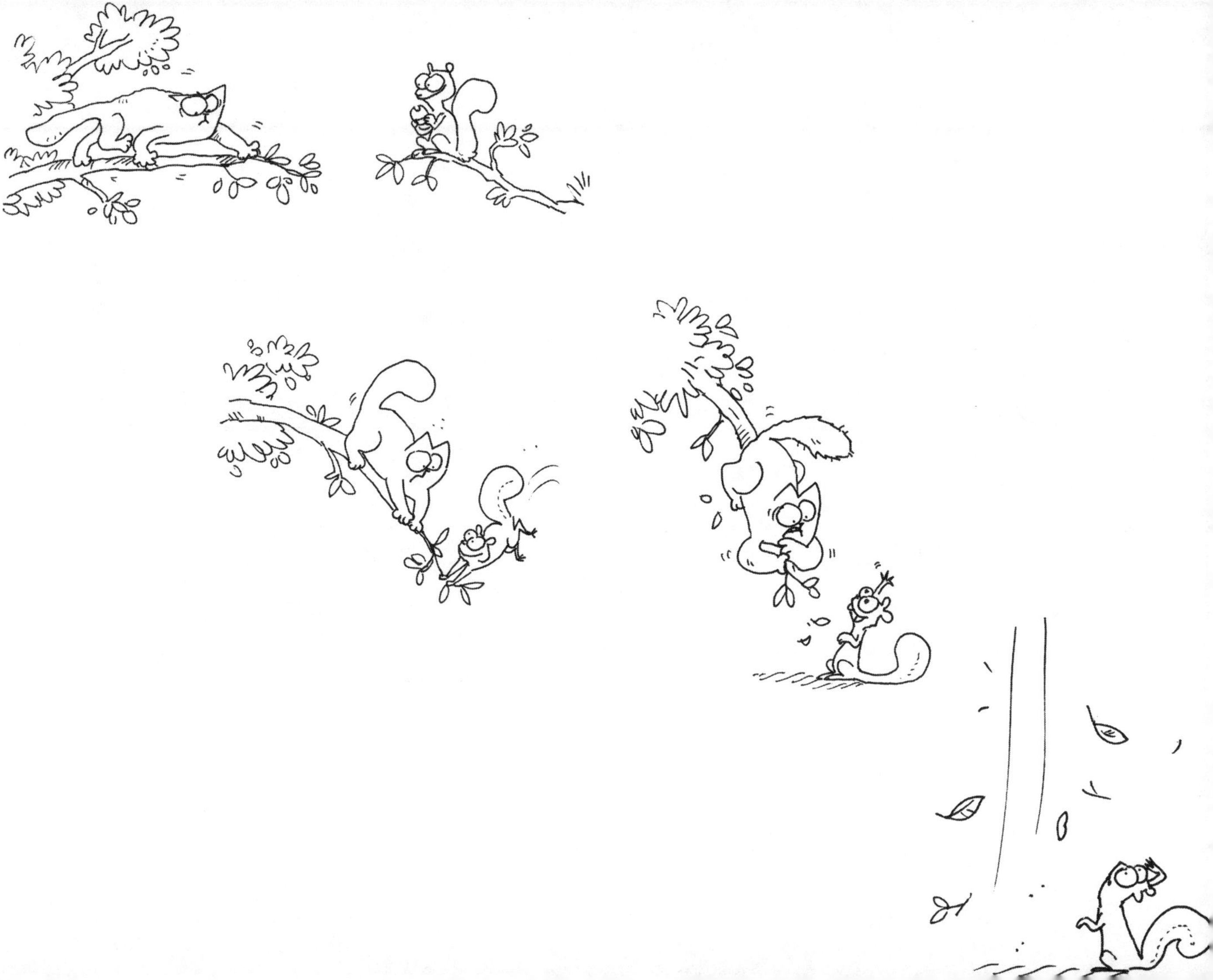

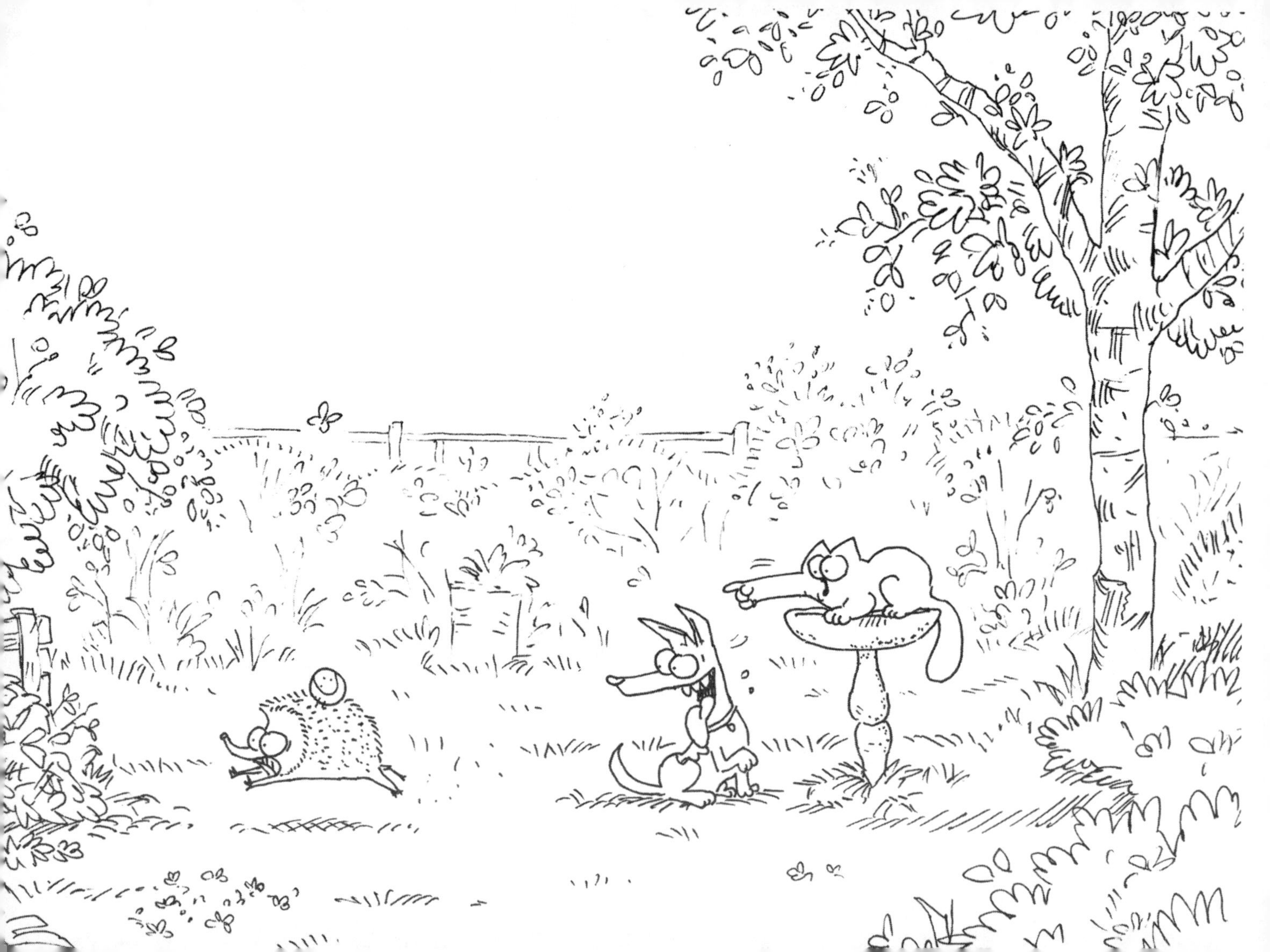

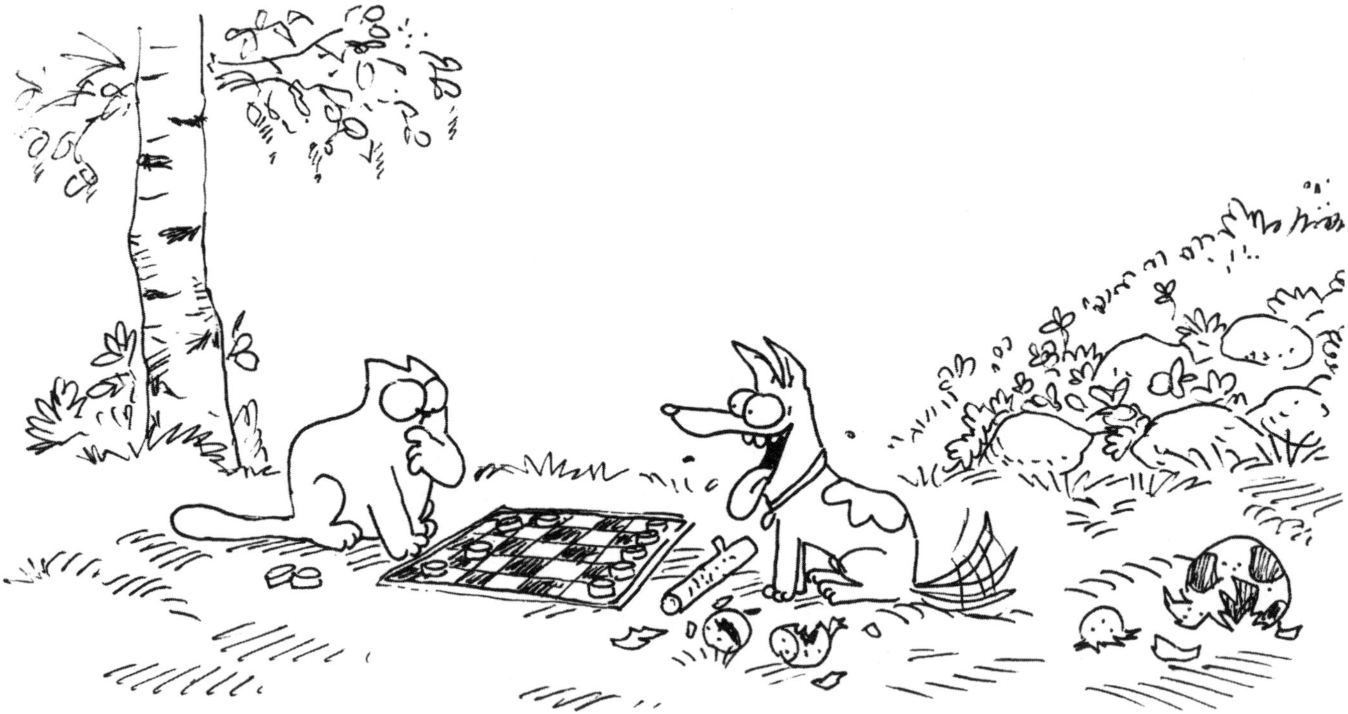

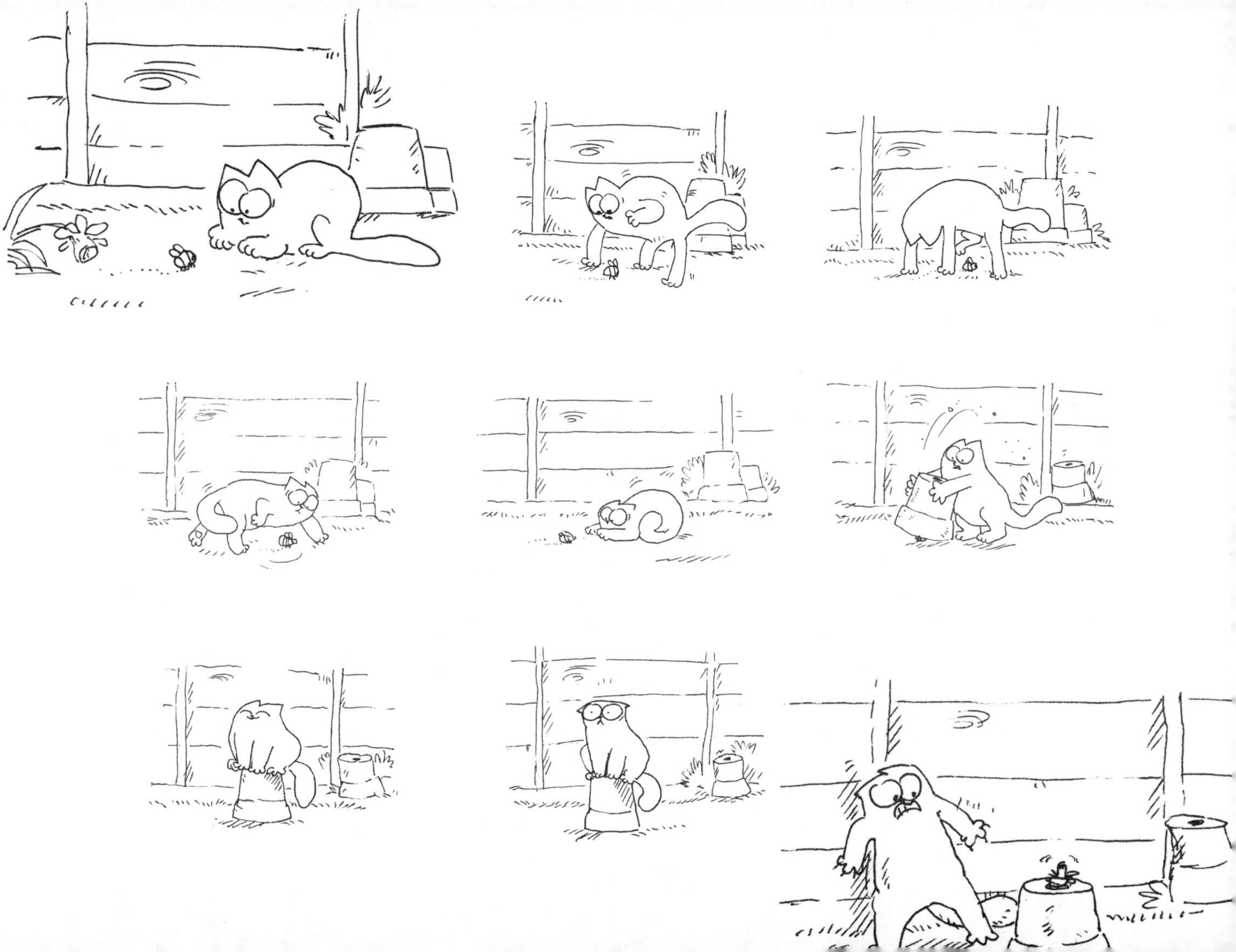

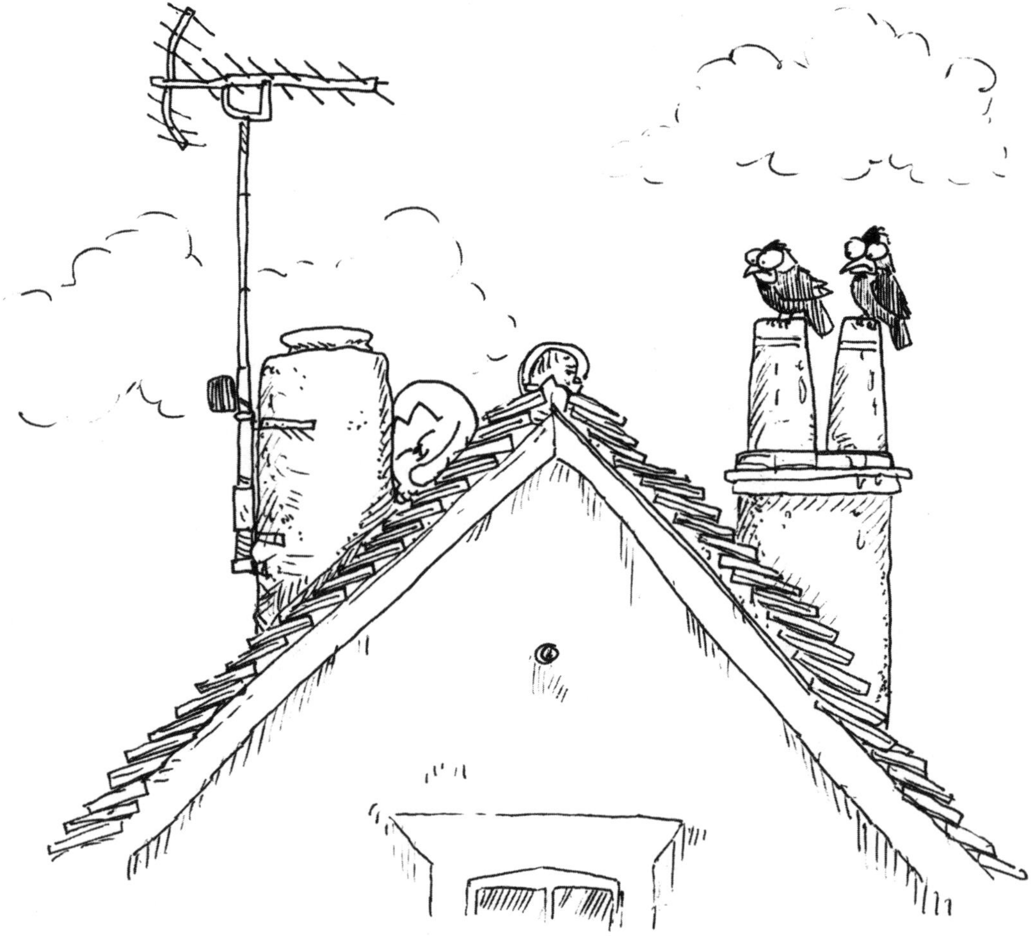

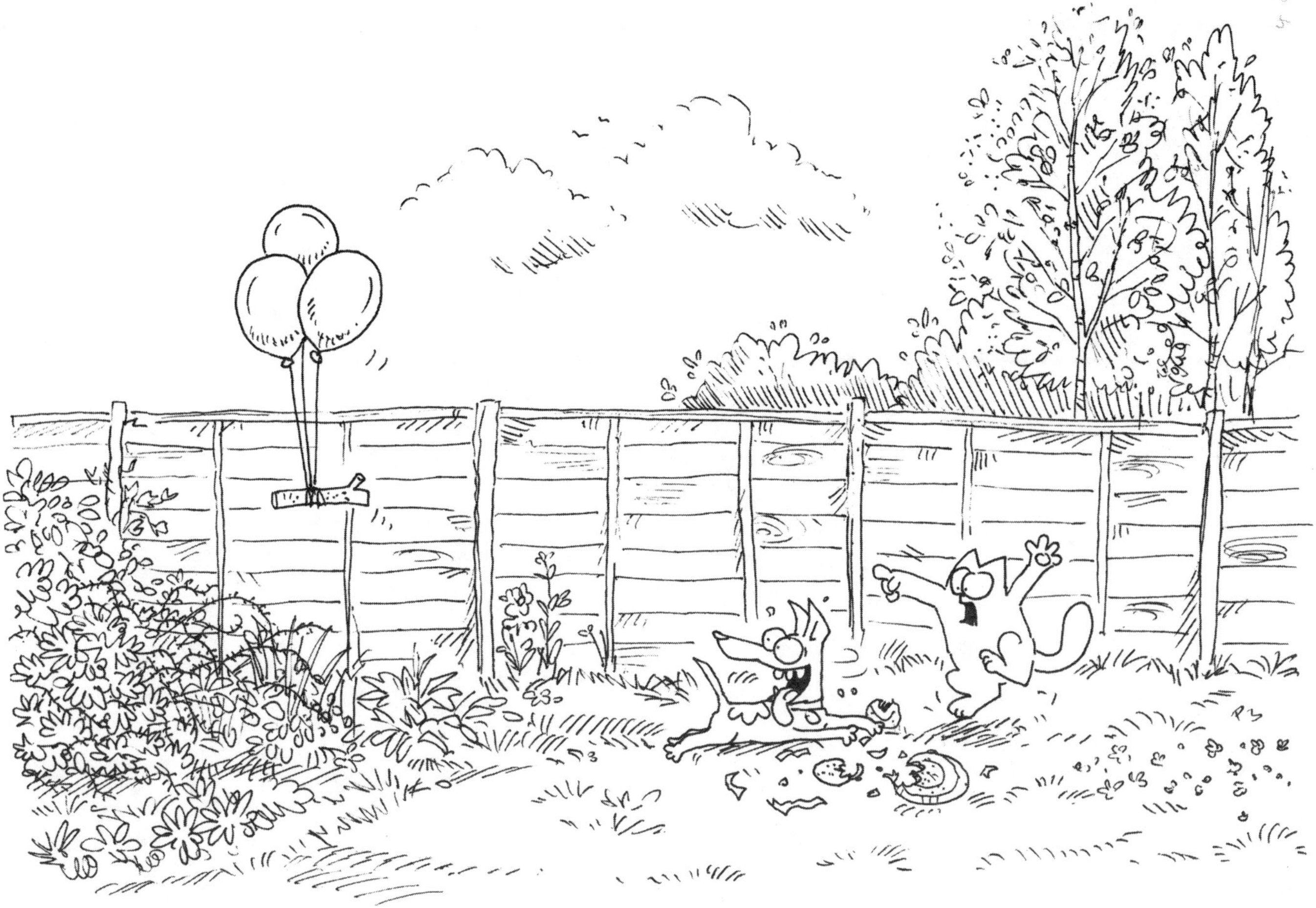

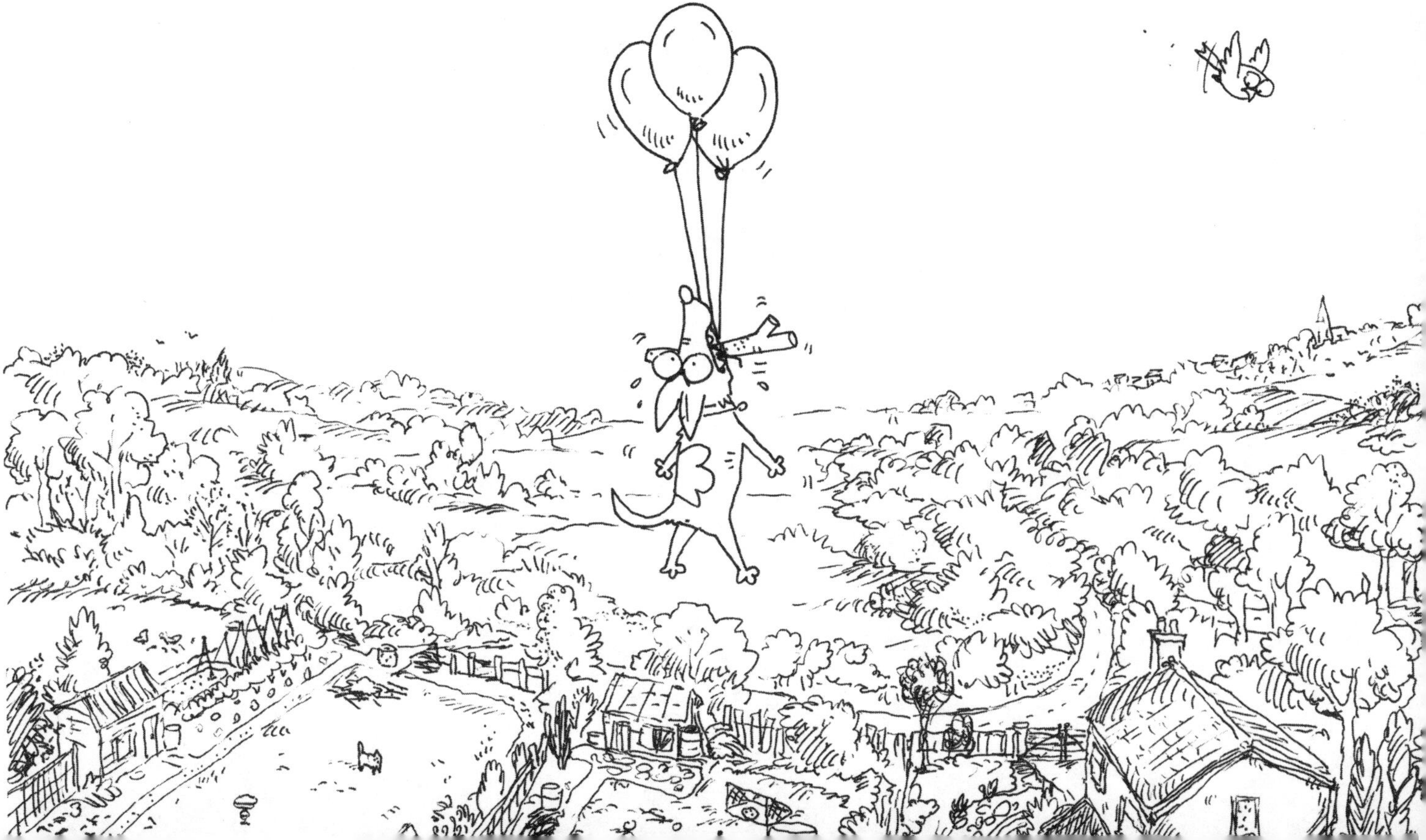

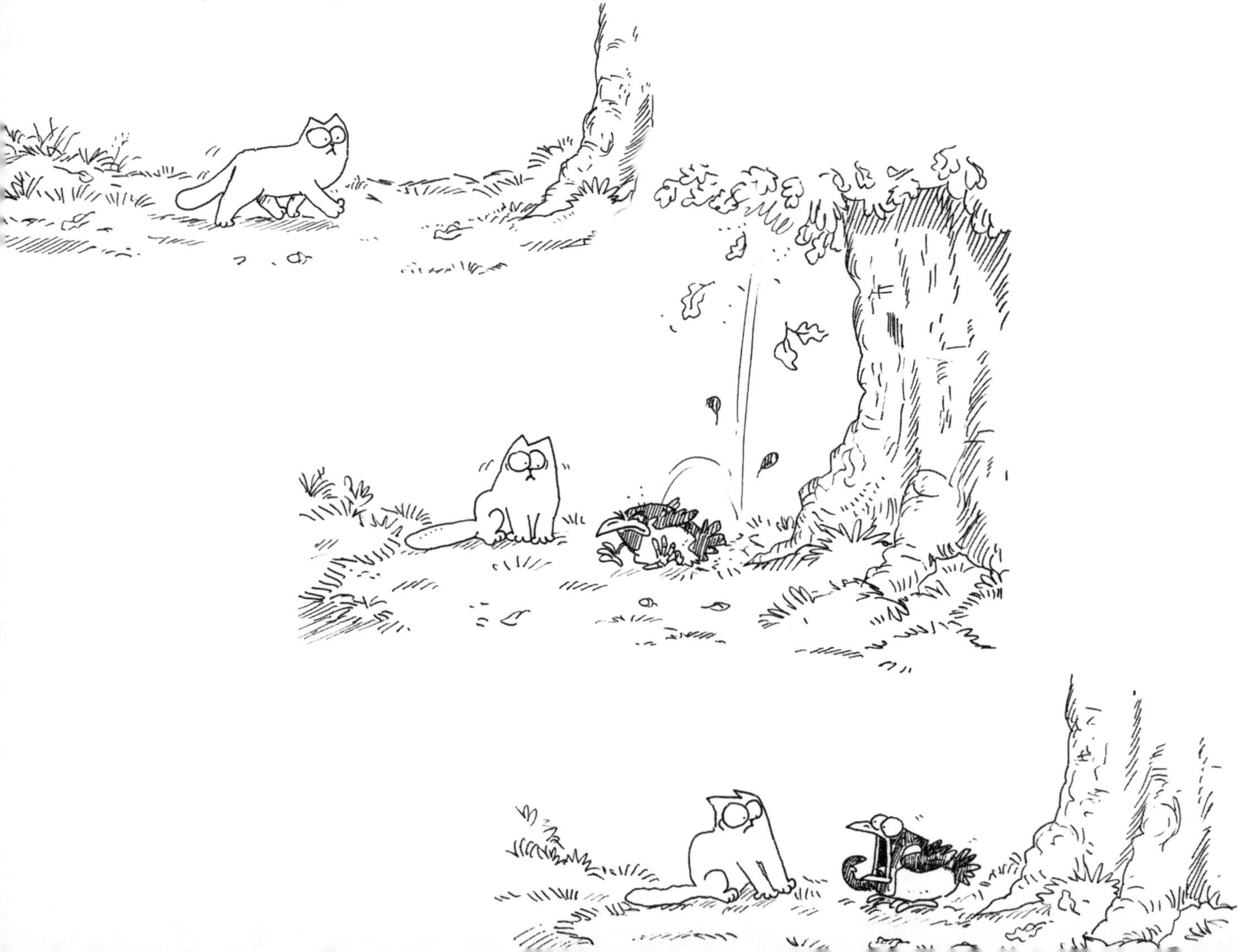

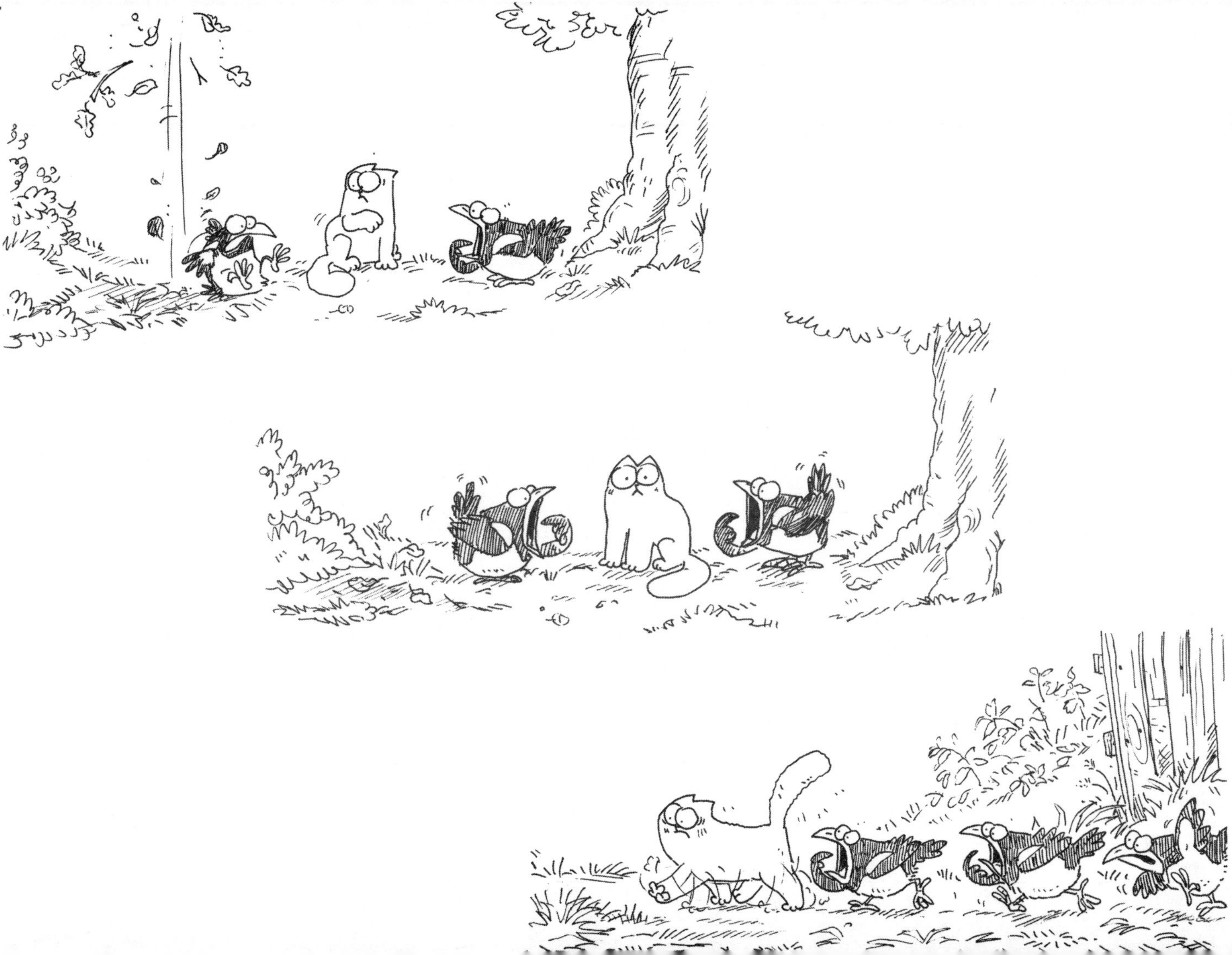

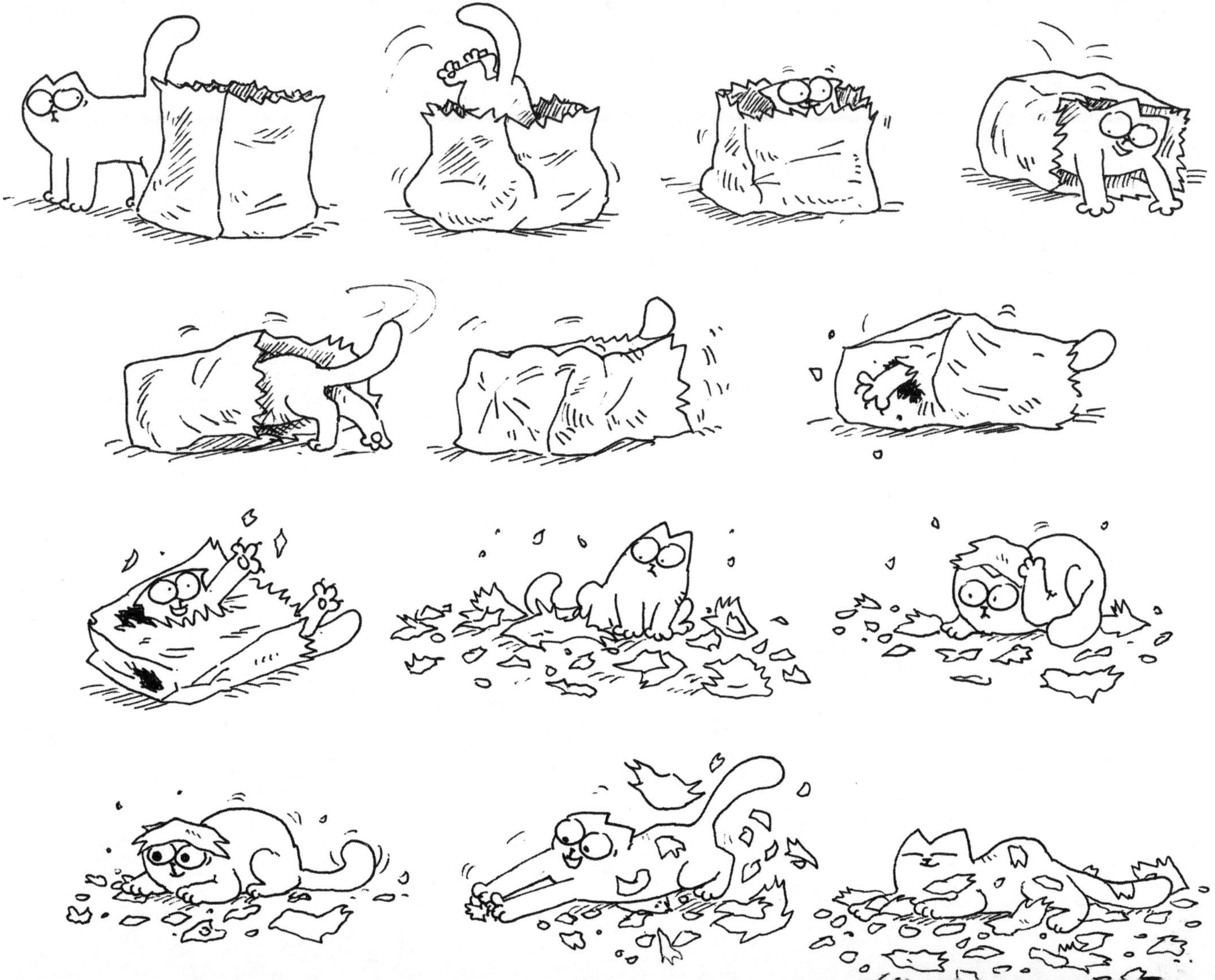

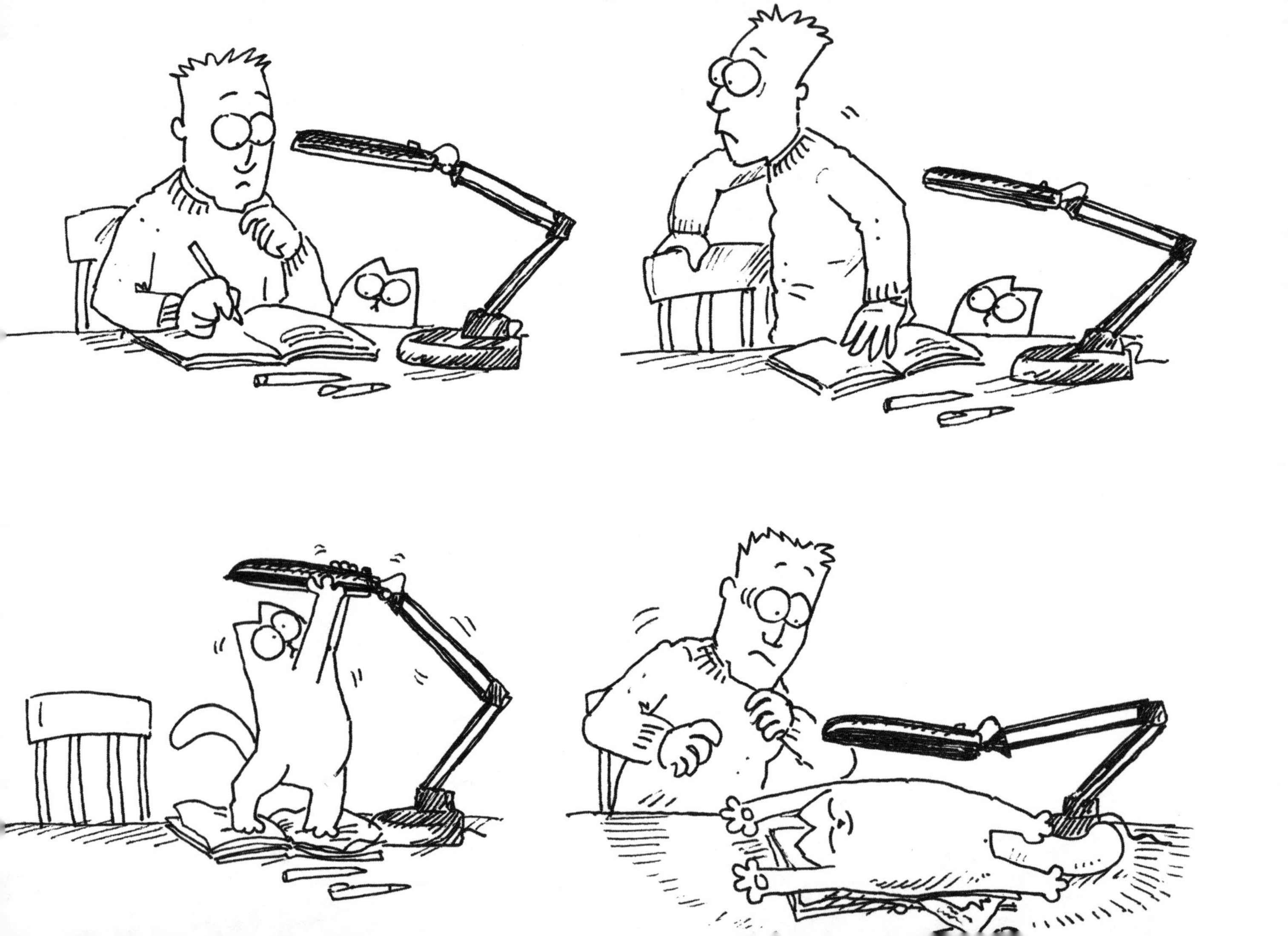

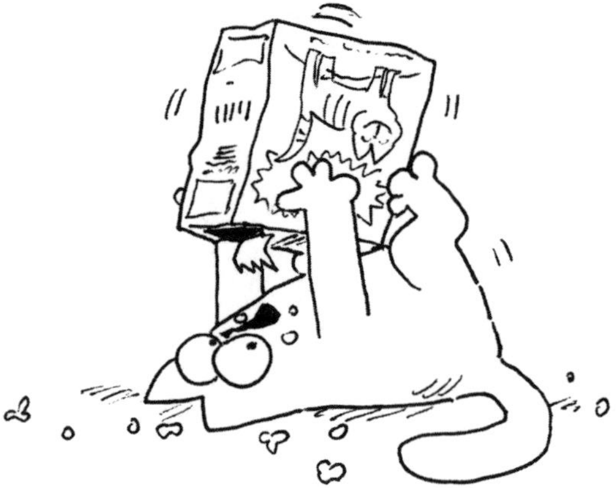
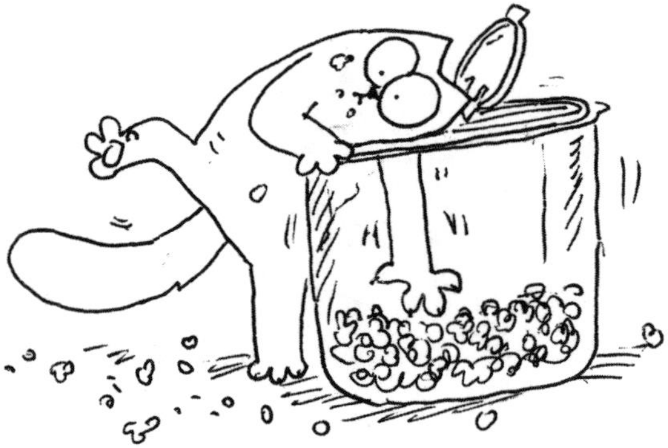
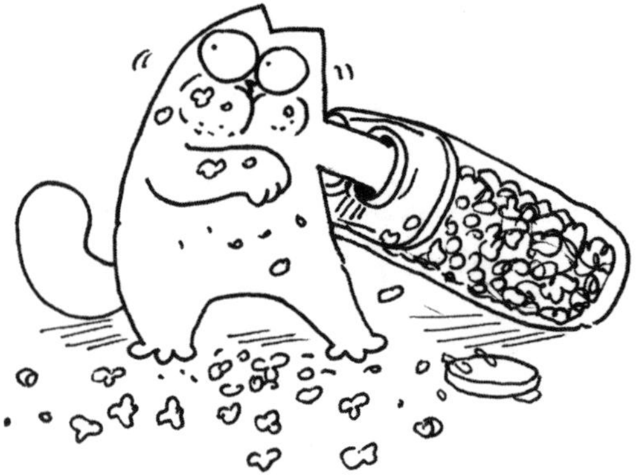
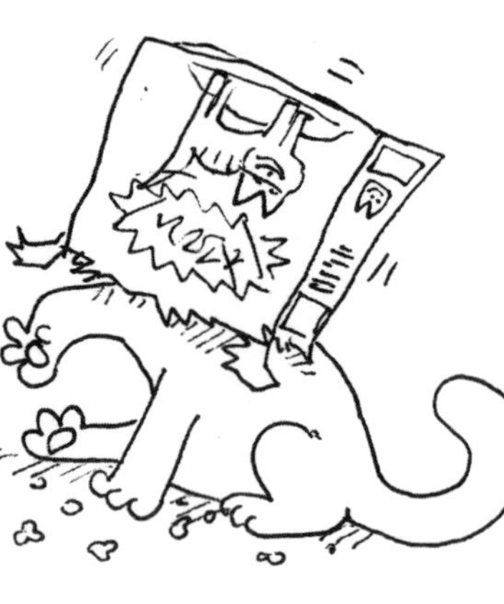

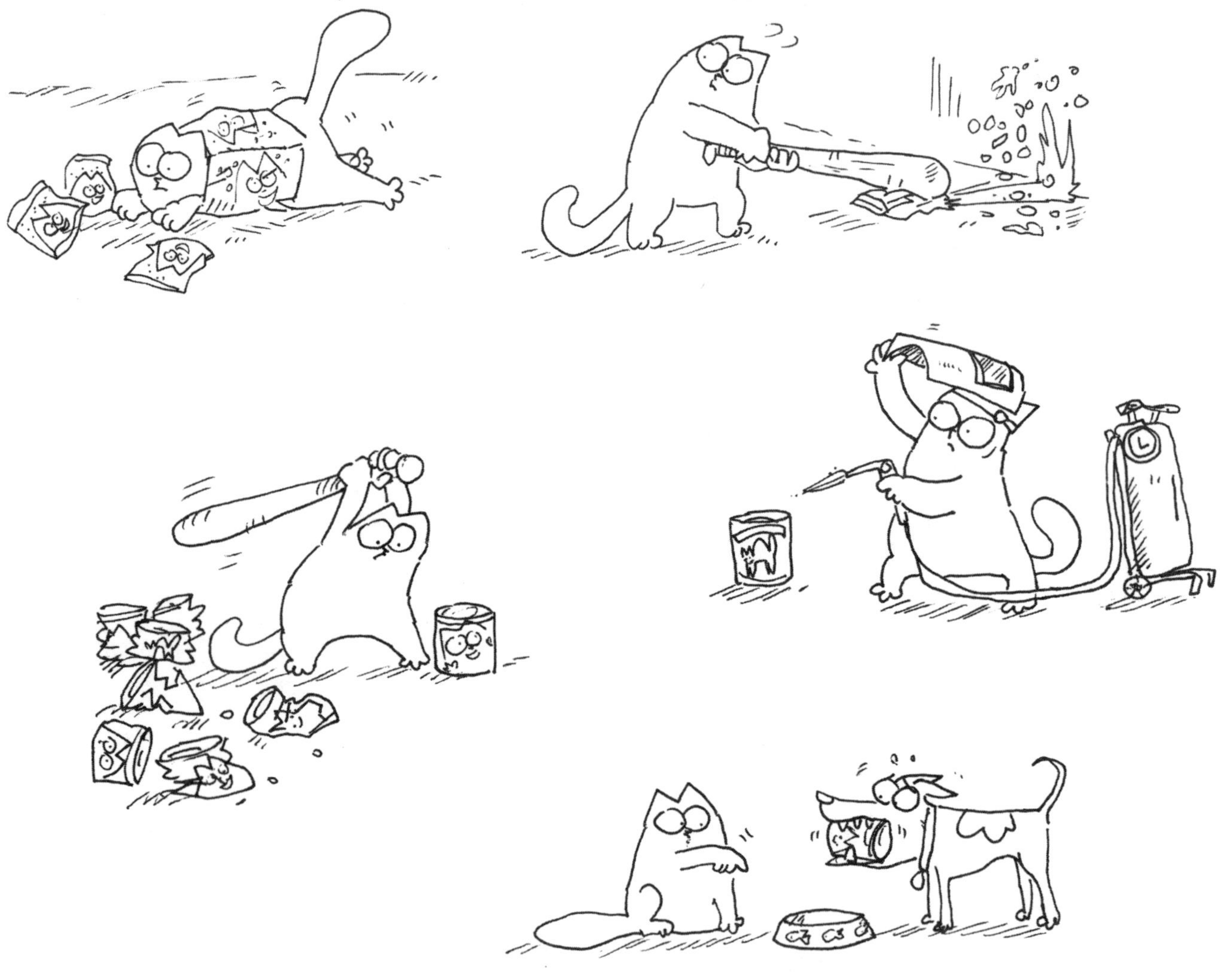

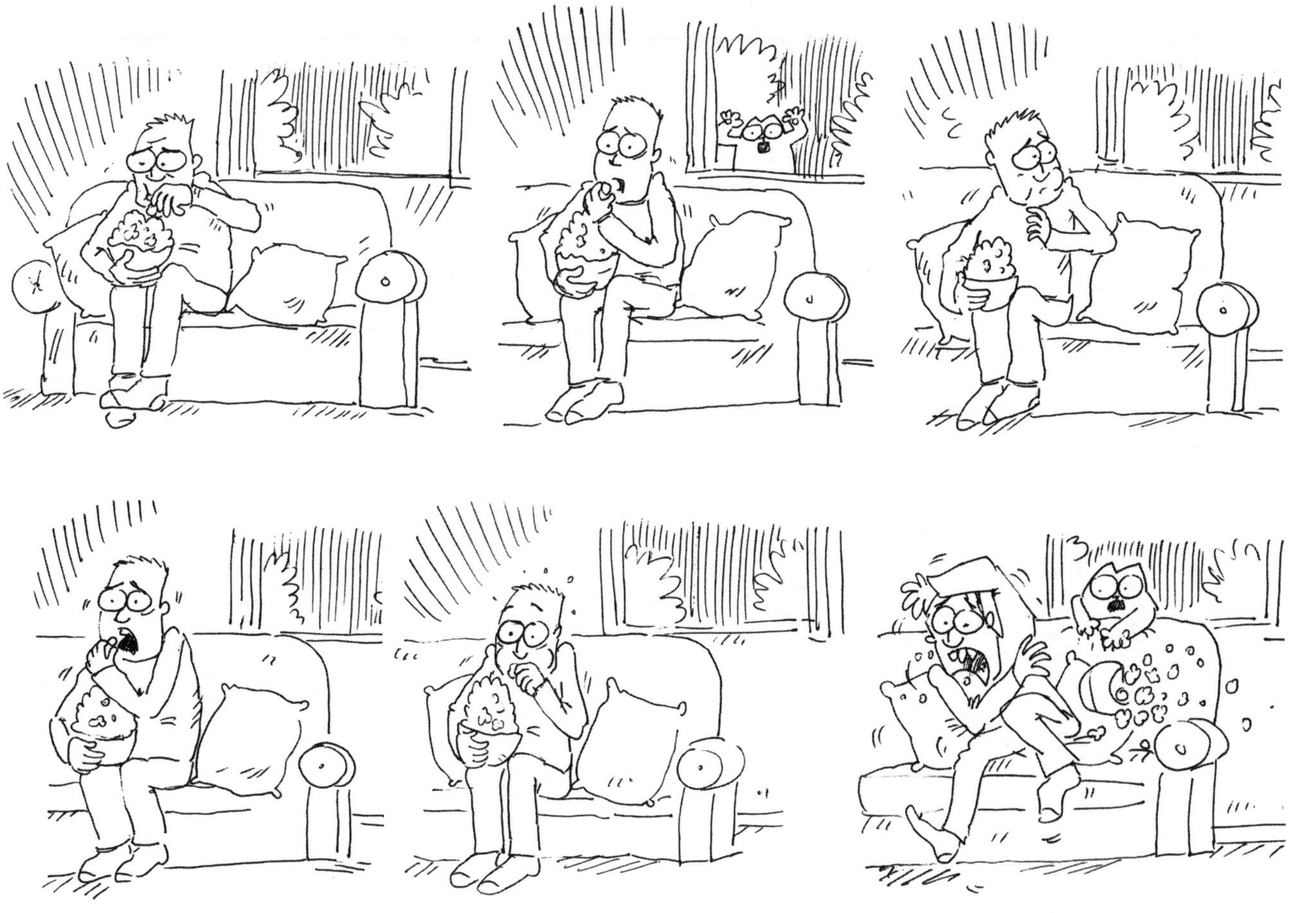

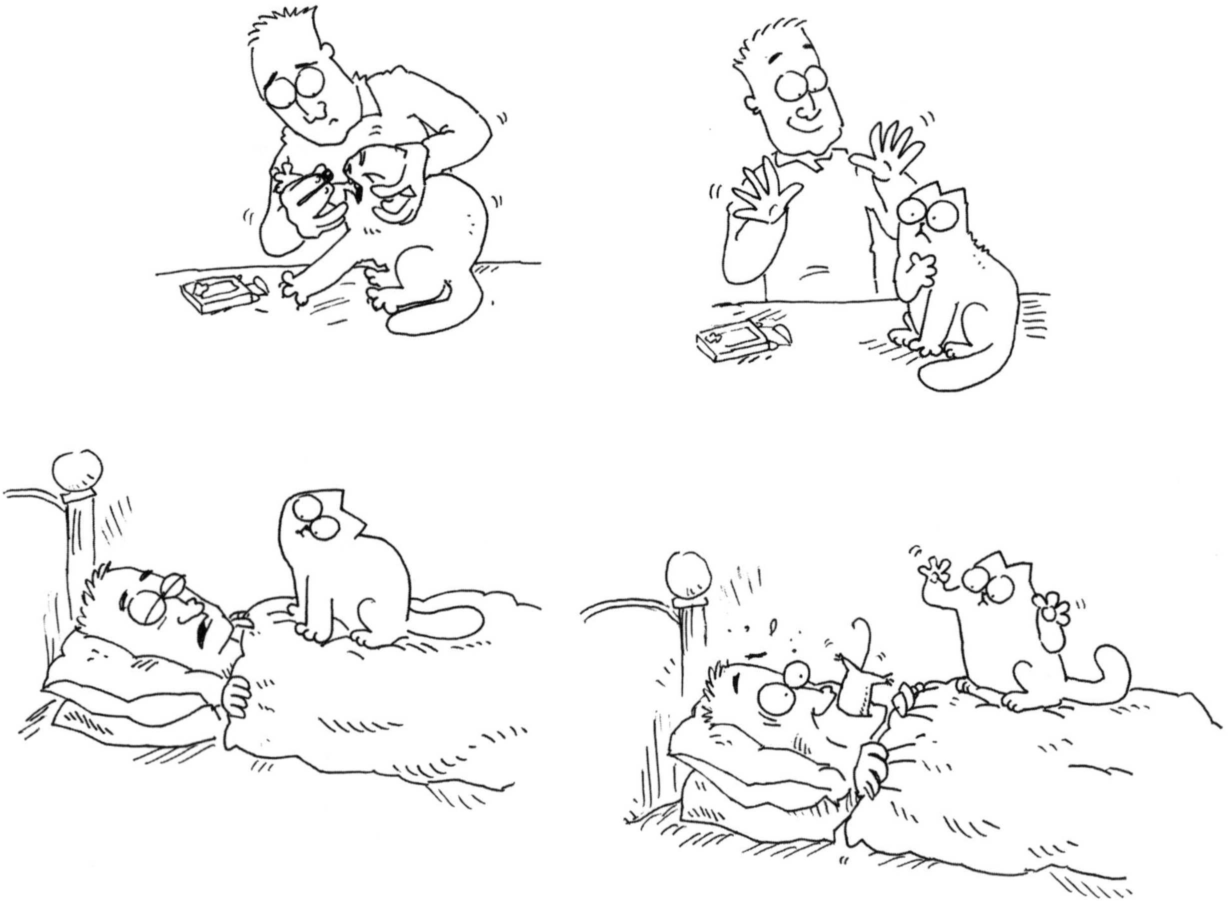

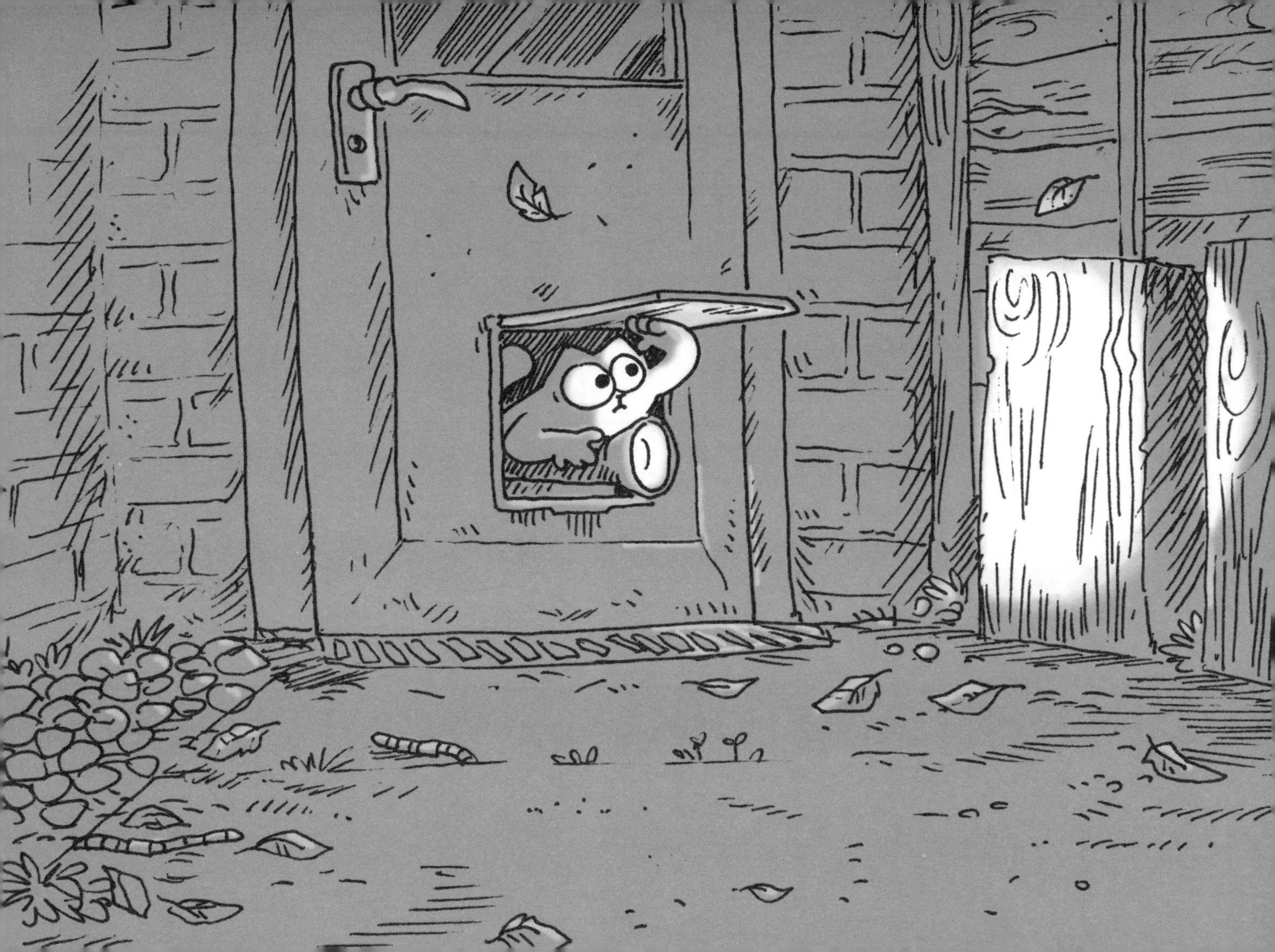

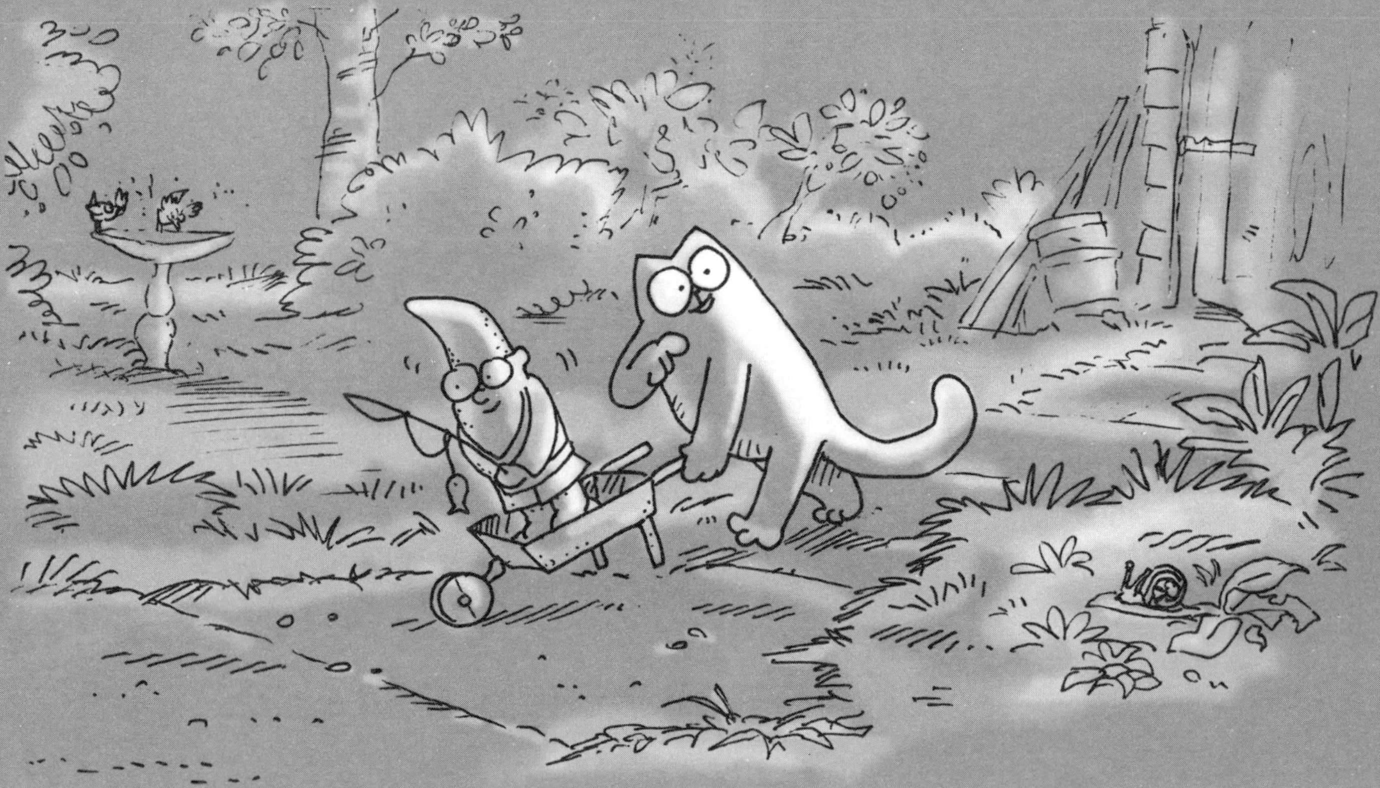

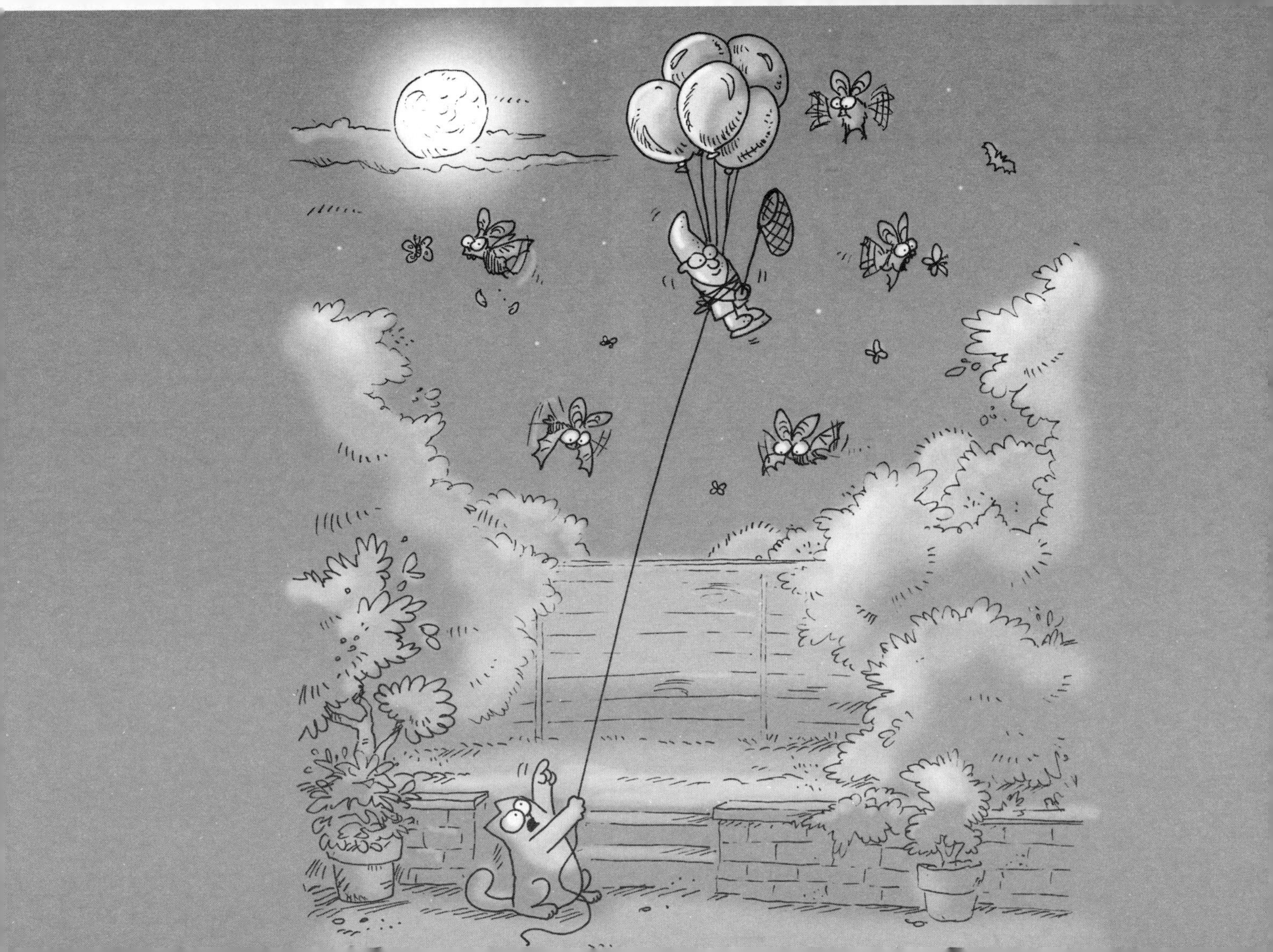

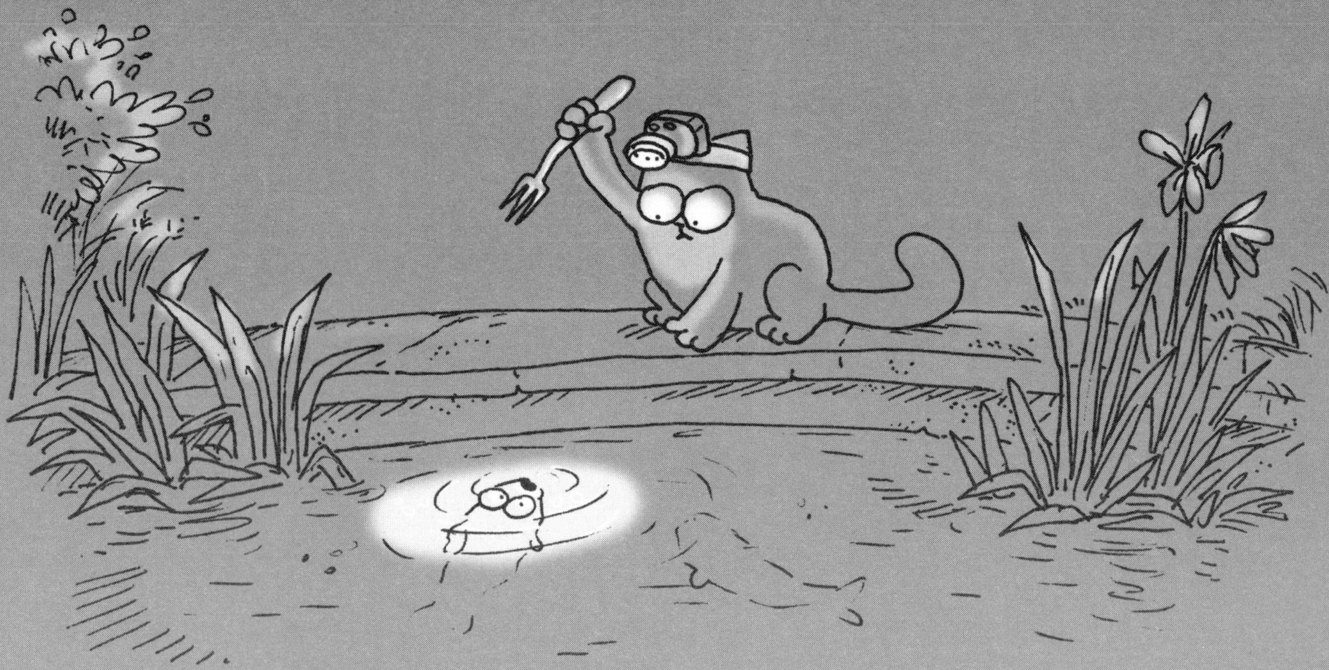

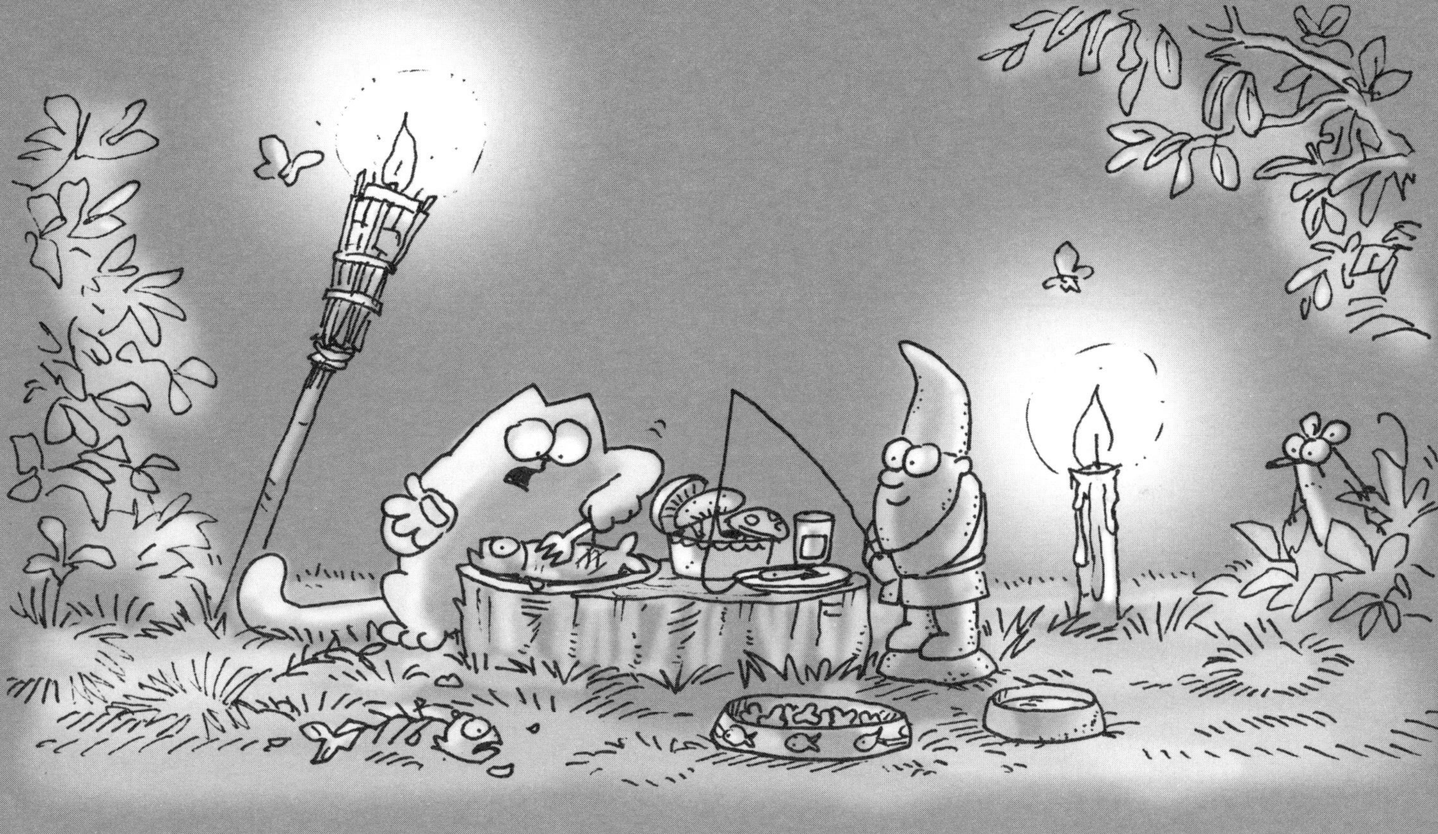

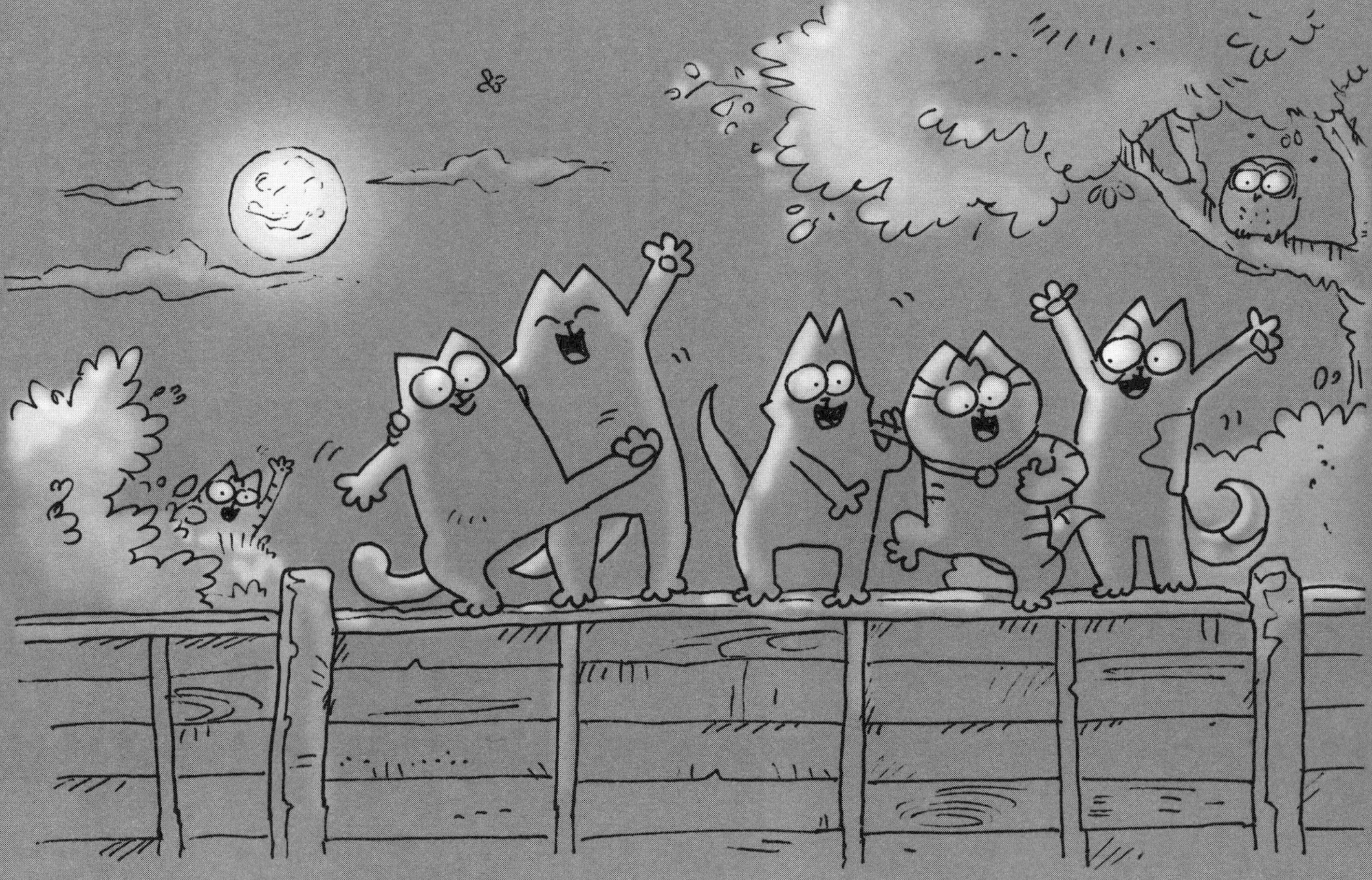

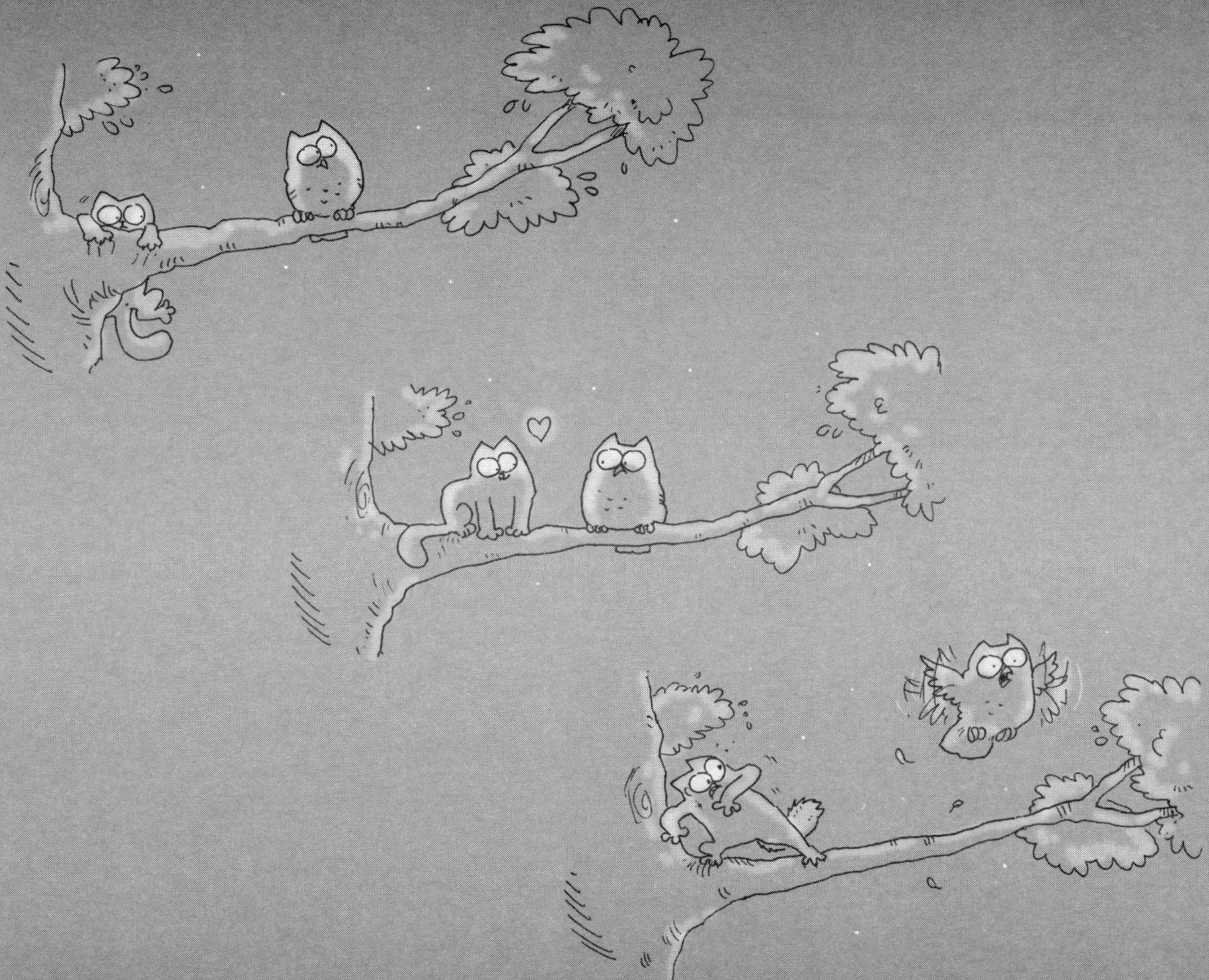

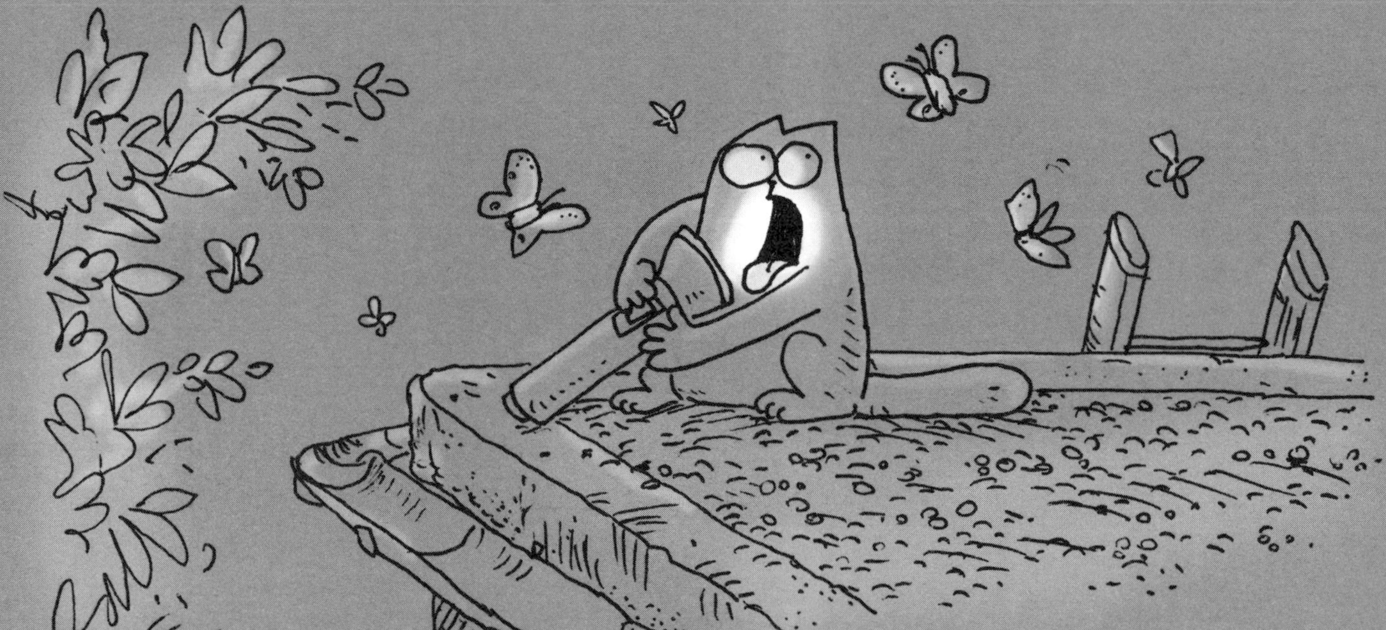

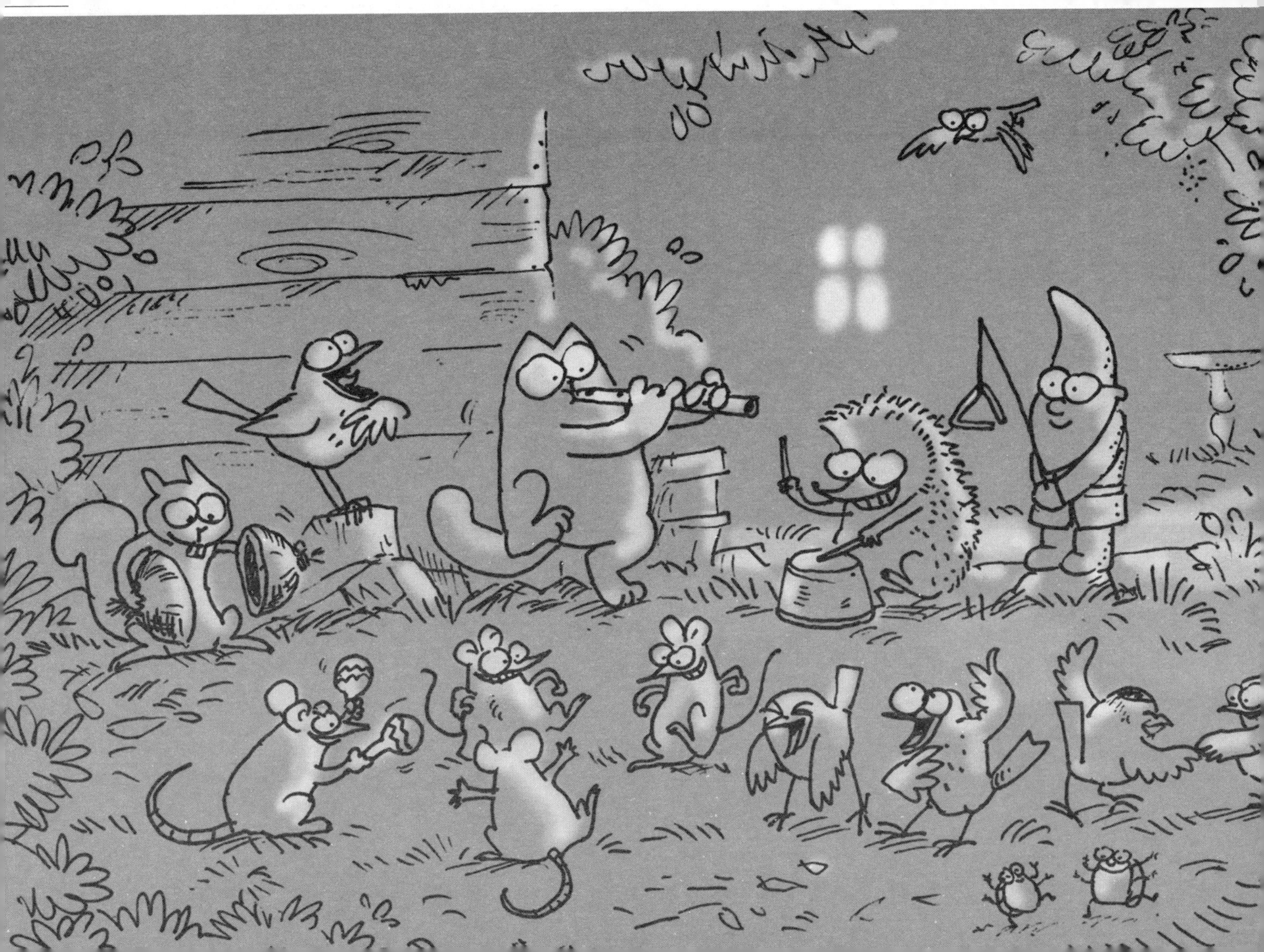

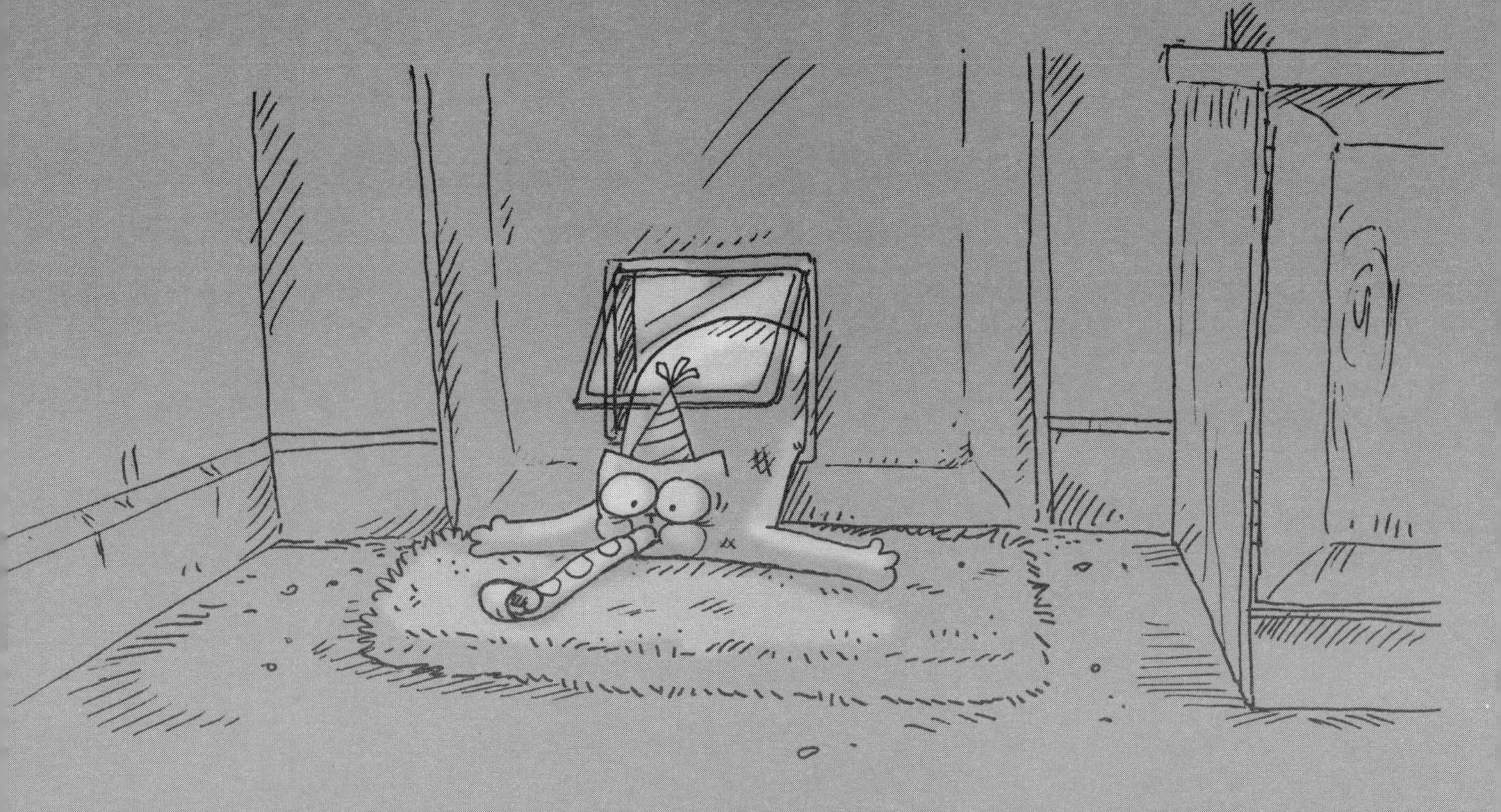

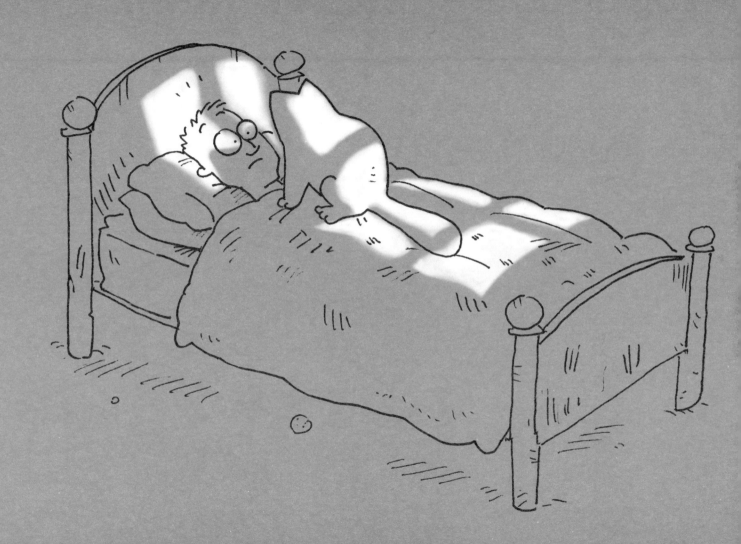

Acknowledgements

Thanks to Mark and Julie Shaw, Victoria Tobin, Nigel Pay, Daniel Greaves, Mike Bell, Richard Tofield, and everybody at Tandem Films for their support. Nick Davies and the Canongate team, Robert Kirby and Duncan Hayes at UA, and my three cats, Hugh, Maisy and Jess for their endless inspiration.